A DERBYSHIRE PARISH AT PEACE AND WAR

South Darley 1925-1955

Keith Taylor and Trevor Brown

COUNTRY BOOKS

Published by:
Country Books
Courtyard Cottage, Little Longstone, Bakewell, Derbyshire DE45 1NN

ISBN 1 898941 59 9

Cover pictures
Front cover: Oker Hill
Back cover: top left, Darley Bridge; top right, The Green and Wensley Hall; below left, The Church of
St. Mary the Virgin; below right, The Bull Ring, Snitterton.

By the same authors:
A DERBYSHIRE PARISH AT WAR: SOUTH DARLEY AND THE GREAT
WAR 1914-1919

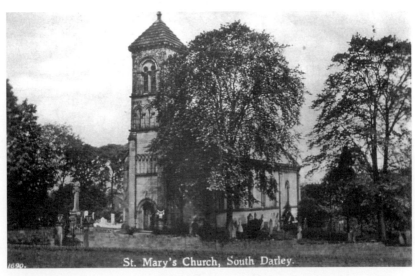

St Mary the Virgin c1938 showing war memorial and war shrine

*To the memory of all South Darley parishioners
who served in the Second World War*

THEY WERE NUMBERED AMONG THOSE WHO,
AT THE CALL OF KING AND COUNTRY, LEFT ALL
THAT WAS DEAR TO THEM, ENDURED HARDNESS,
FACED DANGER, AND FINALLY PASSED OUT OF
THE SIGHT OF MEN BY THE PATH OF DUTY
AND SELF- SACRIFICE, GIVING UP THEIR OWN
LIVES THAT OTHERS MIGHT LIVE IN FREEDOM.
LET THOSE WHO COME AFTER SEE TO IT
THAT THEIR NAMES BE NOT FORGOTTEN

ALFRED LAWMAN	ERNEST EVANS
ERNEST STAFFORD	JAMES RILEY
HERBERT GRIMSHAW	

*A word of appreciation to the authors of this book
from one who served in H.M. Forces
continuously through the war years
and lived to see its publication.
Anon.*

CONTENTS

ACKNOWLEDGEMENTS AND THANKS

A special thanks to Dick Richardson at Country Books for all his help in getting our manuscript and photographs into book form.

Frank Dickens – for computer work
David Millar – for photography
Tony Holmes – for photography
Helen Watkinson and Catherine Wild – for typing the manuscript

Curators of the following regimental museums:
Royal Engineers, Northamptonshire Regiment, Royal Artillery, Cameronians, Northumberland Fusiliers and a special thank you to Cliff Housley at the Sherwood Foresters Museum.

E. Allsop, A. Straw, F. Morton and B. Boam for help on certain aspects of industrial activities.

Special thanks for their time, information, memories and loan of photographs must go to the many residents of South Darley and district, evacuees from the wartime years and relatives of many of the people connected with the life of the parish during the period dealt with by this book. The authors appreciate their kindness, patience and understanding, and their contributions provide the backbone to this historical and pictorial record of the era.

BIBLIOGRAPHY AND SOURCES

Matlock Mercury – 1949-1955 (on micro film) Matlock Local Studies Library
High Peak News – 1937-1947 (on micro film) Matlock Local Studies Library
Derbyshire Times – 1937-1947 (on micro film) Matlock Local Studies Library
South Darley School Log Book – Records Office
Darley Dale County Primary School Log Book – Records Office
Darley Churchtown School Log Book – Darley Churchtown School
Commonwealth War Graves Commission website/internet
Mill Close, The Mine That Drowned, Willies/Gregory/Parker, Scarthin Books
War diaries and Regimental/Battalion Histories
Keep Smiling Through – The Home Front 1939-45 by Susan Briggs, Weidenfeld & Nicholson Ltd
World War Two by Ivor Matanle, Colour Library Books
Second World War by Winston S Churchill
History of the 20th Century, Purnell
Through Limestone Hills – The Peak Line – Ambergate to Chinley by Bill Hudson, Oxford Publishing Company
Derby at War by Hardy and Brown – Quorn
Farewell Manchester by Audrey Jones, Didsbury Press
The War in the Air by Gavin Lyall, Book Club Associates
An Illustrated History of the RAF by Roy Conyers Nesbit, Colour Library Books

INTRODUCTION

The bell rang out from the tower of St. Mary the Virgin on the afternoon of Saturday 10th September 1927 as an invitation to the men,
women and children from Wensley, Snitterton, Oker, Cross Green and
Darley Bridge to attend a sad, yet uplifting ceremony at the parish
church, Cross Green. Sad because it would bring back memories of the
many who had fallen during the First World War, but uplifting because
of the feeling of community spirit generated by such awful losses.
Almost nine years after the cessation of hostilities in the Great War,
South Darley parishioners were to meet at 3pm to witness the unveiling
and dedication of their war memorial, raised by public subscription,
erected within the churchyard and honouring the names of the 22 men
from the parish who had paid the final, supreme sacrifice.

Since July 13th 1919, their names had been inscribed with pride on
a wooden war shrine affixed to the wall next to the entrance to the
church and this had been the focus for the Remembrance Day services
that followed during this intervening period. Now, at long last, the
splendid war memorial we see in the graveyard today had been erected
and the names of the fallen added to a cast bronze plaque on the
Stancliffe gritstone cross and base.

The site around the memorial was thronged as the names of the
fallen were read aloud. The families of those who had fallen and
ex-servicemen from the parish who had served and survived the ghastly
conflict formed the main part of the crowd, for the Great War and its

attendant horrors had impinged on the lives of each and everyone within the parish.

A breeze ruffled the folds of the drape covering the war memorial as Lieutenant Colonel C. Herbert-Stepney, D.S.O., former Commanding Officer of the 16th Battalion, Sherwood Foresters (Chatsworth Rifles) stepped forward to unveil the gritstone cross. Lieutenant Colonel Herbert-Stepney had seen the birth of the 16th Battalion in 1915 as its first Commanding Officer, and had earned the deep respect of the many South Darley parishioners who had joined its ranks. His active participation in the war had ended at Ypres in 1917 when a sniper's bullet had shattered an arm, necessitating its amputation. It seemed only natural that the Commanding Officer of the Chatsworth Rifles should officiate, for his Battalion can be

Lieutenant Colonel C.C. Herbert-Stepney, D.S.O., former commanding officer of the 16th Battalion, Sherwood Foresters, unveiled the war memorial

claimed as the local battalion for South Darley, with at least nine parishioners serving during the war and two members losing their lives.

As the drape fluttered to the ground, revealing union flags positioned on either sides of the plaque, the one-armed Great War veteran gave a moving address. "He was honoured to be present and take a share in their tribute to those departed heroes. No regiment in the British Army stood higher in name during the war than the Sherwood Foresters. Marshall Foch was reported to have asked at one time when there was a particular attack going on who was holding that position, and when he was told 'The Sherwood Foresters', he exclaimed, "Then we shall be all right". It was an easy task to command a battalion of Sherwood Foresters. Courage one expected from soldiers and the records of the war showed the men had that, but what struck one most was the high sense of duty shown by all ranks. Everyone in the battalion seemed to be doing all they possibly could for the common end and welfare, to get on and win the war, and work together as one machine. That was typical of England as a country. The nation and the whole Empire pulled together during those days. They had all been through many difficult times since. Some people said that England, as a country, was going down. The war did not show that, and he did not think that the years since the war had shown it either. Times were still very difficult, but they had only to work and pull together as they did during the war and they could look to the future with confidence."

An impressive silence had fallen over the little churchyard as the Colonel unveiled the monument. Whilst the hymn 'Jesu, Love of my soul' was sung, the relatives and friends of the fallen were invited to lay wreaths of flowers on the memorial, followed by the reading of the dedication and a prayer by the vicar and the haunting notes of the Last Post were sounded by Mr. Goodwin.

Two more hymns were sung, the lesson and blessing said and Reveille was finally played by Mr. Fawley. Memories of the war, tinged with horror and sadness, must have come flooding back to those gathered round the memorial, but South Darley folk had at last honoured their dead. As they dispersed, the thought uppermost in

Unveiling of the War Memorial at St Mary's Church, South Darley 1927

their minds would surely have been that such madness must not and should not visit the next generation.

Unfortunately, by the end of 1939 the parish of South Darley was once again confronted by a world at war and the prospect of more lives being lost in the coming conflagration. The poignant reality was, that the sons of people such as Godfrey (Goff) Taylor, Ernest Allen, Tom Evans, The Potter Marsden family, George Bailey and Harry Flint, people who had fought in the 'War to end all Wars' would find themselves treading the same tragic path as their fathers, just twenty one years later. We can see the sacrifice made by the parish a second time round if we look at the plaque added to the war memorial at St. Mary's in 1950, read the names of the five men who perished and wonder why the hopes of those who returned safely in 1919 were so cruelly dashed.

It is in order to honour these five names and those many other parishioners who served and survived the Second World War that we have written this companion to 'A Derbyshire Parish at War – South Darley and the Great War 1914-1919'. However, although the Second World War period and the 'Home Front' forms the central core of the tale, we also wish to bring alive to the reader the kind of place South Darley was during the period 1925 to 1955 – the places where South Darley folk worked and played and the characters who formed the backbone of the parish. We believe that we have been able to provide a picture of South Darley life throughout these thirty tumultuous years and hope that our account can transport you back to those fascinating times.

Keith Taylor   Trevor Brown   2001

CHAPTER ONE

BETWEEN THE WARS

South Darley gradually returned to some form of normality in the immediate years after the Great War. Most of the families who had lived, worked and played within its boundaries in pre-war years were still to be found in the parish in the 1920's and the familiar names roll off the tongue: the Stewardsons, Gillatts, Fawleys, Chells, Potter Marsdens, Evans, Walkers, Rileys, Harrisons, Bodens, Taylors, Wilmots, Wrights, Vardys, Bishtons, Hodgkinsons, Clays, Needhams, Stevensons, Websters, Flints, Petts, Allens, Hills, Marsdens, Bamfords etc were all involved with parish affairs during the mid and late 1920's, though fresh blood was injected in the form of new families arriving, such as the Grimshaws, Tricketts, Fletchers, Lawmans, Bowlers and Siddalls. The old families certainly provided a degree of continuity but there were dramatic changes as the parish saw new forms of transportation, fresh industrial activities and the arrival of electricity during the late 1920's and 1930's.

SCHOOLDAYS AND DISCIPLINE

Major changes had been witnessed at the Church school, with a change of leadership in September 1924 when David Chapman Parsons replaced George Frederick Porter as headmaster, and it appears that change was necessary. G.F. Porter had arrived at the school in 1890 and had done splendid work there throughout the years. However, in the last few years of his tenure, reports show that the school was in quite a bad way, with shortages in equipment, books and apparatus, inefficiency prevalent and unruly behaviour noted amongst some of the pupils.

Later reports show that David Parsons was able to lead his staff, Miss Minnie Pilkington (later Potter) and Miss Aggie Haynes in "pulling" round the school. He was a tough disciplinarian who came from a teaching background in Borstal establishments and it is true to say that some children feared him and the ever-attendant cane. Sitting at his desk, with one hand cupping his chin and a finger beckoning a child to visit him at playtime, was a sight to bring trepidation to the heart of any child, boy or girl, for girls did not escape the punishment of a strike across the knuckles. The rod was often cut from his own backgarden at Derwent House, Darley Bridge, or from the banks of the River Derwent, and it was not unknown for a lad to be told to climb the wall of the nearby plantation to cut his own means of punishment. Known by the nickname 'Pigeon' Parsons because of the pigeons he kept in that same backgarden, he would cycle up the hill each day to bring knowledge and discipline to the young people of South Darley.

When the morning of Empire Day, May 24th 1925, arrived, a long standing tradition died at South Darley School, Cross Green, for, although stories about Horatio Nelson or David Livingstone were read and appropriate songs sung, the children were not taken across in the afternoon to the grounds of Eversleigh House, where in previous years they had received refreshments, entertainment's and games, kindly provided by the head of the household, Mr. Myles Sleigh. Gradually, as Mr. Parsons set about the task of improving the academic quality of life within the school, this tradition was allowed to lapse, although the children still received a half-day holiday. A few days later, though, on May 29th, the children were still expected to bring in oak leaves or oak apples on Oak Apple Day, set aside on the day of the Restoration of Charles II to the English throne. In past years, anyone without oak leaves could expect to be plagued by boys such as Arnold Wright, armed with nettles, and bare legs could soon receive the painful, telltale rash.

By February 1925, the older lads were expending some of their excess energy by playing schools such as Darley Council School at football in the Whitworth Institute grounds, whilst the senior girls were walking across to Two Dales to attend the Cookery Centre, held in the Church Sunday School (now used by Hayes the bakers). This building was also used by the senior boys for their woodwork lessons, whilst swimming instruction commenced at the pool inside the Institute room that had housed the Red Cross Hospital for wounded servicemen during the First World War.

Teacher Minnie Potter (nee Pilkington), who had arrived at the school in 1918 was of a gentler nature. She was both a fine musician and dance teacher. It was through her keen efforts and the hard work of her pupils that the school began to do well in musical competitions. In early June 1926, sixteen girls were taken to Matlock Bath to take part in

South Darley C. of E. School Choir, in front of Eversleigh House.
Winners of the Greatorex Challenge Shield 1926, Matlock Bath Music Festival.
Back row: Eileen Beckett, Mary Evans, Albert Seedhouse, Sarah Wilmot, May Handley,
Mary Phillips, Tom Concannon, Frances Wilmot, George Taylor, Lily Marsden, Tom
Evans, Ida Wood, Frank Hodgkinson, Sarah Swindell, Billy Marsden, Annie Marsden,
Alice Pashley, Betty White
Middle row: Minnie Pilkington, Mary Spencer, Margery Beckett, Ruth Walters, Dinah
Petts, David Parsons
Seated on grass: Arnold Wright, Jim Taylor

Miss Minnie Potter's dancing group, South Darley School, 1924
Ruth Walters (Wensley), May Handley (Darley Bridge), Connie Pashley (Wensley),
Margery Beckett (Darley Bridge), unknown, Sarah Swindell (Wensley)

the Country Dancing contest and at the same venue a group competed in a School Choir Class at Matlock Bath Festival. The dancing team for those over '12' came third and those under '12' came second, whilst the school choir won first prize and the shield.

Unfortunately, for the school, headteacher David Parsons and the Reverend Edward Augustus Hadfield, vicar of South Darley since 1893, fell out within a year of the headteacher's arrival. By 1926 the situation was so bad that they were not even on speaking terms. Without consultation, Reverend Hadfield or his wife would visit the other teachers' classrooms and when David Parsons sent notes of admonition to the vicarage, or visited, the vicar would not reply and sent the maid/companion, Maude Allen, to say he would not see him. On Remembrance Day 11th November 1926, the vicar was told he would not be allowed to take the short service within the classroom. Despite this notification, Reverend Hadfield arrived and began the two-minute silence, whereupon Mr. Parsons told the class to sit down and begin their composition. The vicar gave way by leaving the classroom reluctantly and Mr. Parsons then observed the silence with the children. Throughout 1927/28 there was great animosity between the two men, though fortunately for the school a truce seems to have been arrived at during the following years and the vicar returned to the school, wearing his familiar mortarboard.

Another area of school life in which the headteacher eventually overcame the opposition of the clergyman was in his wish to introduce new technology to the school. The Reverend Hadfield was against the installation of a wireless set when the issue was first proposed in March 1928 but by January 14th 1929 it had been decided to give the BBC wireless lessons a trial during the coming term. Geography and history lessons would hopefully be enhanced over the airwaves, whilst occasional poetry and music programmes were to be transmitted.

1935 photograph of Reverend Edward Augustus Hadfield, Vicar of South Darley 1893-1937 and Mrs Hadfield

One man who was able to help with the wireless when problems developed with the battery was the local newsagent, Jack Masters, at the house by the side of Wensley Chapel, who, with his wife Connie, ran a battery charging business from their home. His newspaper round went beyond Winster and before buying a car, he was a familiar sight as he travelled the district on his motorbike and sidecar. Jimmy Taylor from Tiersall View, Wensley Square, was one of a number of lads who rode with him and dashed to and fro between sidecar and houses, delivering papers early in a morning. When Jack died in April 1939, both businesses were taken over by his brother-in-law, Harold Hall.

South Darley School c1924. Teacher Minnie Potter (nee Pilkington)
Frank Hodgkinson, back row, first right

Cross Green School, near Wensley, is pictured about 1929
(Back row l-r) Miss Haynes, Jack Flint, R Hodgkinson, Fred Elliot, L Webster,
W Kemp, W Concannon, A Lawman, B Edge, C Wright, E Evans, A Silverwood,
T Naylor, C Hadfield. (2nd row): Miss Pilkington, F Flint, J Hardy, B Gregory,
N Boden, E Corless, M Bonsall, D Hudson, A Marsden, Frances Wilmot, B Webb,
M Tomlinson, J Gregory, M Coleman, C Wright, Mr Parsons (3rd row): Lily Wood, M
Silverwood, M Haynes, M Wayne, M Roose, E Wright, J Parsons, N Corless, V
Webster, M Lawman, M Marsden, E Tomlinson, M Concannon. W Wood, G Naylor.
(4th row): B Devaney, W Sellors, E Wright, A Allen, M Wood, P Hudson, E Roose,
M Hudson, ? Gregory, E Gillatt, ? Allen, Sylvia Marsden, G Fletcher, F Wayne, T
Fletcher.(5th row): B Gillatt, W Hardy, Joe Taylor, G Wayne, K Hardy, G Allen, H
Petts, J Potter, J Devereux, B Sheldon, R Allen, D Marsden, and P Marsden

South Darley School c1925
(Back row l-r) Francis Hodgkinson, X, X, X, X, X
(2nd row) X Dinah Petts, X, X, X, X, X, ? Pashley, David Parsons
(3rd row) Frank Taylor, X, X, X, Margery Beckett, X
(4th row) X, X, X, X, X

South Darley School c1926
(Back row l-r) Jack Flint, Ivan Wright, Fred Elliott, Herbert Wood, Billy Concannon,
Alf Lawman, Luther Webster, X (2nd row) Enid Groom, Eileen Beckett, Betty White,
Mary Evans, ? Clay, Annie Marsden (3rd row) Ronnie Walker, Richard Hodgkinson,
Joe Wood, Luther Turner, Don Taylor, Ben Edge

(Back row l-r) Bessie Gregory, Margery Goodwin, Ernest Evans, Nancy Boden, Alan Silverwood, Lena Lomas, John Potter Marsden, Marion Tomlinson (2nd row) May Lawman, Marion Haynes, Margaret Silverwood, Marion Marsden, X, Lily Wood (Front row) May Wayne, Stanley Phillips, Gwen Taylor

SHOPS AND BUSINESSES

In our modern, supermarket orientated lives we find that nowadays there are no shops within South Darley, but times were very different in the mid 1920's and 1930's. Darley Bridge possessed five shops,

Darley Bridge shopkeepers, blind Billy Needham and his wife Lucy May Needham

Wensley four and Oker was served by one, each shop providing a focal point for provisions and gossip.

By the side of the Three Stags Head Inn, blind Billy Needham's shop still sold general provisions, whilst home-made ice-cream was made in a churn for weekend visitors to the Whitworth Park and yeast was taken round the district on Mondays by Billy, helped by his daughter, Daisy. Every night, Daisy's job was to cut up wads of tobacco twist into tiny packets or 'screws', ready for sale to the Mill Close lead mines on the 9.45 p.m. shift. Daisy stayed up with her father and waited at the kitchen door for the miners, who later paid up at 2 p.m. on a Friday pay-day. The miners believed that chewing tobacco kept their saliva flowing during work. Though Billy was blind, his sense of hearing was sharpened and shopkeeper's son, Graham Neville, was always amazed when he entered Needham's shop and Billy shouted from the next room, "How are you young Neville?"

Albert Fawley, who ran his shop and post office at Derwent House, continued setting up his stall on the pavement of Station Road, selling Darley Dale rock and postcards to the Saturday holiday visitors to the Park. He died in mid September 1928, and five choir boys were allowed by Mr. Parsons to attend his funeral, but the shop continued to be run by his wife Sarah and daughter Cissie until the mid 1930's. However, by 1936 the post-office had been transferred to the Needham's store.

Master butcher, Frank Hodgkinson, lived behind the shop at Number 19, Darley Bridge, and during the Great War and the early 1920's delivered far and wide around the district, including Birchover, in his horse and van. The horse was stabled at the Square and Compass Inn.

Frank Hodgkinson's butchers van at Churchtown during mid 1920's, with Kitty the horse

19

Meat was prepared in his slaughter house near Ivanbrook and a speciality was a delicious potted meat. By the late 1920's however, his horse had died and the van was no longer used. The shop continued to serve as a butchers and local deliveries, carried in a basket, were made on foot until the mid 1930's, when Frank retired and the family moved to a new home when the houses on Eversleigh Rise were built in 1935. The premises were not used for commercial business again until 1950.

'Sconey' Joe and Annie Marsh at Oker in 1930's

Another shop was to be found at No.2, Riverside Cottage, the nearest house to the bridge and from 1920 to 1932 it was the home of 'Sconey' Joe Marsh and his wife Annie. They arrived in the parish from Sheffield after the Great War and set up a bakery and general provisions shop, thus resulting in the locals providing Joe with his nickname. Annie was an expert in making cakes and buns, whilst Joe's expertise was in bread making and icing cakes. The oven was in the outhouse in the front garden and 'Sconey' Joe delivered bread and cakes to the locals in a box on wheels. Later he would travel a wide area with bread and confectioneries in a small blue car with buggy seat attached at the back, under which the goods were stored.

A stalwart of St. Mary's Church, Joe was people's warden for twenty-one years and helped with the playing of the organ at times. By 1932 they had left Darley Bridge when Joe's brother-in-law, Herbert Fidler, began building houses at Oker in 1932/33. A shop front was put in for Joe and Annie at 'Oakerside' and they started up again as shop-keepers, with Joe running the shop for the next 23 years. Joe's former occupation in Sheffield had been in brick laying and he helped Herbert Fidler construct the Oker houses and shop.

Probably the most colourful character in Darley Bridge, Sam 'Fishy'

Riley of Oker View Cottages, was still plying his trade as fishmonger throughout the 20's and 30's, until his death in 1939. Stories still abound of his journeys to Winster, Elton, Birchover and Parwich. His safe arrival home after visiting various hostelries on the journey was only due to the good sense of the horse. Green groceries as well as fish were now being sold from off the cart.

It was his son, Len Riley, however, who now became the mainstay of the business and in the 1930's Len was living at Number 17, Darley Bridge. Throughout the

Sammy 'Fishy' Riley, Darley Bridge fishmonger c1937

1930's and into the 1950's Len ran the business from the front room of his house, and stored the sacks and containers of green groceries there. The horse was stabled in the Three Stags Head outbuildings and Len would collect the fish and ice from off the early morning train at Darley Station.

It would not be too long into his journey that the ice would begin to melt and even into the early 1950's the local lads were gently teasing Len by shouting the same refrain taught by their fathers, "Len Riley sells fish, three halfpence a dish, don't buy it, don't buy it, it stinks when you fry it". Len was not always amused and his red face would get even more colourful. On Wednesdays and Saturdays he delivered to Wensley and quite often he would be going round Wensley at 6 or 7 p.m. and Winster and Elton even later. When reaching Wensley Square, he would bellow, "Green groceries!". The wonderful tale is told of times in the late 1920's when Len was delivering fish to Oker. The fish smelt strongly, for the ice had long since melted and Len would freshen the fish by dousing them in water from the trough by the side of Oker Road.

After Joe Marsh left Darley Bridge for Oker in 1932, the shop was taken over by Charles Bower, together with his wife and son Eric. Charles was a baker employed by Moore's Bakery of Dale Road, Matlock, caterers and makers of confectionery. They provided the catering for the tea-rooms in the Whitworth Institute grounds, supplying meals for the many summer visitors to the park.

Mrs Bower looked after the Darley Bridge shop, which now sold general provisions and its days as a bakery came to an end. By 1938, however, Charles Bower had decided to work for himself and the family moved to Broadwalk, where Bowers Bakery was established. The Darley Bridge shop was not empty for long, however, for Vincent and Mary Jane Bell arrived to take over.

Darley Bridge shops c1937, Charles Bower nearest the bridge,
Mary Neville's with the awning

When Sarah Fawley and daughter Cissie left Derwent House, Darley Bridge, in 1935, Mary and Billy Neville came from Tansley to run the shop for the next nine years. General provisions were sold, whilst Mary had a hairdressing business in the front room, where two hairdryers were kept. Mary Lomas, daughter of farmer John Lomas at Bridge Farm, helped her with the hairdressing during the war years.

There was an excellent trade in cigarettes with the Mill Close miners and Mary installed two dispensing machines outside the shop. Round about six o'clock in the morning the dispensers could be heard jangling as the shifts changed over at 5.45 a.m. at Mill Close Mine. This trade decreased dramatically after the disastrous flooding of the mine in 1938/39. Young Graham Neville remembers lead miner Joe Vardy, their next door neighbour, coming into the shop and saying, "By God, Mary, I thought we'd had it! Water was right up to our necks!"

Mary's husband Billy, was employed as a driver for Tom Smith of Oker Farm. Tom had taken up farming with his brother Fred, but in the late 1920's he bought five or six brown Bedford trucks and used them as milk lorries to take churns of milk direct from farms in the district to the Sheffield Coop dairy. Without doubt, Tom was one of the first in the district to collect milk in this way. Many farmers could now avoid the early morning dash by horse and cart down Eversleigh Rise to catch the milk train at Darley Station. Bill was one of six drivers, including

Left: Mary Neville, shopkeeper, Darley Bridge
Right: Joe Wilmot driving one of Tom Smith's lorries

23

Ben Clay's Morris Commercial lorry outside his green grocer's shop, Main Street, Wensley c1933

Hamlet Bourne of Tansley, Joe Wilmot of Ashton Farm and Charlie Dunn of Oker, and Billy would often wake the residents of Darley Bridge at 6 a.m. whilst arranging empty churns on his lorry, parked near the bridge.

Tom Smith's lorries also carted wood for Gregory's Saw Mill on Old Road. It was a regular occurrence for local green grocers, Len Riley and Ben Clay, to take a lift with a driver to Sheffield market in the early morning and bring their green groceries back with the empty churns, whilst local furniture man, Micky Morris, would bring back furniture on other occasions. During other periods the lorries transported stone, including pulp stones, from the local quarries.

At Wensley in the 1920's Ben Clay and his wife Florence kept the greengrocer's shop where "Peacehaven" is now situated. His sister Hannah served in the shop, which sold most items, including horse harnesses and paraffin, whilst his brother Bill took the horse and cart around Darley. Meanwhile, Ben would travel the top country, as far as

Parwich, in his blue, red and gold Morris Commercial lorry, often late into the evening. On one occasion, young George Wayne was travelling with him, when the carbide lamp failed to light. At the top of West Bank, Winster, he told George to climb out onto the mudguard with a lighted candle under a jam jar and hold on precariously, so that other traffic would know of their presence. "If any policeman's around, we can travel faster than him on his bike!" he shouted to the young lad.

By the early 1930's, the shop had closed and the business moved across the road to a converted barn, still served by Hannah Clay. She was a hard worker, often teased dreadfully by her nephew Billy. The stove in the shop often needed cleaning and on one occasion Billy clambered up to the chimney pot to drop a weighted holly branch down inside without warning her and soot flew everywhere. Ben bought cakes from Gunstone's Bakery and his son would take them to Winster in a converted pram. Any leftovers would be eaten by his friends.

On sunny days Hannah sat by the roadside with a tub of ice cream to sell. The children were often asked to turn the wooden churn, in return for a cornet of ice cream, but eventually a gas driven motor replaced much of the hard work. At Wakes Week in late August Ben would take ice cream on his lorry to Darley Bridge to sell at Timmy Ray's fairground. However, in 1938, Ben, who had been gassed whilst serving in the Great War, spent six months at Walton Sanatorium, Chesterfield suffering from TB and the shop closed down for good. When he recovered, shortly before the start of the Second World War, Ben resumed his green grocery business on a stall at Matlock Market.

Between the wars we have seen that Timmy Ray arrived in his gypsy caravan at Darley Bridge in the last week of August, ready for South Darley Wakes. Two large traction engines called 'Big Sally' and 'Little Sally' drove the roundabouts and attractions in the field opposite the Square and Compass. At the end of the week the two thirsty engines would drain the troughs of water as they chugged up Eversleigh Rise and Toll Bar Hill on their steady progress to Winster and their eventual 'wintering' quarters at Hartington.

Henry (Harry) Martin and his wife Mary Jane kept the Square and

Compass during the 1920's and 30's and the inn's profits rose significantly during Wakes Week. Beer came in enamel jugs and was poured into glasses and people could sit out next to an old fashioned vegetable garden, where the present car park is situated. The owner of the public house, coal merchant Tom Wright, and later his nephew Alfred Smith, would pay Tim Ray to allow the children free goes on the rides and attractions on the last night of Wakes Week. Families from South and North Darley thronged the site on this night.

Unfortunately, Harry and the Square and Compass were not able to escape the fate that has befallen all its licensees. Snow and frost in late December 1927 was followed by a warm, quick thaw and then a blizzard struck and more frosts occurred. By January 5th 1928 another thaw set in and on the Friday a tremendous gale arose, causing the Derwent to overflow its banks, transforming Darley Meadows into one huge lake.

The flood was deepest at the crossroads between Darley Station and South Darley. St. Helen's churchyard was flooded and the water entered the church. The walls on both sides of the road leading from Four Lane Ends to South Darley were demolished by the force of the water. The

Square and Compass Inn c1908 landlord Harry (Henry) Martin

Wheelwright and publican of the Square and Compass, George Hodgkinson and his wife, Nell, taken in 1955.

house that suffered most was the Square and Compass Inn, where, at the flood's height, there was a considerable depth in the lower rooms. Several of the houses at Darley Bridge were also inundated and the cricket ground was completely covered. Nothing ever seems to change through the years at South Darley when nature is at its wildest.

Harry Martin was a wheelwright by trade and employed Sam Edge from Oker and Harry's nephew, George Hodgkinson, to operate the business from a yard situated through the archway of the pub. They had a forge, and when putting a heated metal rim on a wheel for a farm cart, the wheel would be rested on two props above a trough of water. The props were removed and the wheel dropped into the water, quickly cooling the heated metal. The wheelwright's business was dwindling as rubber tyres for motorised transport became more common and George Hodgkinson would often act as blacksmith for Darley Bridge garage and haulage contractors, George Cooper and George Hothesall. He helped them with riveting and concentrated on making the wooden bodies for lorries and vans. When Harry Martin died in September 1937, his nephew George and wife Nell took over the tenancy until 1957 and concentrated more and more on the public house trade.

During Wakes Week the Royal Jubilee Lodge of the Manchester

Royal Jubilee Lodge walk – Wensley Square, August 1928

Royal Jubilee Lodge walk, August 1928. Gathering at Crown Inn, Wensley

Carnival, Wensley Square 1928

Wensley Carnival, August 1928

Hannah Chell. Wensley 23rd August 1926. Pony rides provided by striking Derbyshire/Nottinghamshire coalminers

Unity of Odd Fellows (Friendly Society) still marched, with members wearing blue sashes and banner held aloft, from Wensley Square to Oker, along the Wenslees to Darley Bridge, before holding a short church service with Reverend Hadfield, and meeting in the Lodge Room at the Crown Inn, Wensley, for a meal. Money collected on the day would help to pay for any club member's stay in hospital, before the days of the National Health Service, but by 1939 the event was becoming a shadow of its former self and was not resumed after the interval of the Second World War years.

Throughout the 1920's and 30's, however, it remained an important social event in the parish calendar and Wensley Square became a colourful scene during carnival week. Extra interest and excitement was generated for many attending in the square on August 23rd 1926 when, during the National Strike, coalminers from the Derbyshire and Nottinghamshire coalfields brought their pit ponies and raised money for the cause of the strikers by selling pony rides along Main Street, Wensley.

Returning to Ben-Clay's business, we find he was not the only shop-keeper in Wensley. Miss Harriet Watts had dealt in haberdashery from being a young woman, selling buttons, cottons, wool, silks, needles, embroidery, stockings and underwear from the front room of her cottage next to Wensley post office. In her early days she had travelled in a pony and trap around the district and for a short period used one of the lock up shops where Button Cottage is now situated (workmen found a large collection of buttons when the buildings were converted). For most of the 20's and 30's and 40's, however, she ran the business from her home, even when she moved to the top of

Former lock-up shop belonging to Edgar Wildsmith in 1920's/30's. Now the site of Button Cottage. HM The Queen in the car

Wensley cobbler John Devaney in front of his house and shop, Blindwell House, Wensley c1932

Holmelea, Main Street, Wensley. Post Office until 1910 run by Mrs Harrison, before it moved to John Keane Colman's grocery shop, the Square, Wensley

the square, next to Hillcrest Cottage. Harriet was very hard of hearing and in the 1940's she could be found taking a suitcase of her wares around South Darley and Stanton Lees, a label attached to her coat with the word 'Deaf' written on it.

Another Wensley shopkeeper was the cobbler, John Devaney, who lived at Blindwell House and had a small workshop attached to the building. He had arrived in England from Ireland to join the army and fight in the Great War. In Manchester, he had met Phoebe Gillatt who came from the Dale, Wensley, but was in service in the city, and when they married at the end of the war they set up home and a shoemaker's business in Wensley.

His family in Ireland was well established in the shoe making business. John was a tall, red haired Irishman who liked his whisky and could often be found at the Crown Inn and especially the Red Lion. His skill as a cobbler was well recognised. Horace Smith, the well known Two Dales cobbler was apprenticed to him and Roy Gillatt, his nephew, although working eventually at Mill Close Mine, was also apprenticed to him as a youth. The Mill Close lead miners, themselves, also recognised his skills and many who preferred clogs for working in the wet conditions underground, came to him. His daughter Kathleen could often be found delivering boots around the district. Unfortunately, for the Devaney family, John was knocked down by a car and killed near Gurdhall Farm whilst returning from Winster on the night of 11th September 1934 and the business ended with his demise. However, it is true to say that a considerable number of Wensley men knew the rudiments of shoemaking and often did their own repairs in the 1930's.

Wensley post office and grocers had been run for many years by John Keane Colman, before being passed on to his son, John junior. A change came in 1930 when Richard Hodgkinson arrived from Derby to take over the business. He had retired from a very good civil service job in the employment of the Indian Railway and on the day the family arrived with their belongings, a large chest was handed down from the wagon. Mr. Hodgkinson told the carriers to be careful for it had crossed the Red Sea and Indian Ocean many times.

As in John Keane Colman's day, the post office and groceries were in separate halves of the shop and Richard worked usually in the post office. Daisy Taylor, of Tiersall View, served in the shop during the 1940's and acted as post woman for the village. In those days parcels and letters arrived at the post office very early and he and Daisy sorted them out before she delivered them to Wensley homes. Although an affable man, Richard Hodgkinson was quite prepared to place the names of those who owed him money in the shop window, a case of 'naming and shaming'.

Edgar Wildsmith, a retired master tailor from Sheffield, arrived in the village to live at 'Marie Knoll' in 1925 and owned the barns across the road from his home. For a short while Harriet Watts used part of these battered premises for her haberdashery business, as did Gerald Fletcher, a pork butcher, for a few years from 1932, but from 1928 until his death in 1940 Edgar Wildsmith kept a shop there, selling general provisions. It was not a complete success as Edgar was far too trusting and some of the local lads had many ruses to fox the shopkeeper into allowing them to have goods without paying for them. These old buildings have of course now been converted into Button Cottage.

MOTORISED TRANSPORT

Shops and businesses within South Darley provided a fine service to its inhabitants but a considerable improvement in the lives of many South Darley residents came about in the mid to late 1920's because of the development of a new form of transportation. A motorised bus service developed which provided people with a greater choice, allowing them to visit other villages and neighbouring towns to do their shopping and also enable them to look for work a little further afield.

James Smith Nurseries provided probably the first motorised passenger transport in Two Dales, when, during the evening a works lorry was cleaned out, wooden seats placed on the back, and passengers transported to Matlock. Freddy Wilson on Park Lane, Two Dales,

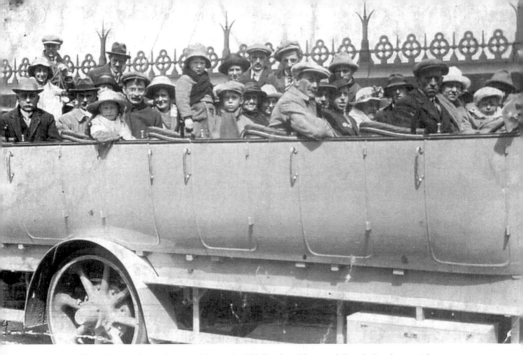

Charabanc trip to the seaside early 1920's for Oker and South Darley residents, including Mr and Mrs Sam Edge, Mr and Mrs Hadfield and Grace Greatorex

Tommy Slack's bus outside Needham's shop late 1920's, Darley Bridge

operated the first charabanc, called 'Bluebird' and Tommy Slack from Green Lane, North Darley, arrived at Darley Bridge with the first motor bus in the 1920's.

However, it was another Green Lane inhabitant, James Henry Woolliscroft, who eventually came to be most influential as far as passenger traffic was concerned. He acquired a Model-T-Ford for his business at a green grocers shop on Green Lane at the end of the Great War and this doubled as a taxi and a makeshift charabanc. It was parked in the Stancliffe Stone Quarry yard

Silver Service bus driver, Vic Brightmore, on the Matlock to Youlgrave run in 1934. AEC Reliance bus

and painted silver, resulting in the name 'Silver Service' being given to his bus company, a name for ever synonymous with passenger transport in the Darley area.

Silver Service, late 1930's. David Lowe (driver) Sid Gibbs (mechanic)

35

1927/28 Silver Service 'Blackpool Express' REO No.5

Before the 1934 Traffic Act was passed, there were no set regulations and competition was fierce. The 'pippin service' was the order of the day. There were no official picking up points and buses from different companies would vie for trade! If one bus picked up a fare, the other buses would race ahead to win the next fare, or 'pip' them to it, and frantic driving was commonplace in those early days. On more than one occasion a bus company would come before the magistrate on dangerous driving charges. The 1934 Act resulted in a number of small services finishing, such as Freddy Wilson's, and Silver Service came to the fore. Even before 1934, however, the company had established a regular service through Matlock, Rowsley, Youlgreave and Friden brickwork's, whilst Wensley and Winster were served by Alfreton Transport in the mid 1920's, which was then taken over by Silver Service and the route extended to Birchover and Bakewell by the late 1920's. In 1928/29 the Company moved from Stancliffe Yard to a purpose built garage at the junction of Hackney Lane with the Main A6 (containing Milner Conversions at the time of writing), where repairs were effected.

The first saloon bus, a 14 seater, was acquired in 1924 and in the same year the first regular schedule services were begun with a 20 seater Dennis bus. Colin Hadfield, as a child in the 1930's, remembers the Silver Service buses slowly grinding their way up Eversleigh and Toll Bar Hill. Small external ladders on the back of the bus led to the luggage compartment, and foot holes were set in the bodywork. Children would run after the bus and place their hands on the ladder and feet in the holes and cling on for a ride up the hill.

Traffic was specialised and distinctly thin, except for early morning buses for the quarrymen and market day transport from the villages into Matlock. By the year 1929 larger vehicles were adopted, including 37 and 39 seaters. By 1939 the fleet consisted of eleven vehicles and regular services were established to Blackpool (for 15 shillings) and other sea side destinations.

OKER TRUST

AND THE COMING OF ELECTRICITY

1928 saw a major change in land ownership and social history within the parish when the Oker Trust sold the whole of Oker Hill to Captain Charles Blythe Ward of Dale View, Sitch Lane, Oker in May of that year.

The origin of the Oker Trust was a piece of common land (Oker Hill) on which all ratepayers had rights of grazing. In the early part of the 19th century, considerable portions of this land were unfortunately being encroached upon. As a result, it was decided to promote an Act of Parliament in 1819 to enclose and administer the Estate on behalf of the ratepayers of the parish. Every fourteen years, at the Red Lion Inn, Wensley, parishioners who wished to supplement their incomes by keeping a few animals could bid for each of the nine 'lots' of common or waste ground called Oker Hill and Cross Green, totalling 97 acres, and the rents of each successful bidder were applied in aid of the Poor Rate for the parish (to help the poor). Fences and walls were built on

Oker Hill to separate the 'lots' of land, whilst cowsheds were constructed and meers laid to provide water. Any surplus money left after helping in the relief and maintenance of the poor was to go towards the repair of the parish highways.

Captain Ward, a director in Ward's Sheaf Brewery in Sheffield, had bought Dale View in 1919/20 and developed it into a splendid large dwelling in landscaped gardens for his wife Eva, and later, his children Ann and Dulcie. He became a benefactor to the parish when he purchased a First World War army

Sam Edge, wheelwright of 'The Yews', Oker, with his wife

hut and had it erected on a portion of the Trust's land at the junction of Aston Lane and Oker Road in April 1921 and the Oker Trust agreed to widen and improve the road next to the site. This hut became Oker and Snitterton Institute and was to benefit the parish over the next thirty years. Levi Dakin and his brother were dry stone wallers from Oker. They put in the foundations for the hut and Sam Edge, wheelwright and joiner from Oker, erected the hut.

Finally in 1928, Captain Charles Ward offered £2800 for the charity's lands and Oker Trust accepted. The money was invested in high-class gilt-edged security Government War Bonds and the yearly interest would be used to continue in the relief of the parish rate. However, an era had come to an end, with the tenant smallholders no longer farming the familiar slopes of Oker Hill.

The selling of the Oker Trust's land resulted in electricity being introduced into the parish more quickly. During 1924/25 the Derbyshire and Nottinghamshire Electricity Company had negotiated with the Trust to bring overhead cables across Oker Hill to Darley Bridge and on

Herbert Chell, chauffeur for Captain Charles Ward of Dale View, Sitch Lane, with an Armstrong Sidley

to Mill Close Mine. The Trust wished for the power to be brought underground instead, and stalemate resulted throughout the next few years.

However, with the purchase of the land by Captain Ward, negotiations resumed and the Electricity Company was given permission to go ahead. It also meant that Dale View would no longer have to rely on power from the generator, situated within the grounds, and tended to by Captain Ward's brother-in-law, Laret Duke.

The cable was laid underground between Matlock and Snitterton, but from there, pylons were erected over the slopes of Oker Hill. Harold Petts of Oker remembers a team of two horses pulling the cable up the steep hillside from pylon to pylon.

By 1931/32 electricity cables were being laid on Eversleigh Rise and Toll Bar Hill. The power line was placed underground and the difficult task was undertaken by Irish navvies. Between Wensley Hall and the Red Lion Inn the village was built on solid limestone rock and therefore the trench had to be blasted out. A series of holes were drilled, the charges placed in, and then the section to be blasted was covered with metal sheets and railway sleepers.

One group of parishioners who were not to benefit from electricity for many, many years were those living in The Dale, in the four cottages belonging to the Haywood and Phinney Charity. These cottages were provided rent-free for widows in the parish. During the 1920's and 30's Mrs Degge lived in the bottom cottage, next to Edith Knowles (Gillatt), with Elizabeth Taylor in the topmost one. However, Esther and Bill Marsden, with children Marion and Peter, were allowed to pay rent for the fourth cottage, in order to live next door to Esther's mother, Elizabeth Taylor. Not only did the widows live rent free in The Dale, but they still received from the Charity once a year, a piece of flannel material that could be made into warm vests.

The cottages consisted of one room downstairs and one upstairs. Lighting came from paraffin lamps downstairs and candles upstairs, whilst cooking was undertaken in a simple, small oven, heated from an adjacent open fire. There was no kitchen sink, since water for drinking and washing purposes was collected from the well, opposite, supplied by a sough from the old leadmines on Wensley hillside. The water was hard and difficult to lather, whilst in winter a covering of ice had often to be smashed.

Esther Marsden with children Marion and Peter, in Wensley Dale, c1927

Until the reservoir was built behind the Red Lion Inn in 1909, people obtained their drinking water from the village pump at the White House, or trailed down to Dale Well in Wensley Dale. Coming back up Stone's Croft they would often rest their buckets on a stone paver, set into the banking for that purpose. For washing clothes, large stone troughs and barrels were placed near the gutter pipe from the roofs of the cottages, in order to collect rainwater.

When the reservoir was constructed, the water flowed in a 3-inch cast iron pipe, under pressure, from Stanton Moor, near the hamlet of Stanton Lees. It rarely ran dry and replaced the pump and Dale Well. However, even into the 1940's some cottages in Wensley still only had a cold water tap in the kitchen.

SPORT AND LEISURE

Leisure time activity throughout the 1920's and 30's, especially for the menfolk of the parish, was provided for by Darley Dale Cricket Club, Oker and Snitterton Institute, Wensley Reading Room and Wensley Red Stars Football Club.

The Cricket Club was formed in 1863 when James Smith (Nurseries) levelled the riverside ground at a cost of £6.12 sh. 0d. In 1904 the new pavilion was built at a cost of £254, replacing a tiny corrugated iron structure erected on what is now the car park, at a cost of £15. In the early days, venues were close to the railway line running along the Derwent Valley, for ease of transportation, and even in the 20's and 30's Derby, Duffield, Belper, Bakewell and Buxton still provided the main opposition.

By 1930, brothers Alfred and Fred Smith of Bank House, Eversleigh, and later Warney Lea, Darley Dale, were the main benefactors of the club, and their word was law. The first and second eleven's played at Darley Bridge, whilst Charlie Hallows from Two Dales ran the third eleven on the Whitworth Institute ground and a nursery group of under 15's were allowed to attend practice sessions free of charge, as long as they behaved themselves. By 1928, one in sixteen of the local South and North Darley menfolk were involved with the club and reports were given in the local press that the ground was the best small club ground in the county.

Excellent South Darley cricketers such as Herbert Grimshaw, Reg Boden, Joe Wall, Joe Wilmot and Cyril Taylor played regularly for the club during the 1920's and 30's. Reg took over the wicket keeping gloves in 1919 at the age of 17, when the other two regular keepers were injured on an uneven pitch that had been neglected during the match free years of the First World War. He never looked back and was to remain the first team keeper into the late 1950's.

My uncle, Cyril Taylor, was a fine self-taught left arm leg spin bowler who regularly became the leading wicket taker for the club. For example, during the 1931 season, Herbert Grimshaw, Arthur Morton and Cyril Taylor were the most successful bowlers in that order. Cyril Taylor, however, took 70 wickets, or 17 more than those of Herbert and Arthur

Cyril Taylor holds the ball with which he took all ten wickets for Darley First Eleven in the home match against Sheffield Collegiate on 26th July 1930

added together. 72 wickets were taken by him in 1929, 74 in 1930 and 70 during 1931. Even by present day standards this was an incredible performance, for in those days there were less games played during the season. The crowning glory came on Saturday July 26th 1930 when Cyril produced the best bowling analysis of his career by taking all ten wickets for 42 runs against a strong Sheffield Collegiate side at Darley Bridge. His twin brother, Wilfred, who was the scorer for Darley Dale during the 1930's was able to proudly record this fine achievement.

Reg Boden, wicket-keeper, worked at Stancliffe Stone Quarries office and when his friend Cyril Taylor was on the 5.45 a.m. to 1.45 p.m. shift at Mill Close Mine on Saturdays, Reg would go up to the mine in his car to fetch Cyril so that he would be ready for the next

Darley Dale Cricket Club's First Eleven mid 1930's
(Back row l-r) Alfred Smith, X, Joe Wilmot, Joe Wall, Herbert Grimshaw, X (Front row
l-r) Frank Unwin, Louis Jacques, Noel Jacques, Reg Boden, Les Marples, Cyril Taylor

Darley Dale Cricket Club Second Eleven 1936
(Back row l-r) Fred Smith, George Holland, Herbert Taylor Norman Lees, Joe Wilmot,
Cyril Taylor, Wilfred Taylor (scorer), John Siddell (Front row) W Mitchell, Barry
Sharman, Charles Lymn, JR Taylor, Alfred Smith, A Bland
Played 17 matches, won 11, lost 2, drew 4

The picture is of the opening of the Darley Dale Cricket Club scoring pavilion by Judge- E. H. Longson. The pavilion, which is built of Stancliffe Stone and has cost over £800, was presented to the club by Mr A. H. Smith, Warney Lea, Darley Dale.
In the picture are (left to right): Rev. R. Griffiths (Rector of Darle Dale), Mr. Fred Smith, Judge E. H. Longson, Mr. A. H. Smlth, Mr. W. Jacques, Mr. J. W. Hibbs, Mr. C. R. Lymn (chairman), Mr. G. W. Burton, Mr. Noel Jacques (captain), Mr. F. A. Gregory.

match on time. There were also occasional local matches at night between the Stancliffe Stone and Mill Close teams, with Reg and Cyril now playing on opposite sides. In one such match there was a dispute and anger was generated between several of the rival players. Cyril heard at work the next day that certain Mill Close members were planning to tip Reg's car over on the following Saturday when he arrived to pick him up, so Cyril left a little early and they got away safely. The Mill Close team members of those days obviously took their sport seriously.

By 1938 the club was in a healthy condition. In the previous season, 1937, the Darley ground was being used by Derbyshire 2nd Eleven to play two matches, each of two days duration, and Alfred Smith had provided a splendid new scoring pavilion (score-board) in the same year, opened by Judge Longson on May 12th 1937 in commemoration of the coronation of George VI and Queen Elizabeth.

As a postscript, it could be added that, healthy though the club's position may have been, there was a distinctly unpleasant smell in the air when the wind was in the wrong direction. From the 1920's until the early 1960's it emanated from a green corrugated iron shed that stood on the site of the present Darley Bridge Picnic area, adjacent to the cricket ground. The culprit was the Hide and Skin (Sheffield and District Hide and Skin Company), managed by Mr. Sharman. Lorries arrived with the carcasses of cattle, which were cut up to obtain the offal and bones, whilst at a later stage the skins were cured. As the doors were opened, the smell could be dreadful. When no one else was looking, one or two of the locals had an arrangement to go round the back to collect dripping to be used in the cooking of very tasty chips. Salt petre and sand were placed in layers around the hides to dress and cure them. One man cured and dressed sheep and pigs' intestines for sausage skins, and bones were collected before being delivered to Sheffield.

Oker and Snitterton Institute was the focus of many South Darley social functions and events during the 1920's and 30's, before the building of South Darley Village Hall at Cross Green in 1952. The young men could play billiards, cards and darts, the Women's Institute met on a regular basis, whist drives were well attended, South and North Darley people were attracted to dances, wedding receptions could be held and concert parties and pantomimes entertained the local parishioners. Tobacco and cigarettes could even be purchased on the premises.

The Institute was opened on the 1st April 1921 with a whist drive, the winners being Joseph Potter from Wensley and Mary Dakin of Oker, whilst in lovely weather on the 12th April, it was the venue for the wedding feast at the marriage of George Hadfield and Rosa Petch. It was not until the 9th June 1921, however, that the formal opening took place with a tea given by the Trustees' wives, Mrs. Lomas, Mrs. Fiddler and Mrs. Harrison.

During the following years the hut became a well-loved outlet for social occasions, as we can see in the years 1938/39, leading up to the Second World War. The September meeting of South Darley W.I. in 1938 held a rummage sale in aid of a Folk Dance Fund and it was decided to form confectionery and keep fit classes. On Friday 31st December 1938, a very happy evening was spent when members' children were entertained to a Christmas party and fancy dress dance. Frank Hodgkinson's Band supplied the dance music and winners of the fancy dress prizes were: – 1.Shirley Chell 2. Doris Wright 3. Pauline Watson 4. Sybil Watson and George Wright. Before the party broke up the youngsters were presented with chocolates, oranges, apples and other sweets.

On Wednesday 18th January 1939 the annual New Years' Party for the Women's' Institute involved games and dancing and the dramatic section of Darley Dale Townswomen's' Guild presented a sketch "False Alarm". A month later there was a demonstration on 'Dress designing', with Mrs. Bowser of Wensley Hall Guest House giving the vote of thanks. Classes in 'Rush seating' were to start soon and the Folk Dance team was again to enter the W.I. Competition. Mrs. Annie Marsh, the baker from Oker, judged a scone competition won by Mrs. F. Farmer of Snitterton, whilst the tea hostesses were Mesdames Laura Duke (Two Dales Café), F. Farmer and Mrs. Bowser.

March 7th 1939 saw a billiards supper being held in aid of funds, with 70 people attending. They were entertained by Mr. J. Briddon's Concert Party of Tansley and later there was dancing, for which F. Hodgkinson supplied the music. The Garden Party of the Women's' Institute on Saturday 15th July, just six weeks before the start of war, should have taken place at the garden of Mrs. Board's home, Snitterton Hall, but poor weather caused it to be relocated to the Institute Hut. Mrs. Davie of Stanton Hall opened it. There were stalls, with teas

*South Darley Women's Institute meeting at the Oker and Snitterton Institute, late 1930's
(Back row l-r) Mrs Stewartson, Mrs Annie Pepper, Norah Bark, Connie Masters, Mrs
Wright, Mrs Duke, Mrs Watson, X, X, Mary Spencer, Mrs Naylor, Miss Gladys Walker,
Mrs Hewson (Second row) Betty Thompson, Mrs Sheldon, Mrs Watkinson, Mrs Frances
Harrison, Mrs Hudson, Mrs Groves, Mrs Hadfield, Mrs Wood, Mrs Viney, X, Mrs
Annie Marsh, X (Front row) Mrs Siddell, Mrs Bertha Rouse, X, X, Mrs Ellison, Mrs
Fidler, Mrs Bagshaw, Patsy Morrisey, Mrs Edith Marshall, X, Mrs Morrisey*

*Pantomime in Oker 'Hut', Christmas 1932/33
Joan Kenyon, Jean Smith, Barbara Barrow, Hilary Duke, Muriel Duke, Anne Ward,
Dulcie Ward, Margaret Wilson, Jean Kenyon*

Fancy dress in the Oker Institute c1937
(Back row l-r) Mrs Lucy Siddall, Miss Walker, Ethel Hole (nee Wright), Mrs Norah
Bark, Mrs Ward, Muriel Duke, X, X, X, (Front row) X, Zoe Bark, Hilary Duke, X, X,
Sybil Watson, Mrs Watson, X

Wensley Red Stars football team (formerly 'The Wuffits') 1921-22 season
(Back row l-r) Herbert Chell, Cyril Taylor, Doug Marsden, Reg Boden, Steve Riley,
Fred Walker, Stanley Stone, Jim Wood (Front row) Wilfred Taylor, Cyril Flint, Billy
Chell, Roy Gillatt, Jack Boden

served and in the evening displays of folk dancing were given by South Darley Women's' Institute team and the North Darley Girls' Friendly Society. Mrs. Minnie Potter was the accompanist and £14 was raised. If 1938/39 is anything to go by, many happy hours had been spent in the old First World War army hut, throughout the inter war years.

Wensley Reading Room, provided in 1892 by local man 'made good' and parish benefactor, Manchester brewer Joseph Taylor, was an outlet for men and youths. Joseph Taylor also provided land for the graveyard at St. Mary's in 1890, helped to provide for the extension of the parish school in 1892 and built Oaker Terrace and Eagle Terrace in the early 1890's, the latter named after Taylor's 'Eagle Brewery'. In winter, a great roaring fire welcomed members to the Reading Room, where they came to play billiards, dominoes or cards, whilst a substantial library of books and newspapers were available, supervised by librarian Joe Slack. Newsagent Jack Masters was Chairman of the Committee for a number of years and Council roadman George Tomlinson was Secretary.

Meanwhile, the youths within South Darley could work off excess energy during the winter months by competing for Wensley Red Stars Football Team against opposition from as far afield as Brassington. Formerly known as the 'Wensley Wuffits', their home matches were played in the field behind the Red Lion Inn, next to the reservoir. Herbert 'Starr' Marshall, cab proprietor of Cross Green, provided horse drawn wagons to take the team to away matches in the early 1920's but by the late 1920's motorised transport had taken over.

NEW ENTERPRISES AND OLD HOSTELRIES

Engines required maintenance and mention has been made earlier to the garage of George Cooper at Darley Bridge during the 1930's, on the approximate site of present day 'Waters Transport'. A garage has therefore been on this site for seventy years. Whilst visiting friends in the parish, George Andrew Cooper met the sister of Ben Clay's wife,

George Cooper's garage at Darley Bridge during mid 1930's. Jim Hardy, Frank Hodgkinson, George Cooper

married her and settled down in South Darley. He was an excellent mechanic and for awhile he worked on Ben Clay's Morris Commercial lorry and taxi.

George then started up a business of his own in a small garage at the top of Wensley. Just beyond the Red Lion Inn and Keswick Cottage is a stile leading down into Wensleydale, and by the road side a concrete base was laid and corrugated iron shed built, in which George serviced the few local cars. His own vehicle was a M.G. sports car named 'Will of the Wisp', with leather belts strapped over the bonnet.

Steam lorry crash at Darley Bridge, September 1929

A few years later he moved to Darley Bridge and Herbert Fidler built a large garage for him, from where he ran a small fleet of lorries and serviced other vehicles. Jim Hardy and Frank Hodgkinson were employed as drivers.

When George Cooper fell

into financial difficulties, George William Hothesall, from Sheffield, who had retired to Number 6, Oker Road, put money into the garage, which was re-named Cooper and Hothesall. George Hothesall also ran an Austin taxi from his Oker Road home and eventually bought George Cooper out in the late 1930's.

Nowadays, the old bridge over the Derwent at this spot seems to be damaged by passing lorries every few months, but it is interesting to note that the first such incident happened on the 24th September 1929 when a steam tipper lorry from Mill Close with gravel on board, destined for Manchester, failed to negotiate the bend and crashed through the parapet. An unsuccessful attempt was made to haul it out with horses from Gregory's wood yard but eventually Twiggs from Matlock were called to winch it out with steel cables.

The early 1930's were the 'Depression' years, with industry in the doldrums, and yet house building appears to have been a 'boom industry'. This is borne out if we look in particular at several parts of South Darley.

Flint Lane witnessed the construction of Cross Green Cottages by Tom Wright, coal merchant, in 1929, and in 1932/33 Herbert Fidler began to build the houses opposite Oker Chapel, including a shop for his brother-in-law, Joe Marsh, with Joe and council roadman George Tomlinson providing labour in their spare time during the evenings.

The appearance of South Darley was changed considerably when Alfred Smith employed R.A. Twyford, house builders from Two Dales,

to start construction of the houses on Eversleigh Rise, using Stancliffe Stone. The first villa was completed in 1934. This development resulted in the demolition of Bank House Cottages, three old cottages set well back from the road, opposite Bank House. Ernest Allen , nursery-

Construction of the bottom villa on Eversleigh Rise in 1934

51

man at James Smith's nurseries lived at the top cottage, Joe Needham, mine deputy, in the middle one and Stephen Wagstaffe, cart driver for Alfred Smith at the bottom cottage.

The four villas at the bottom of the hill were built first and then the rest of the development in stages, but when Twyfords ran short of money, Wildgooses of Matlock had to complete the job. At roughly the same time, Alfred Smith started on the construction of St. Mary's View, whilst Herbert Fidler began work on the pebble-dashed houses nearby. We can see therefore, that between 1929 and 1936 sixty-one houses had been constructed in a sparsely populated parish, changing dramatically the visual impact in the space of seven years.

New housing certainly brought fresh blood into the parish, but the long established hostelries of the Three Stags Head, The Crown Inn, Red Lion and Square and Compass still catered for the liquid needs of

In front of the Red Lion, mid 1920's
(Back row l-r) Fred Bishton, X, John Devaney (cobbler), Mrs Cauldwell (landlady),
Alec Wood, X, X (Front row) Jack Hallam, Len Riley, George Eaton, Billy Masters

their regulars. We have already visited Harry Martin at the Square and Compass, but at the top of Wensley, Jess Cauldwell was landlord of the Red Lion Pub, after arriving in 1924 to take over from George Degge.

Jesse was also a farmer, whose wife looked after the inn. He ran a butcher's business and the horse and trap would be taken to Chesterfield market by Mrs. Caudwell on a Saturday, where she sold meat from a stall. The pub was old fashioned, with hessian mats on the floor along with the traditional spittoon, and it smelt of the farmyard. Inside Mrs. Caudwell's kitchen, the farmyard hens wandered around and found inconvenient places to lay their eggs. The Red Lion was a Free House, with the legend of fine beer and a plentiful supply.

Working for Jesse Cauldwell on the farm was a well-known South Darley character by the name of 'Little Roger', a tiny person who worked all hours for the Cauldwells and slept out in the barn. He was believed to have come from a Manchester orphanage, Crumsel Workhouse, and was an affable person, though sometimes teased by the local lads. George Oliver, or "Little Roger", was a hard working farmhand, clothes often caked in 'cow muck' and smelling of the same. Everyone who remembers 'Little Roger' remarks about his speciality of 'singing for a pint'. He had quite a good singing voice and whether in the local pubs he visited or in people's homes, he would be asked to perform his party pieces such as 'Isle of Capri'. By the end of the evening he would often be drunk and start wending his way back to the Red Lion cow barn, his home in Wensley.

Crown Inn c1926
X, Florence Ellen Briggs (landlady),
Sybil Marsden, X

The Cauldwells seemed to have a policy of 'Open all hours', as did the landlady at the Crown Inn from 1921, Mrs. Florence Briggs. It was in the upstairs Lodge Room of the Crown Inn that the Royal Jubilee Lodge of the Manchester Unity of Odd Fellows met, and sales of ale were plentiful on such occasions.

A tale, with possible embellishments, is told of Wensley drinking companions, Alec Wood, Joe Slack and Arthur Devereux setting off to enjoy the conviviality of Bonsall Wakes. Having washed down a few draughts of Bonsall's finest ale they arrived at a competition comprising an upright greasy pole with a large ham tied to the top. After one or two unsuccessful attempts at claiming the ham, they thought better of such unrewarding methods and returned some time later with a hatchet. As they attempted to chop the pole down, they were taken away before any real damage could be done.

Joseph William Marsden, landlord of the Three Stags Head 1923-1930

Joseph William Marsden arrived from Sheffield as landlord of the Three Stags Head, Darley Bridge, in 1923, with his wife Sarah and family, and ran the pub for seven years. The tenancy did not always provide a sufficient living and Joe therefore took on a second job as game keeper for the Davie Thornhills on Stanton Estate, where he was also in charge of the trout hatchery, producing fish to stock the local rivers.

In 1930, Walter Stevens took over the tenancy and Joe Marsden went to live with his wife at Oaker View, next to Sammy 'Fishy' Riley. Walter Stevens had lost a leg during the Great War. His son, Wally, was deaf and dumb, whilst his wife was never seen inside the pub itself because she was also deaf. Instead, her sister, Miss Walker, lived with them and helped Walter run the establishment.

FARMING CHANGES

Drink of a non-intoxicating nature could be provided from many quarters within South Darley, for supplies of milk were required daily. The larger farms sent most of their milk to the city dairies in churns but at Wensley, milk could be bought from Frank Hardy of Thorntree House, whilst mole catcher George Diamond Stewardson kept a few

cows for milking as did Robert Fawley across the road from Field Farm and Tom Wigley of Eagle Terrace kept animals on land near Gurdhall. Frank Hardy was still walking around Wensley during the 1930's carrying milk in two buckets suspended from a yoke slung across his shoulders and Grace Greatorex from Oker was doing the same in the late 1920's.

James Tissington Trickett and wife Mary,
in 1948

However, changes were taking place in the supply of milk in the 1930's when we look at the modernisation taking place on the farm of James Tissington Trickett at Eversleigh House, Cross Green. James Trickett was a gentleman farmer who had occupied Cowley Hall, South Darley, in the early 1920's. By 1928 he had moved to Eversleigh House to start farming after the Sleighs left South Darley. He carried on the Sleigh's tradition of offering his gardens for Church fetes and other fund raising events.

A large orchard of apple and pear trees, together with barns converted into farm buildings, were surrounded by a high wall running the length of Flint Lane and round Kirby Lane, from Eversleigh House to Eversleigh Cottage. Mr Trickett was a good-natured man who, on occasions, would stand near the school with a basket of fruit and offer them to the children. Mr. Sheldon of Eversleigh Cottage acted as farm bailiff.

It was in the selling of milk, however, that James Trickett began to

Express Dairy lorries near Rowsley sidings in 1930's

The Wain family haymaking in Wensley Dale in the 1920's

'move with the times'. By 1936 he had introduced a small glass bottling plant in one of the farm buildings, each bottle capped with a cardboard tag. Crates of milk were sold on Eversleigh Rise and children at Cross Green School drank Trickett's milk before the start of the Second World War. This operation contrasted sharply with the yoke and ladle method of distributing milk.

For farmers such as Joe Hardy at Green Farm, Joe and Ethel Clay at Field Farm, Joe Greatorex at Lobby Farm and Tom Wigley near Gurdhall, farming was at a low point during the late 1920's and early 1930's.

In 1928, the farms and land belonging to Snitterton Hall were sold and split up, with Joe Greatorex coming to live at Lobby Cottage (later Farm) and renting 90 acres with hay barns and stirk sheds. His brother Arthur stayed with their mother Grace at Oker, and whilst Joe earned extra money working at Constable Harts Quarry, Matlock, Arthur worked on the farm. Joe's son, Ron, remembers that their first horse was called 'Owd Joe', a commandeered war-horse from the Great War that had once pulled gun carriages.

During these years, South Darley farmers found it difficult to sell all their milk and would either send it to the cheese factory at Gratton, near Elton, during the summer months, feed it to the pigs and beef calves or sell it to local households in the parish. The salvation for all the local farmers was the setting up of the Milk Marketing Board in 1933/34 and Tom Smith at Oker Farm could take it by lorry to Sheffield Coop Dairy or George Siddall and Shirley and Proctor delivered it to the Express Dairy at Rowsley.

Left: Frank Ernest Hardy, Wensley milkman
Right: Burley Derbyshire, farmhand for the Hardy's

Joseph Hardy had arrived at Wensley from Chesterfield in 1930 to take over Green Farm after the death of his uncle, whilst his brother Frank looked after the milk round. Dairy cattle and beef animals were kept, with some land near the farm ploughed for oats and hay. At harvest time there were always four or five large stacks built on the Green.

Wensley hillside was a difficult area for providing water for the cattle and they therefore used water from the local mineshafts. A large ten-gallon corn bin was transported to the hillside and water was drawn up from the bottom of the shaft by means of an old-fashioned horse gin, operated by turning a wheel. The shaft was 65 feet deep with another 65 feet of water at the bottom, and when tested, the water was found to be free of lead. Frank kept his cattle for milking on the Barnyard Field and Barley Close and the two brothers, together with their farmhand 'Burley' Derbyshire, helped each other in their farming and milking operations.

Meanwhile, at Flatts Farm, Darley Bridge, Arthur Gadsby arrived from Brailsford with this family in March 1938, bringing with them two or three cattle, that were eventually built up to a dairy herd of 45 animals. As they moved in, the Square and Compass Inn was being refurbished for the new tenant, George Hodgkinson, after the death of Harry Martin.

Three horses were used on the land before the first tractor was used in 1950 and hand milking lasted until the late 1940's. At harvest and threshing time, Mrs. Gadsby catered for up to 17 men for dinner, including those farm hands lent by other farmers, and apple pie or jam roly poly was served first as the main course, to stop the men eating too much dinner. The tractor and threshing drum came from Slaters at Winster. All the haystacks were thatched and the finishing touches were almost like works of art.

Another farmer, Tom Wigley, lived at Eagle Terrace during the 1930's and kept dairy cattle on rented land near Gurdhall, on the Winster road, supplying milk to the locals. However, he also acted as a carter and one necessary but unpleasant task was to take away the 'night soil', mixed with ash and cinders from the earth closets of the Wensley residents. It was shovelled into his cart and taken to the main rubbish tip for Wensley, on Wigley's land between Gurdhall and Clough View, or to the tip at Lumb Ditch, between Lumb Cottages and the top house on Eversleigh Rise. Both tips were colonised by large numbers of rats. In the days before such collections were made, the 'night soil' was simply buried in each resident's garden.

Farming on a smaller scale, in order to provide milk for local people, was undertaken by George Diamond Stewardson from Toll Bar Hill. He was the well-known molecatcher, whose expertise with his small mole catching spade was appreciated on farms and estates at Chatsworth and as far north as Millers Dale. He kept about ten cows for milking on twenty acres of land known as Thunderpits Farm, with a hay barn and shed for hand milking, in fields between Wensley and St. Mary's Church.

Molecatcher George Diamond Stewardson with moling spade under arm

Ploughing late 1920's between Gas Cottages and present day Hooley's Estate

Right: Wensley farmer Joe Clay of Field Farm with Reg Boden's son Raymond about 1935, next to Oker Road

Below: Harvesting near St Elphin's School in late 1920's

WENSLEY HALL

Possibly the most imposing building in Wensley was the Hall and in the late 1920's it was the home of Mrs. Edith Marshall and her husband, Arthur. She was the daughter of Sydney Bowman, a member of the well-known Quaker family of Monyash. She was born at Monyash, but at

Wensley Hall, home of Mrs Marshall, and from 1933 Wensley Hall Guest House run by Mr and Mrs Bowser

the age of six the family moved to Yorkshire for the next thirteen years before arriving at Wensley Hall in 1900.

Edith had a strict upbringing but she was lively and had strong determination. In 1907, at the age of 26, she eloped to get married to Arthur Marshall, a man 34 years her senior, but eventually she became reconciled with her father, Sydney. It had been in 1916, during the desperate days of the First World War, that Sydney Bowman travelled to France in his car and offered both himself and the vehicle for

Mrs E.H.M. Marshall

ambulance duty, just before the Quakers organised their own ambulance service. During his time near the front line, his car was twice damaged by shellfire and forced off the road.

The Marshalls lived at Wensley Hall until the early 1930's, when they had Garden Cottage built and rented the Hall to the Bowser family. Newly widowed in 1934, Mrs Marshall was always busy. She had already started a poultry farm in the field across the road from the Hall and also in her orchard, where hundreds of birds were kept.

61

The eggs were pickled and sold to the Matlock catering firm of Moore's Bakery on Dale Road.

Within a short time of the Hall being advertised, Eric and Muriel

Wensley Hall Guest House
Top: Eric and Muriel Bowser seated to the right with friends and guests 1934
Left: Eric and Muriel on their wedding day in 1933
Middle: Eric Bowser
Right: Ruth and Eleanor Bowser with greengrocer Len Riley's horse 'Dolly'

Bowser arrived in the village to begin a new venture, Wensley Hall GuestHouse. Muriel had recently returned from Madagascar, where she had been headmistress of a school and Eric had been deputy head-teacher of a private boy's school in England. Both were out of work when plans were being made for their wedding in Liverpool in 1932. They answered the advertisement about the Hall and Muriel attended a short catering course in preparation for the new experience.

Instead of a honeymoon, they set off for Wensley on motorbike and sidecar and were soon involved in catering for the needs of their new guests. They had met in earlier times whilst attending Holiday Fellowship gatherings in the Lake District, with Eric leading the walks throughout mountain and lakeside scenery and Muriel acting as a hostess. They now attempted to bring the tone of such Fellowship holidays into their own Wensley setting. Many friends and acquaintances had been made by Eric and Muriel in their visits to the Lake District and these people would often come to stay as paying guests in this beautiful region of Derbyshire.

As many as twelve guests had the freedom to roam the countryside by themselves or go on guided walks, but would meet during the evening meal and socialise as a group. The Silver Service bus route was often taken to places such as Birchover or Youlgreave and a stimulating walk would return the guests to the friendly atmosphere of the Hall. Eventually, Eric replaced the motor bike with a car and was able to collect guests from either Darley or Matlock stations. Meanwhile on Sundays, a room at the Guest House became a Quaker meeting room, for both Eric and Muriel were members of the Society of Friends.

DISASTERS AND LOSS

Meanwhile, the years 1936, 1937 and 1938, which led inexorably towards war on the international scene, saw disaster and problems rear their heads locally, especially at nearby Mill Close lead mine, the largest provider of jobs in the area. In 1937, Bert Boam and Jim Wood were working on a top ledge of the 129 fathom level, whilst down below them, Harold Mayall and Vic Littlewood were loading a wagon with the broken ore. Without warning, a huge slab of the roof crashed down onto Harold and Vic, with Harold being killed instantly. Vic Littlewood, though injured, was protected by a projecting rock.

Joe Needham, the deputy, was brought to the scene and asked for volunteers to uncover Vic. Vernon Wild of Winster and Bert Boam began the task of picking the rocks from off the injured man. Harold Mayall was carried out first. Vic was tied to a plank with fuse wire, taken to the shaft and placed into the cage in an upright position. Lifted to the 70-fathom level, he was then taken by locomotive to the main shaft. When he recovered some months later, Vic was set to work on the surface.

In 1936, flooding from the Pilhough Fault had occurred at Mill Close, causing many miners to be laid off for several weeks, but the problem had been overcome. However, more depressing news came on Friday afternoon, 25th February 1938 when a shot, drilled by Fred Boam of Winster, blasted into the Pilhough Fault and an underground reservoir on the 144-fathom level. 500,000 gallons of water cascaded into the mine in two hours and the miners rushed to the surface, many only just escaping with their lives after the water level rose to their chins.

Sometime later, two employees of the mine were rewarded with bravery certificates and silver salvers by the Andrew Carnegie Hero Fund Trustees for the work they had performed in helping to rescue the underground workers. The account in the paper at the time reads:–

"Facing death amid rushing waters that threatened to sweep them away in the underground workings of a lead mine, Alexander McCall, mine surveyor, of Warren Carr, South Darley, and Ernest Devaney (son of former Wensley cobbler John Devaney) of Green Lane, Darley Dale, rescued many of their comrades.

Yesterday their heroism was recognised by the Carnegie Hero Fund Trustees in Dunfermline, who presented both men with an honorary certificate.

Water was pouring down a shaft at the rate of 20 tons per minute, to a level which contained a number of men and McCall was lowered 50 feet down this shaft. He located the trapped men and led them to safety by an alternative route, but he was severely injured in doing so.

Pumpman Ernest Devaney became anxious for the life of an isolated pump man at work 48 feet below the affected part. He went 2000 feet against the rush of water, which thrice swept him off his feet and with the aid of other miners was lowered to where the pump man continued at his post. Both were hauled to safety".

Some four hundred miners were laid off work and although through-out 1938 and 1939 many miners returned to work, this was really the beginning of the end. By June 1939 rumours abounded that the mine was to close, for the directors had made the decision to clear out the mine's remaining reserves and cease operations. This came about by June 1940 and after that only the surface plant was operated for the retreatment of residues of zinc in the surface tips. After six weeks of salvage operations deep underground, the mine finally closed in August 1940, and in 1941 was sold to its present owners, H.J. Enthoven and Sons Ltd. The treatment plant remained in use throughout the war, supported by the Ministry of Supply, but in 1945 was sold to Matlock steel merchants, William Twigg. The end of an era had come about in South Darley by 1940 as five centuries of lead mining in the Wensley area came to a close.

Another tragedy was only just avoided on the evening of Wednesday 4th May 1938 when John Gregory's timber yard, Victoria Sawmills, Old Road, was almost completely gutted and a neighbouring mill and petrol depot were in considerable danger in a disastrous and spectacular fire. Fourteen workmen left the premises at 5.00 p.m. but by 5.30 p.m. flames were noticed arising from a pile of wood in the yard. Matlock Brigade turned out in a few minutes but a large section of the yard and several buildings were alight, a mass of roaring flames. The Brigade tried to prevent flames spreading to the flour mill next door, which was formerly occupied by Bakelite Ltd. The wind was blowing 50 feet high flames in the direction of the buildings, and a few yards further away was the big petrol depot of Shell Mex Ltd., where about 60,000 gallons of petrol were stored. The fire brigade obtained a good supply of water from Warney Brook and soon after 7.00 p.m. the Chesterfield Brigade arrived. At the time of the fire an express train had passed by on the nearby railway and suggestions were made that a spark could have been the cause of the fire.

Smoking ruins of Gregory's Woodyard, Old Road, after disastrous fire on 4th May 1938

A sad loss was felt by South Darley parishioners with news of the death of their vicar, Reverend E.A. Hadfield on Saturday 16th January 1937 and his burial on the 19th January. Readers of 'A Derbyshire Parish of War – South Darley and the Great War 1914-1919' will have seen how strong a personality he was within the parish, especially in the dreadful years of the First World War. The vicar had arrived at St. Mary's in 1893 and was to be the incumbent for the following 43 years. When he first arrived at South Darley the church was lit by oil lamps and he installed first gas, then electricity.

A sad postscript to this loss was the news of the death of Ben Marsden (aged 51) of The Square, Wensley, on the afternoon of the vicar's funeral. Ben was cycling down Toll Bar Hill on his way to work as a shunter at Rowsley sidings when overtaken by another cyclist. The machines collided and both fell into the roadway, with Ben receiving a

Crown Inn, Wensley, 1937
L-r: Jim Wood, Mrs Briggs, X, Elsie Withey, Bill Taylor (carrying Jimmy), Arthur
Devereux, with Ken Marsden in the front

fractured skull. He was a prominent member of the Church choir and a few hours before the incident he had acted as a bearer at the funeral of Reverend Hadfield, after changing his shift at the sidings, for that purpose. Ben Marsden left a widow and three children.

Throughout the previous pages we have attempted to give a flavour of South Darley life between the wars through the lives of some of the main characters in the parish, including shopkeepers, innkeepers and farmers and by looking at a number of the organisations that played a crucial role in their day to day existence. However, for most adults in South Darley during this period, their lives revolved around the need to earn a living for themselves and their families. Except for the few who went to grammar school and on to higher education, the children of the parish left school at fourteen and had to 'grow up' very quickly. Money was scarce, and, as we shall see in the following chapter, a job was vital if the family was to survive.

Red Lion Inn, Wensley, 1937
Mrs Stone and son Graham, Jim Wood, Polly Flint, Joe Webster, Bill (Goff) Taylor,
George Farnell, Sarah Flint

Planting of tree on Oker Hill, Coronation Day, 12th May 1937
Back row l-r: Walter Marsden, Joe Wilmot, X, George Wood, Mrs Fidler, Barbara
Barrow, X, X, Mrs Wood, Mrs Seedhouse, Sam Edge, X, X, X, X, Mrs Duke, X, Muriel
Duke
Front row: Ron Greatorex, Norman Peach, George Wright, Ivan Greatorex, Grace
Greatorex, Dulcie Ward, Ann Ward, Joe Greatorex, Desmond Watson, Hilary Duke,
Jean Peach, X, Pauline Watson

Carnival time in 1930's at Matlock View Cottages, Wensley (now demolished)
Left: Gwen Masters, Joan Masters, Doreen Webster, Jim Taylor, Ciceley Wood, Emily
Wood Right: Ciceley Wood, Emily Wood, Jim Taylor, Jim Wood

CHAPTER TWO

EARNING A LIVING

When mention is made of the 1930's, thoughts immediately turn to the onset of the 'Depression'. As the bottom fell out of the Wall Street stock market of late 1929, investment faltered, people had less money to spend, factories lacking markets closed down, men were thrown out of work, and, unable to buy, helped to reduce demand still further. As people tightened their belts the farmers found that no one could afford to buy the food they had grown. Great Britain finally abandoned her policy of free trade. International trade virtually collapsed, whilst more factories, shipbuilding plants and industries were closed down and more men were thrown out of work.

However, in South and North Darley, although the farming economy was at a low ebb and more people than usual were out of work, the main ravages of the Depression Years that visited the industrial cities and ports did not strike such deadly blows in this mainly rural area.

South Darley and neighbouring parishes were fortunate to retain Mill Close Lead Mine as the largest employer of labour, whilst the numerous limestone and gritstone quarries required large numbers of manual workers to provide stone for the only business that was booming in the 1930's, the building industry. Meanwhile the L.M.S. activities at Rowsley Sidings were expanding and the old established nurseries of James Smiths and Sons still needed a substantial workforce. Although certain of these jobs were low paid, it was often possible to move from one to another as the need arose. For example, between 1917 and 1940 my uncle, Cyril Taylor, worked first at Mill Close, then at Twyfords, the Two Dales based house-builders, then spent a few years at Stancliffe Stone quarries before returning to Mill Close for its last nine years before flooding caused it to be closed.

If ever an employer provided a 'bridge' through the terrible trade slump of the 1930's it was MILL CLOSE LEAD MINE. Well over 600 employees were provided with a reasonable living for themselves and their dependants. In 1922 'Consolidated Goldfields' had taken a major interest and under that Company's expertise there was a large injection of capital, which allowed technical equipment to be updated. However, in the mid 1920's the mine was largely unchanged, with the three powerful steam engines, 'Jumbo', 'Baby' and 'Alice', still pumping out the vast amounts of water. Deep inside the mine, gantries or bridges were used to cross the cavities they found and hand haulage of wagons was still necessary in the upper levels of passageways, though at the 70 fathom level an electric battery locomotive was in use with batteries by the Bakewell D.P. Battery Company.

Between 1920 and 1929 dozens of minor joints and veins to the west of the main vein were worked, under and beyond the hamlet of Stanton Lees, where considerable amounts of ore were found.

There were three shifts running throughout each day of the week: 5.45 a.m. to 1.45 p.m., 1.45 p.m. to 9.45 p.m. and 9.45 p.m. to 5.45 a.m. The men would arrive at the stripping coe at Lees Shaft, next to the steam pump. Warm, hard wearing moleskin trousers, bought from the 'Army Stores' at Matlock Green, were often worn and a type of clog was much favoured by the miners. John Devaney, the cobbler at Wensley Square, would convert old boots by cutting off sections and attaching wooden soles, with clog nails and clippets added.

At the nearby office the head deputy sat at the open window, ready to hand out 5 tallow candles to each miner, a total of almost 2000 candles a day. Old candles were often used by miners to grease their clogs, whilst at 'snap time' a bottle of tea was laid over two stones and warmed by the flame of a candle flickering below. If work was to be done on the 62fathom level, safety lamps were handed out, for gas was a danger on this level. The paraffin lamp was often tied onto the end of a scarf and, when worn by inexperienced miners, it swung around and often went out. If they knocked '1,2,3,4,5,' on the air pipes running along the level, a person would come along to relight it.

The men would enter the cage, four at a time, and be lowered into the depths to the 70fathom level, where they walked a mile or so to some steps if they wished to get to the 62 level. Planks and steel loops supported the roof of the 70fathom level, leaving room for the locomotive to run. Riding on the loco was forbidden, although some drivers allowed men to ride in the tubs. The water would often be ankle or knee deep and when, at times, the pumps failed they could be walking chest deep through the level in order to get out.

Although the shifts were long, considerable amounts of time were spent walking to their places of work. It could be as much as two miles to the workplace, with winzes (shafts) to climb down and several hundred feet to climb up, and this journey had to be repeated at the end of the shift. On most levels, the only lighting was at the bottom of the shafts, otherwise it was dark.

Some of the best miners worked as 'developers', driving a tunnel for exploration or shafts to open out the ore bodies, using Ingersoll drills. The holes were charged with dynamite and the safety fuse lit. One such 'firer' was Ben Walker of St. Mary's View. After the explosion an air hose was left open in the heading a while to clear the fumes and 'snap' time was taken by the driller and his mate.

The fallen ore could either be brought down into a chute, to be fed under gravity to tubs in the haulage level, or to the ground for hard shovelling. Such work could be precarious, for the men were standing high in the roof on a single plank. Later, in the life of the mine, the work was very simple in the large cavities on the 129 fathom level, where picks were used to break the ore before shovelling it into tubs. It was still dangerous work, though, for there was great pressure on the heavy cross-timbers supporting the toadstone roof.

Wagoners on the 62 level pushed their small wagon loads of lead and stone to a chute and tipped it down to the 70 fathom level, where it was taken by the locomotive, often driven by George Harrison of Darley Bridge, to the main upshaft. Sometimes the little wagons came off the rails and the men could hardly manage between them to lift them back up.

Some of the toughest and most skilled jobs were connected with the sinking of shafts or equipping them with timber for compartments and cage guides. The main winding shaft was timbered by George Shimwell of 4 Oker Road. For young lads fresh from school, however, there was still plenty of hard work on the picking belt at the surface dressing plant, picking out the stone from the lead ore, before moving on later to underground work.

It seems that although parts of the mine were affected by gas, there was a relatively free and easy attitude towards smoking. Safety lamps were carried in the upper workings but on lower levels candles were used and safety fuses lit by matches for blasting. Maybe because of this, smoking of cigarettes was not unknown, by any means. Miners sometimes 'lit up', for they could always tell when a deputy was coming in the darkness, for he always carried an electric torch. They quickly extinguished their cigarettes and deputy Joe Needham of Darley Bridge, who was like a father to many of those on his shift, would remark, 'What a nice scent you are wearing!'"

By 1929 most of the ore had been exploited and if the mine was to continue working profitably it was necessary to sink a shaft (winze) at the northern end of the workings on the 70 fathom level. Old Mill Close miners considered it wise to follow water, believing it led to the next ore-rich area. At this northern end of the workings a strong flow of water had emerged and a decision was taken to sink at the "boil up", as it was called, to the 103 fathom level and levels 84 and 93 fathoms soon found rich ore. Eventually, more levels were developed down to 144 fathoms. However, the water problem increased and electric pumps had to be installed, with only the old 'Baby' and 'Alice' steam pumps remaining on standby.

The appearance of the mine changed as two 500 ton steel bins were erected high above the buildings situated over the Jumbo engine house and shaft, one being used for Haddon ore and one for Stanton. Mill Close was mined under land belonging to Stanton and Haddon Estates, each being paid a royalty of £1 per ton. The wagoners below ground had to put special sticks in each wagon, marking under whose land the material had been mined, showing whether it was connected to the Davie-Thornhills or Haddon Hall. Some of the sticks had been bounced out of the wagons by the time they reached the surface and the miners had to guess which sticks to put back in.

Jumbo shaft was refitted to allow the cages to bring up material from the 70 fathom level, whilst Lees Shaft was now used only for man winding and some equipment. On the 129 fathom level a main cavern was found four hundred feet long, forty feet high and 100 feet wide containing not only deposits of lead but considerable amounts of zinc blend, enough to make recovery a profitable matter. As a result of this a flotation process was added to the dressing plant on the surface. Mill Close Lead Mine had become by far the most modern lead mine in existence in the country. This development and modernisation, took place between 1929 and 1935, at the height of the 'Depression Years' and enabled many families in South Darley and surrounding areas to be shielded from the worst aspects of lack of work and pay.

Jumbo engine house at Mill Close Lead Mine

Although QUARRYING was generally less highly paid than lead mining and had the drawback of workers being laid off during extremely cold and frosty periods, it

Working on the surface 1930. Bill Blackham, Arthur Vardy, Herbert Heathcote, Bert Webster, Les Flint, Thomas Webster, Chris Stone, Harry Taylor

Waiting to go underground at Lees shaft during the 1930's

still provided regular employment for many people in the area and it was always reassuring to hear the hooter sounding lunch break from Stancliffe Stone Quarry yard, at Darley Dale. Numerous other smaller operators were quarrying in the 1920's and 1930's, for this was a period of rapid house building development and stone was obtained from Knab Quarry (Sydnope Hill, Two Dales), Farley, Stanton, Birchover and the Matlock quarries. Virtually all South Darley quarrymen worked for Stancliffe Quarries or at the Matlock quarries.

Leadminers at Jumbo engine house late 1920's
Back row: Harry Walker, Jim Taylor
Front: Percy Boam, Isaiah Walters

Quarrying in the 1920's and 1930's was still labour intensive and provided work for many people at Stancliffe. The scene in the 1930's was certainly very different from that of today. In 1897 Stancliffe Estates Limited had been formed and its owners decided to extract the large gritstone outcrop north-east of the A6, north of Church Lane, by connecting the quarry workings with the main line of the Midlands Railway by means of a three mile long standard gauge railway track. A small sidings had already been constructed in 1848 opposite the Church Inn. It was always stated by the Stancliffe Company that quarried stone could be loaded in the yard and off-loaded at its destination with no intermediate handling.

This branch line passed by the present day Broad Meadow Sheltered Housing Complex, passing underneath the A6 road by what is now called 'Twiggs Tunnel', a pedestrian subway, and then running in what used to be a cutting behind Peakland View and under a small footway bridge into the Stancliffe masonry yard. Passing through Stancliffe Yard buildings (now Molyneux Engineering Works) to cross Whitworth Road and travel along what is now Sir Joseph's Lane, the line eventually reached the Stancliffe Stone Quarry area. At Stancliffe Yard, near the footbridge, another line ran up the hillside to Halldale Quarry. This line was used for the disposal of waste stone. Round the area still known as the "Tipping", three spurs allowed the whole area to be covered with stone. This was later taken over by the Council, thinly covered with soil and used as a recreation area. At the top of the "Tipping", a junction near the bottom of Moor Lane allowed the line to climb 200 feet in half a mile on an embankment, and cross Hallmoor Road into Hallmoor Quarry, from where the famous pink sandstone could be obtained.

In both quarries, cranes for loading huge blocks of stone onto flat trucks for transport to the yard, were placed along the track. The yard itself was dominated by two large steam cranes, one of which was operated by Doug Marsden of 8 Oker Road, South Darley. Building stone, pavers, pulp stones, cut stone and ornamental stonework were produced and used in all the major cities and towns of the United Kingdom as well as abroad. Building sand and grit was produced for the building trade by a huge crusher at the entrance of Stancliffe Quarry, whilst one of the first artificial stones, 'Stancrete' was developed and used to build the shops at Broadwalk, Darley Dale.

Two brown painted saddle tank engines operated on the line, one called 'Henry Dawson' and the other 'Sir Joseph Whitworth', whilst a loco called 'Canada was used when the others were being repaired. Four empty trucks could be hauled up to Hall dale and two fully loaded ones brought down. However, by 1936 the Halldale Quarry was nearly worked out and it became clear that the two engines could not be maintained for much longer. Before the war began in 1939 the track was dismantled and the engines replaced by lorries until the quarry closed in 1977. I can still remember, however, the old lines sunk into the tarmac of the Halldale road in the late 1950's.

Stancliffe Quarries was of course a large quarrying company and yet in the first few years of the 1930's a number of much smaller quarries, each employing a handful of men, could be found in the Darley area and a good example was Knabb Quarry, on Sydnope Hillside, Two Dales. From 1930 it was rented by the Pearson family, Ben and his two sons Harry and Harold, from Park Lane, Two Dales, and worked from 1931 to about 1936/37. Before 1914 their father, Ben, had worked at Knabb for Mr. Palmer, together with many other quarrymen. At that time, it was commonplace for two men to come down the hill to one of the three pubs in the area to collect a barrel of beer and roll it uphill to the quarry where they were sometimes joined by the women from nearby Loskar Row. A tune would be struck up by Tommy Norton on his accordion and impromptu dancing took place in the quarry bottom.

In 1931 pulp stones for the wood pulping mills of Scandinavia were obtained and grind stones (needle stones of up to four feet) were sent to Sheffield. Ben and Harold got the stone out and cut it up and then it was turned over to Harry for dressing. Everything was done by hand and a pulp stone of up to 6 feet in diameter could be got out, dressed and a hole put in it within 3 days.

Ben and his sons often used to go to the quarry at 3 in the morning and finish at 1 in the afternoon to miss the heat of the summer afternoons. The brothers related that quarrymen at Stancliffe and Halldale also followed this practice. The Pearsons took their 'snap' with them but Mrs. Ada Pearson would always bring them their hot dinner in enamel pots. Harry would meet her at the bottom of Sydnope Hill. She would eat with them and then collect eggs from 200 hens that they kept below the quarry.

Knabb Quarry stone matched up with good Stancliffe Stone, with a colouring of white, brown and pink. Some of the other quarry stones were pink and mottled and stained the paper. Buyers knew where to get the various colours and qualities when they arrived every Spring and Autumn. One such buyer was Mr. N.A. Eie who came from Norway and always stayed at the Peacock Hotel at Rowsley.

The stone from Knabb went to Darley Station whilst Farley stone was transported to Matlock. Upto the late 1920's, local farmers such as

Industry Exhibition Showground at Stanley Park, Blackpool 1929 showing Stancliffe Quarry Estates stand

Stancliffe Stone Yard. Pulp stones being loaded for Norway. Locomotive (0-4-0 saddle tank) Henry Dawson or Sir Joseph Whitworth is in the bottom right hand corner

Stancliffe Stone Yard c1920. Locomotive Henry Dawson or Sir Joseph Whitworth in the distance

Knabb Quarry, Two Dales, in 1930's showing Harry and Harold Pearson

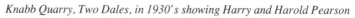

the Wagstaffes came to take the stone to the Station yard on horses and drugs (flat carts). A 'slipper' (steel cup) slung beneath the cart, was used to hold the cart back whilst travelling down Sydnope Hill, digging up the road in a dreadful way and causing a screaming sound that reverberated across the valley. By the late 1920's and into the 1930's lorries were being used. However, by the end of 1936 there was a downturn in the trade in stone with Scandinavia and the Pearson brothers finished at Knabb. Harry transferred to Stancliffe stone masons yard and then to Twyfords Quarry, Birchover. Harold went to Wildgooses Quarry at Lumsdale and eventually Harry joined him.

Meanwhile ROWSLEY SIDINGS was another important outlet for employment in the district. In 1849 the line to Rowsley from Derby was officially opened and by 1867 the line was opened from Derby to Manchester and became the Midlands trunk route from London and the Midlands to the Northwest. The Derbyshire and Nottinghamshire coal-fields used the line to send its coal to the industrial centres and ports west of the Pennines, whilst northern industries used it as an outlet to the south for their industrial products and imports.

By 1874 the present Darley Dale station and additional sidings had been built and became an important dispatching point for local stone and timber. After the Great War passenger traffic increased rapidly to almost 200 per weekday per year. Most journeys were local but an increasing number of passengers travelled regularly to Derby from the early 1920's. By 1935 there were ten down and eleven up trains calling at Derby per weekday, two in each direction being Derby-Manchester bound.

However, it was Rowsley Sidings that had become the largest employer of railway men in the locality. The opening of the line through to Manchester resulted in an increase in traffic and the need for assisting engines as far as Peak Forest. The depot was considerably enlarged in 1878 by the addition of a new shed. Freight traffic increased in the early 1870's and needed to be sorted out before climbing over the Peak. Rowsley was the most suitable site for such sidings and in March 1877 the sidings were opened for traffic. There was a marked increase in the number of men employed there and work was begun on the blocks of cottages and by 1898 the housing stock in Rowsley had increased by a half in 12 years. A new signal-box, the busiest on the Derby – Manchester line, was opened in June 1915 and in 1924 a main shed building was completed to provide a new motive power depot at Rowsley.

Locomotive servicing was now dealt with and new sidings opened in 1929 which allowed standing room for an extra 193 wagons plus space for 33 crippled wagons. One siding served the Express Dairy and was opened in 1933, with space for a milk cooling depot, spray, pond condenser and filter plant. In the first year of operation the carriage value of milk from Rowsley was £16886, with milk tanks attached to the 5.18 p.m. local to Derby for Cricklewood, or the 10.15 p.m. express to Brent.

Rowsley had now become one of the most important locations on the L.M.S., for much of the freight from the Midlands and the South East to the Northwest was sent over the Peak. 17,000 wagons per week passed through the yard. Loaded minerals were sorted on the downside and empties on the up, during the day, and merchandise on both sides during the night. The modern engine shed was designed to accommodate 60 locomotives and was fully equipped with offices, stores and accommodation, enabling engines to move to and from the yard without using the main line, and rapid turn round times were achieved daily. With this development during the 1930's, more opportunities for employment locally on the railways was provided for the people in the nearby parishes, including South Darley, where, for example, the young Ron Allen from Eversleigh Rise secured a job as a fireman.

In the 1920's there were seven NURSERYMEN and market gardeners in and around Darley Dale, employing a considerable number of local people, and all of these Nurseries made use of the railway. The largest of these was the firm of James Smith and Sons, Darley Dale Nurseries, established at Darley in 1827. Nowadays, the only connection with this industry is the fine garden centre of Forest

10.52 Toton to Rowsley
Mineral train passing through Darley Dale Station on 29th September 1938
From ER Morton collection

9.46 Chinley to Darley slow passenger train enters Darley Dale Station. Note in the
background, wagon standing in Stancliffe private sidings
From ER Morton collection

8.15pm Rowsley to Chadderton freight train at Church Lane crossing, Darley Dale on 14th September 1957

From ER Morton collection

North end of Rowsley Shed 27th June 1957 with engines waiting for turn of duty

From ER Morton collection

Women workers recruited for loco cleaners during WW2
Back row, l-r: Madge Wilmot, Rose Mackley, Dorris Holmes, Harriet Pinder, Pat
Esplin, Doris Rudd, Daphne Evans, Mrs Evans, ? Boden
Front row: Epzilan Parkey, Annie Hiden, Doris Wager, O Fearn, Jack Hibbs, Edna
Watkin, Celia Middleton, Madge Elliot, E Boam
From Henry Marsden

Earlier days at Darley Dale Station Yard. Tom Wright's coal cart.

Nurseries, Darley Dale, Ltd, run by the great grandchildren of Matthew Smith, a relative of James, who broke away from the family firm, and set up his own business at Sydnope.

James Smith and Sons Nurseries covered 250 acres and some of this was over 1100 feet above sea level. One of these nurseries, on account of its exposure was named Siberia and its stock was as hardy as could possibly be obtained, devoted to rhododendrons, hardy heaths and American plants.

A large staff of men and boys budded and grafted, hoed and weeded in various quarters of the scattered nurseries. Spacious packing sheds were built near Wheatley Road, Two Dales, where all trees and shrubs were unloaded and packed undercover. The firm supplied the British monarch, Kew, The Royal Botanic Gardens in Edinburgh and Dublin and numerous customers abroad.

The nurseries were especially famous for the cultivation of hardy heathers, including the lucky white Scotch heather. Tons of blooms were dispatched each year to all corners of the United Kingdom and to America. Siberia, about 100 acres in extent, was the largest of fourteen branches of the nurseries. The other 13 branches were named Home, Siberia North, Canada, Butcher's Lane, Station, Churchtown, Hall Moor, Bent, Hill Top, Wheatley Roundhills, Willsitch and Hall Dale nurseries. Land was difficult to obtain in the neighbourhood and so areas varying in size were taken as they fell vacant.

James Smith grew heathers specifically for use in the packing of iron tubes and pipes for safe transit. Large amounts were sent in sheeted wagons from Darley Dale Station to Stanton Iron Works and wagon loads of spent hops came into Darley sidings from various breweries, ready for composting and being used as a fertiliser.

Also very close to Darley Dale Station and sidings was JOHN GREGORY, TIMBER MERCHANTS at Victoria Mill, along Old Road. The owner was John Gregory, or 'Honest John', who got his nickname, the story says, when on one occasion whilst felling a large stand of trees, he had a contract that he would pay when he had removed the last tree. The story goes on to relate that he never removed it and so he

James Smith and Sons, Wheatley Nursery, growing heather

never paid. He had arrived at Darley from Tansley at the turn of the 20th century to set up a bone-pulping mill and saw mill. John Gregory employed a considerable number of men in his timber yard, including in the 1920's Tom Evans from 3 Oker Road.

Travelling bands of men would be sent to fell trees that had been purchased over a wide area of the West Midlands, especially in the Ashbourne, Hardwick Woods and Hardwick areas. They would travel with horse and carts and be billeted in local farms in the area. Timber was taken to the nearest local station by the gangs, where it would be

Consignment leaving Darley Dale Nurseries for Germany

Gregory's Victoria Saw Mill, Old Road, Darley Dale c1910. These buildings were destroyed by fire in 1938. Joe Senior, S Middleton, J Burnett, X, J Bucontez, J Jenkins, JW Gregory (son of owner)

Gregory's Saw Mill c1920. John Gregory ('Honest John') in bowler hat, Tom Evans (Wensley) 2nd from right, front row

Timber for Gregory's Wood Yard 1920's. In the sidings at Wingerworth Junction, near Clay Cross

Gregory's woodmen getting timber from Ashover Butts area 1920's

Wingerworth Sidings February 1924

sent to Darley Dale Station for seasoning and cutting. Everything over 9 miles away, the distance a horse could deliver and return in a day, was sent by rail and the station master would visit John Gregory each day to see how many rail-wagons would be required. The timber yard supplied pit props to collieries over a wide area, and wood to wagon builders, house builders and joiners.

Next door neighbours to the sawmill was a company called BAKELITE LIMITED. In the early 1920's, a company was formed at Sheffield called Mouldensite Ltd., but in 1924 all activity was transferred to a site at Darley Dale, (now Johnson's Mill, on Old Road), next door to John Gregory's woodyard. Phenol Formaldehyde resins (plastics), moulding powders and mouldings were manufactured and in 1927 the company was renamed Bakelite Limited, with a main branch in Birmingham. At Darley the production of laminates was introduced and proved to be a very satisfactory operation, the maximum usage being in the electrical and radio industries. British Petroleum tankers could be conveniently brought into Darley Dale sidings.

A major decision was then taken to concentrate all manufacturing on a new 80 acre site at Birmingham in 1932, resulting in some job losses in the area as the company and a number of employees were transferred.

From 1932 the former works at Old Road were used by Sydney Johnson to manufacture cattle cake and feeding stuffs production but after the start of the German Blitz on industrial areas in 1940/41 the Darley Dale site was requisitioned for war production by Bakelite in March 1941 and was reconverted within a month, providing employment for nearly 40 people. Manufacturing facilities were quickly installed for materials used by the armaments industries and particularly for laminates used in aircraft manufacture. Mosquito fighter-bombers were designed around the capability of wood faced Phenolic laminates to be the main body reinforcement. The Hengist and Horsa gliders were made on a similar basis and most bomber and fighter planes had Bakelite insulation generally, in addition to control panels.

The production process made use of both resin and varnish. A solid synthetic resin, when mixed with inert materials, could, subjected to heat and pressure, be moulded into a variety of products.

A synthetic varnish was also manufactured to impregnate a variety of materials such as cotton sheeting, asbestos sheeting or stiff brown paper sheet. Dependant on which board was to be fabricated, each sheeting was passed through a trough of varnish, then into an oven where the material became solid but still chemically active. This sheeting was then passed under a guillotine to cut the correct size. To build a board, so many pieces were stacked together and the pile heated under great pressure, so bonding the sheets together. The Admiralty and other sections of the War Office sent their own inspectors to check the materials ordered for their use.

Darley Dale certainly contributed to the war effort but the Darley Dale site could not be embodied into the company's plans in 1946, after the end of the war. Bakelite severed its links with Darley a second and final time, with many employees going to the Birmingham base. Once again the Old Road factory was to become a centre for producing animal feed for the farming industry.

Finally, on a much smaller scale, we can see how the area coped with the economic decline of the early 1930's when we look at the enthusiasm of certain people who diversified and used their energies to open new businesses that provided work for people during a difficult period. One such person was Mrs. May Charlesworth of Brook Side, next to the Plough Inn, Two Dales. She would try her hand at anything, including making ice-cream with the help of her husband Jobie, and selling it alongside the A6, close to the Whitworth Institute, at weekends and Bank Holidays during the 1920's and 1930's.

However, for a few years during the 1930's, she provided work for six to eight women when she started an eiderdown factory in a corrugated iron shed next to the Plough Inn. Six electric sewing machines were installed and an experienced 'cutter out', Mrs. Gilberthorpe of Hackney, cut the material into strips that were sewed together. Inside the shed was a large blower, used for filling the

The Plough Inn, Two Dales c1935. The eiderdown factory shed can just be seen immediately to the right of the pub

eiderdowns with feathers and the whole process could be quite dusty with feathers flying in all directions on occasions. Work was let out to women working in their own homes and then it was brought in to the shed. For these difficult years of the early 1930's the business provided useful money to supplement the family income of women such as Una Lane, Annie Grafton (from Rycroft), Marjorie Saunders (from Broadwalk) and Hannah Charlesworth.

As the families from South Darley and Darley Dale struggled through these difficult times towards the end of the decade, the political climate in Europe was changing and dark clouds loomed on the horizon. In a number of countries, the strain imposed by economic collapse and the bitterness or disappointments caused by the outcome of the Versailles Peace Treaty imposed in 1920 had found their democratic institutions wanting. Fascist and Nazi regimes had won favour in a number of countries, with scant regard for democratic niceties, and were determined to push their aggressive foreign policies in the belief that the remaining democracies were weak-willed and ill-prepared to defend their rights.

The Spanish Civil War of 1936-1939 seemed to many to encapsulate the battle between Fascism and Democracy and the victory of Fascism on the Iberian Peninsula emboldened still further the aggressive plans of Nazi Germany. As the year 1938 progressed, many people in South Darley would possibly think back to the period of the Great War and wonder if the madness of those times could be returning to haunt them.

CHAPTER THREE

WAR AND SACRIFICE

The threat of war was tangible during 1938 as General Franco's forces gained the ascendancy in Spain and a German ultimatum led to the appointment of several Nazi Germans as ministers in the Austrian cabinet. On March 11th German troops entered Austria and the Anschluss, or forbidden union of Austria with Germany, was established.

As the year progressed, tension increased in other areas of Europe, especially in Czechoslovakia, where Hitler demanded the handing over of areas of Bohemia to Germany, particularly those occupied by Sudetan Germans. Under pressure from France and Britain, Czechoslovakia agreed to this demand, whereupon Hitler at once demanded further considerable concessions by October 1st, in default of which Germany would "march". The Czech army mobilised on September 23rd, 1938, France on the next day.

In Britain, territorial AA and coastal defence units, the Observer Corps and Auxiliary Air Force were called up on September 26th and the British fleet was mobilised on the 28th. Gas masks were distributed to civilians and provisional air raid shelters were dug in London parks.

It was during this period of tension that a local cricket touring party, known as the 'Leather jackets' including Darley Cricket Club members, had to curtail its annual weeks cricket tour of North Wales because a number of the party were recalled to their positions, due to the mounting international crisis.

Prime Minister Neville Chamberlain visited Hitler at Bad-Godesberg and Berchtesgaden, without result, and on September 28th Hitler invited the British and French premiers to meet with Mussolini at Munich next day. At this meeting, to which no Czech representative was admitted, it was agreed that German occupation of the areas demanded should proceed in stages between October 1st and 10th. Chamberlain was able to return to London, claiming 'Peace in our time' and most of Britain breathed a collective sigh of relief. Appeasement had apparently 'won the day'.

During this period, the Matlock area had joined in the preparations for a possible war. In early March, N.C.O.'s of 359 AA Company (TA) were being trained in the drill hall and on Sunday March 13th three searchlight positions were taken up in the vicinity of Monyash and a plane was hired to travel above the area, first with lights on and then without, as the AA Company used their sound locator. The Town Hall, Matlock, witnessed 42 members of the St. John's Ambulance Brigade passing the ARP certificate at the end of March and there was a gas decontamination squad at Darley. It was suggested that Matlock shopkeepers who had cellars would offer to have that accommodation available to pedestrians who happened to be in the streets at times of sudden air raids. During the Munich Crisis large numbers of men offered their services as Air Raid Wardens and gas masks were stored at the Town Hall.

Relief turned to concern, when, in March 1939, Hitler ignored certain conditions of the Munich Agreement and occupied Bohemia and Moravia, without British or French government intervention. Sensing a weakness of resolve throughout the European democracies, Hitler turned his attention to Poland during the summer months. War clouds were looming once again over Europe, for at last, Chamberlain spelt out clearly in Parliament British condemnation of Hitler's latest aggression and made it clear that an attack on Poland would not be tolerated. On April 26th Britain reintroduced conscription.

In April 1939 there was a test of air raid sirens throughout the Matlock district and it was said that at Darley Dale the general opinion appeared to be that the test was a 'washout' from the point of view of hearing. Eventually, three months later, three sirens were introduced in an attempt to improve the situation. By the end of April it was also recorded that 1267 households had voluntarily undertaken to receive unaccompanied children in connection with the evacuation scheme.

Unfortunately, by July 1939 it was being reported that there was a shortage of Air Raid Wardens. In the Munich Crisis of 1938 large numbers had volunteered but since then interest had dropped and few were undergoing training now. At the end of July an ARP exercise took place in the whole district to test the blackout. Wardens and special constables were called out at midnight on Thursday 20th July and patrolled the areas. In late August 1939 it was reported by Frank Taylor, the chief ARP warden for Darley Dale, that action had been taken to obtain wardens for South Darley, but without much success.

The weakness displayed by Britain and France in Munich was Hitler's most powerful incentive to plan the attack on Poland, first for August, then for September 1939. He believed that Poland could be defeated in isolation, as Czechoslovakia and Austria had been before, especially when, on August 23rd Germany and Soviet Russia signed a Non-Aggression Pact. Hitler's way to Poland seemed open, but on August 25th the signing of the Anglo-Polish alliance was announced in London, and Hitler realised that his attempt to isolate Poland had failed.

The biggest contrast between the Great War and the Second World War was the unprecedented fear in 1939 of devastating air attacks and that there would be immediate 'danger and horrors' in store. E.M. Forster wrote 'The 1930's are apprehensive of war and are carried towards it'. In the year between Munich and the outbreak of war it began to be felt increasingly strongly that there was no other outcome than war, and almost everyone was ready in September 1939.

During August, people were grimly determined to enjoy the peace-time summer activities that might soon become a distant memory, although for the first time ever, four consecutive Darley Dale weekend cricket matches had to be cancelled in July/August due to rain. Family photographs of mid August 1939 show my parents relaxing in the familiar setting of the Whitworth Park and on the beach at Skegness, with war only 14 days away. Yet in the week before the announcement of war, it was reported in the High Peak News that Matlock had almost a wartime appearance at night, with its extinguished street lamps, darkened windows and white painted kerbs and posts, whilst on Friday 1st September gas masks were distributed at the Burton Institute, Winster, and many other points in the Matlock district.

'Getting away from the tension'. Wilfred and Elsie Taylor and daughter Maureen on the beach at Skegness, two weeks before war was declared

At 11.15a.m. on Sunday September 3rd 1939, Neville Chamberlain announced to a hushed nation that Britain was at war with Germany. It was the beginning of the greatest conflict the world has yet seen and it was not long before the people of South and North Darley learned that they would not be spared. On 1st September, two days before war was declared, three Royal Navy submarines departed Rosythe naval base in Scotland, en route to patrol the North Sea naval bases of Nazi Germany and the Skagerrak, the narrow entrance to the Baltic Sea.

On board H.M.S. Oxley was Chief Stoker John William Jackson of Hall Moor Road, Darley Hillside. On the day he sailed, news had arrived of the birth of his second son. Just three days into the war the submarines were in position on the surface, when, in the darkness, currents caused one to become detached. A failure in the signalling equipment resulted in a torpedo being fired at the Oxley, believing it to be an enemy vessel. The submarine, hit by 'friendly fire', sank to the seabed with only two survivors being plucked to safety. The horror of war had been brought home to the people of Darley, for John Jackson left a wife Bertha and two sons, Geoffrey and baby John. John Jackson was the first Darley man to be killed but it would not be too long before South Darley would also be mourning the loss of one its parishioners, John Alfred Lawman.

Private John Alfred Lawman, 2nd Battalion Northamptonshire Regiment
(Died 22nd/23rd May 1940

Alfred was born to John and Beatrice Annie Lawman on April 18th 1919. Beatrice Stevenson lived at Cliffe House, Wensley and met John Lawman in Derby whilst she was in service and he was in the army, serving in India during the Great War. John had lost an eye whilst fighting in the Boer War.

They lived at Keswick Cottage, Wensley, where a daughter, Doris May was born in 1920 and then moved to other cottages in Wensley before finally living at No.2 Oaklea, in the newly constructed houses at Oker.

Alfred Lawman of 2nd Battalion, Northamptonshire Regiment. Killed 1940 near Dunkirk

Alfred Lawman and his sister, May, (now May Flude), c1939

John Lawman worked at Constable Harts Quarry, Matlock, but by the late 1930's he had been made redundant and Alfred became the main breadwinner when he left school and went onto the flotation plant at Mill Close Lead Mine, before working underground. To raise more money for the family, Mrs, Lawman started a little tea-room in the front room of her house in the 1930's, where tea, sandwiches, cakes and even poached egg on toast were served. A sign outside the house advertised 'Teas with Hovis'.

Alfred, a member of the Church Choir, was a good musician who, in the 1930's, had private violin lessons with the church organist, Mr. Chandler. Later he became very proficient on the piano accordion and mouth organ and would often practice at the bottom of the garden.

By November 1939, Alfred would arrive home from work each day and ask if his call-up papers had arrived, although his father, a local ARP warden, did not wish him to go, partly because Alfred had become the chief wage-earner for the family. However, by mid January 1940, he was posted to the 2nd Battalion, Northamptonshire Regiment, and, with his accordion and mouth organ packed, he departed for Northampton. His training was brief, lasting just ten weeks, and on his second home leave he returned to Oker with his accordion since he knew he would soon be off to join the British Expeditionary Force in France.

The Battalion had long since been in France, and, stationed north of Lille before Christmas 1939, they were building machine gun posts disguised as chicken houses, barns or even haystacks. A small amount of individual training was carried out throughout the next few months and on Alfred's birthday, April 18th 1940, he and other members of the Battalion crossed the Channel to join their comrades in France. His mouth organ accompanied him.

On 29th April, Alfred and the full strength Battalion left by train to Bolbec, near the port of Le Havre. Preparations were immediately made for a move by sea and Norway was to be their destination. After the motorised transport had been loaded and had reached the docks, the sea move was suddenly cancelled and his Battalion returned inland to the Poix region, South West of Amiens, to carry out training.

May 10th saw the German invasion of the Low Countries and the Battalion prepared to march, travelling 25 miles to Bernaville, near Abbeville. They billeted for the night, although slit trenches were dug in case of an air attack. For the next four days they marched, but on the 15th May, motor lorries picked them up, and at 3.30p.m. they started what was to be an all night move via Bethume, Tournai and on to Ninove, twenty miles west of Brussels, which was reached late on the 16th, as refugee traffic on the roads hindered them. They were ordered to cover the Brussels – Halle Canal.

By 10a.m. on 17th May they had dug in, and there was great enemy air activity throughout the day, with many low-flying machine gun attacks made on the Battalion. Fortunately no causalities were occurred and cheers were raised when Sergeant Major Turnbull (AA Platoon) brought down a German aircraft.

At 8.30 a.m. on the 18th the Battalion withdrew, though no contact had been made with the enemy, and marched to Grammont, where the bridges over the canal were being blown. Lorries then carried them to Ascq, along roads jammed with traffic, but owing to RAF fighter patrols, no air attacks were made on the convoy. At dusk they marched on but were picked up by lorries at 2 am on the 21st May. With 35 men to each 3 ton lorry plus equipment, they moved to Lens and then marched through the Great War battle site of Vimy Ridge and dug in a defensive position in a wooded area, covering the River Scarpe. It was now the 22nd May and at 1.00 p.m. they spotted twelve German tanks and 6 armoured carriers 3000 yards ahead of them. Soon after 3pm the wood was subjected to heavy shelling and many casualties resulted from the shells bursting in the trees.

During the night 'D' Company were attacked and the enemy gained a foothold in the village but 'A' Company retook the position. A tank attack was beaten off, but, as the French on their right withdrew, the enemy gained a foothold in the wood and at 6pm the Battalion was commanded to withdraw in order. During this action, lasting two days, over 352 casualties had been sustained, including Private Alfred Lawman. His comrades later reported to his mother that they had seen him wounded and placed aboard an ambulance that departed from the battle zone. They believed that as it withdrew it was attacked by enemy aircraft and those on board were killed. However, in the heat of battle there could be no confirmation of his death.

Orders were now received to move with the greatest speed to Douai and Seclin, where they reorganised, and the convoy moved on to the Ypres – Comines Canal. As the enemy attacked in strength, the position grew more serious and by 10 p.m. on May 27th the enemy drove them back to occupy the ridge. At dawn on the 28th the Battalion counter-attacked, but due to inadequate artillery support the attack failed, with causalities sustained, and the position grew worse.

A very strong enemy attack came in and broke through to Battalion H.Q. Heavy machine gun and artillery fire was by this time covering the whole area. 'A' Company was completely cut off from the rest of the Battalion and fought on until overwhelmed by sheer force. A mere trickle of 40 NCO's and men was able to get out of this position when the Battalion was ordered to withdraw by lorry to Driridders. The gallant remains of the 2nd Battalion were joined by groups from other Regiments to make up a composite battalion, with only six serviceable vehicles. They moved back to the sandhills north of Moeres and the vehicles were destroyed. The German Air Force had mastery of the sky and dive-bombing continued all day. At 4.30 p.m. on the 31st May the men moved by route march to Dunkirk Jetty, embarking at 5am, 1st June, on H.M.S. Malcolm.

So ended the campaign with the B.E.F. They had been decisively beaten by the German Army, not through lack of courage and tenacity on their part, but owing to the enemy superiority of tanks, size of force and air support.

News reached the Lawman family that Alfred was missing but the uncertainty of whether he was alive or not was to haunt them for a number of years. In February 1941, Mr. Lawman died and people believed that a 'broken heart' was a contributory factor. It was not until 1944 that the War Office informed them that they had concluded he was killed in action on or shortly after the 20th May 1940. During the intervening years Mrs. Lawman lived in hope that he may have recovered whilst a prisoner. It is almost certain that Alfred was killed in the action against the enemy on the 22nd or 23rd May 1940 and his name can be found on the Dunkirk Memorial in France. He proved to be the first parishioner from South Darley to die fighting for his country during the Second World War and it brought home to South Darley folk that the 'Phoney War' was over.

Private Ernest Evans,
Gunner in the Royal Marines
(Died 16th June 1942)

Ernest James Evans (sometimes known as Sam), was born on the 1st June 1920, the second son of Tom and Emily Evans of Wensley, and from 1936 the family, including his sister Phyllis, lived at Leafield, 3 Oker Road. He had been named after Ernest Chell, the brother of his mother Emily, who had been tragically killed in May 1918 during a major German offensive in the Great War.

His father, Tom, had himself been a veteran of the First World War, serving from 1915 to 1918 with the 16th Battalion Sherwood Foresters, throughout the terrible conflict in France and Belgium. Together with his father and elder brother Tom, Ernest worked at Mill Close Lead Mine. Emily cleaned the church, vicarage and school to earn extra money, whilst Tom senior, acted as the Church sextant, with the occasional assistance of his two sons. Ernest was a popular member of the South Darley community.

Gunner Ernest Evans, Royal Marines 1940. Died 1942

In early 1940 Ernest enlisted and was sent for training in the Royal Marines at HMS Eastern Kings, at Plymouth. Eventually he specialised as a gunner, trained to fire the powerful turret guns on board Royal Navy warships, and in early 1941 was posted via Glasgow, to join the light cruiser HMS Hermione, stationed with the Home Fleet at Scapa Flow in the Orkney Islands.

Cruiser HMS Hermione 1941 as part of 'Force H' running convoys between Gibraltar and Malta. Ernest Evans is first on the left, back row

On May 21st 1941 the German battleship Bismarck and heavy cruiser Prinz Eugen were ordered to sail from Bergen, Norway, to journey out into the Atlantic and raid the vital shipping lanes. The Home Fleet left port but the German ships evaded the chasing group, after sending HMS Hood to the bottom of the sea off the Greenland coast.

Admiral Somerville, Commander of Naval Force H, based at Gibraltar, left port for the Atlantic and eventually took part in the destruction of the Bismarck. However, during the action, Fleet Air Arm Swordfish torpedo aircraft from Somerville's chief warship, the aircraft carrier Ark Royal, mistakenly attacked and damaged one of their own ships, the cruiser HMS Sheffield. This ship had to divert to an English port for repairs, and the Admiralty decided to send HMS Hermione to Force H at Gibraltar as a replacement.

Ernest therefore found himself based at Gibraltar from June1941 to January 1942 as part of Force H of the Mediterranean Fleet (along with HMS Ark Royal and Renown) and was constantly in action fighting the convoys through from Gibraltar to the island of Malta. Under constant attack by German and Italian planes and with the ever present threat of attack by submarines and E-boats, the task was difficult and dangerous. Ernest writes home on one occasion to report that they had rammed and disabled an Italian submarine.

During one such convoy run from Gibraltar to Malta in 1941, an account was sent back to Britain by the war correspondent of the Daily Express, on board the cruiser HMS Hermione.

'For twenty seven hours on end we were subjected to continuous attacks by high level, dive and torpedo bombers as well as 'E' boats, as we protected a convoy of six merchantmen steaming through the "Med" to Malta.

All the merchantmen got through. HMS Renown and Ark Royal were with us on the first day. Ark Royal's fighters took off soon after breakfast and bombs plop into the sea a hundred yards to starboard, spouting water 30 feet high and as we open fire the deafening cracks of the main armament mingle with the thunder of Pom Poms, which sound like a man beating a big kettle drum. A column of black smoke rises from HMS Fearless as she is hit by a bomb astern.

An Italian plane swoops into the water and two Italians clamber into their rubber boat. The second wave of Italian planes cannot face the terrific barrage and drop a hail of bombs two miles away and flee, pursued by the Ark Royal's fighters. Far astern, Fearless blows up as she is torpedoed by another destroyer after the survivors had been rescued.

For the next two days and nights we were without the Ark Royal and Renown. At 7pm Torpedo bombers attacked to starboard, skimming over the water towards us, shells bursting all around them. The torpedoes slide past 15 yards to starboard. At 7.45pm another big formation attacks and soundless columns of water rise around us.

We had a lull until 'E' boats attacked at 3am next day. In inky

Cruiser HMS Hermione in Mediterranean Sea as part of 'Force H', 1941

'Force H' Western Mediterranean, 1941. Warplane from HMS Ark Royal takes off to help in protecting the convoy run from Gibraltar to Malta

1941 'Force H' including HMS Hermione, is attacked by German and Italian planes whilst protecting the convoy en route to Malta

blackness, ships open fire at the dim targets. A searchlight flicks on for a few seconds and an 'E' boat scuttles across the water like a beetle to escape the shells. It twists and turns but flying woodwork means a direct hit. A minute later there is a big explosion astern as the merchantman 'Sydney Star' is torpedoed, but she carries on and we and the destroyer 'Nestor' are detached to assist her.

At 7.20am eight Junkers 87 dive-bombers come screaming out of the sun to deliver two attacks. The 'Sydney Star', plodding along with a heavy list, swings away just in time. Our guns are still firing and the air is filled with the stench of burnt cordite. Empty shell cases fill the

105

wash houses and overflow into the crew's recreation space, as we steamed slowly into Malta, applauded by soldiers on the quay side'.

After bringing Admiral Somerville back to England in January 1942, HMS Hermione sailed round the Cape of Good Hope to Durban, a few months later, in preparation for the proposed attack on the Indian Ocean island of Madagascar, off the coast of East Africa. Japan's advance into the Indian Ocean and Vichy French control of the island raised fears that Madagascar might be handed over to the Japanese, complete with the important naval base of Diego-Suarez, which controlled the Mozambique Channel.

Allied landings (Operation "Ironclad") on May 15th 1942, supported by Hermione, eventually resulted in the surrender of the Vichy French forces. A party of Royal Marines from Ernest's ship had formed part of the landing troops and these remained on the island when Ernest and HMS Hermione proceeded to Alexandria, in Egypt.

The vital Mediterranean island of Malta was in desperate straits and could not survive much longer without replenishment. Starvation for its inhabitants was close at hand and fuel was almost non-existent. Fortunately, a total of 198 Spitfires had been flown in from air-craft carriers for defence purposes and a major effort was decided on to get supplies through to the island in June of 1942.

Convoys would be run through from east and west in a simultaneous operation. From Gibraltar would come six cargo vessels escorted by aircraft carriers, cruisers and destroyers in an operation code-named 'Harpoon'. At the same time from Alexandria in the east, a convoy of eleven freighters would set out, covered by the Mediterranean Fleet cruisers and destroyers, reinforced by three cruisers and some destroyers from the Eastern Fleet in an operation code-named 'Vigorous'. Within this force was HMS Hermione and Royal Marine, Ernest Evans.

The danger for both expeditions would come from inevitable attacks in the Sicilian Channel and the notorious 'Bomb Alley' but also from the Italian surface forces grouped around the modern battleships Vittorio Veneto and Littorio, based at Taranto, only 19 hours steaming time from the route of the 'Vigorous' convoy.

At dawn on the 14th June 'Harpoon' force was about 120 miles S.W. of Sardinia whilst the 'Vigorous' force was well inside 'Bomb Alley'. Ernest's force had been protected by RAF fighters from the North African coast and proceeded unmolested until late afternoon when it passed out of range of British held airfields. However, one freighter had been damaged by dive-bombers and diverted to Tobruk, together with one that was too slow. This freighter was sent to the bottom of the sea when set upon by forty dive-bombers.

At 2.30pm the Italian Naval fleet sailed from Taranto to intercept the 'Vigorous' convoy. On the result of this contest could depend the survival of Malta and perhaps the whole struggle for the Middle East.

Meanwhile, 'Harpoon' had proved a costly operation for the British but eventually two freighters got through and Malta was saved at a time when starvation was near. The island's condition, however, would have been better if the 'Vigorous' convoy had not failed in its enterprise.

Its escort consisted of seven cruisers, including Hermione, and 26 destroyers, but no battleship to oppose the Italian battle squadron should it intervene. By nightfall on the 14th June, the 'Vigorous' convoy had undergone seven air attacks by a total of some 70 Stukas and JU88's and the freighter Bhutan had been sunk. Nightfall brought little respite for aircraft illuminated the ships with flares and German E-boats prowled on the outskirts.

The commander of 'Vigorous' knew he could not hold off the Italian fleet during the long summer day ahead and asked Alexandria whether he should retire. He was told to hold on course till 2am to see what might happen. In the confusion of such orders and the difficulties of completing such a manoeuvre by 50 ships, the E-boats saw their opportunity. The cruiser Newcastle and destroyer Hasty were both torpedoed.

Four Wellington bombers had taken off from Malta at midnight and nine Beauforts three and a half hours later to raid the Italian Fleet but a smoke screen prevented the Wellingtons doing any damage and the Beauforts did not fare much better.

The convoy was once again ordered to turn back to the east. This marching and counter marching in 'Bomb Alley' extracted its toll, for

20 Stukas attacked and disabled the gun turrets of the Birmingham. In the afternoon 12 dive-bombers picked out the small destroyer HMS Airedale and she went to the bottom.

The Italian Fleet was still coming after the convoy in undiminished strength, despite an attack by American Liberator bombers. Around the British convoy, air attack followed air attack with scarcely an interval between them, and ammunition stocks were falling low. It was decided to continue heading back to Alexandria.

The effort to relieve Malta from the East had been a dismal failure. Before the squadron reached Alexandria, it suffered further casualties south of Crete. The cruiser Hermione, with Ernest on board, was torpedoed and sunk by submarine U-205 during the night whilst the Australian destroyer Nestor had to be scuttled.

So ended a desperate and gallant episode in the battle for the Mediterranean. Only two supply ships out of a total of seventeen managed to get through to Malta, with a cargo of 15,000 tons, at a heavy cost in ships, aircraft and lives. However, these cargoes were just enough to keep the Maltese people and garrison meagrely fed until another convoy could be fought through. The one vital task of the Italian Navy was to eliminate Malta and so protect the supply line to Libya. An essential preliminary was to prevent supply ships reaching the island. In this they failed.

During this action we have seen that at 1.27am on Tuesday 16th June 1942, HMS Hermione had been sunk and the crew found themselves swimming for their lives in the sea. Ernest was apparently not seriously wounded but whilst in the water is believed to have swallowed and inhaled diesel fuel and oil from the sunken ship. Although plucked to safety by another ship and transferred to a hospital in Alexandria, he died on the evening of that same day, June 16th, aged 22 years. His birthday had been celebrated on the 1st June, just 15 days prior to the battle and a letter and a card sent by his Aunt, Hannah Marsden from 8 Oker Road never reached him in time for him to read. The unopened letter was returned to Hannah a few weeks later and reads: -

Dear Ernest,

Just a few lines, hoping this reaches you in time for your birthday, and finds you OK as we are at present. I feel that you are very far away from us, but I hope you will soon be coming nearer. I have been very anxious about you these last few weeks, but I am hoping we shall hear from you soon. How I have wished that I could only come and be with you sometimes. Just a word from you now and again to satisfy myself you were all right. Of course I never say these things to your mother. I always try to cheer her with the best story I can think of. We have Tom with us at present. Wouldn't it just be ideal if you were here too. Let us keep hoping that it will happen soon.

Everything is beginning to look lovely here, the blossom, and bluebells and forget-me-nots. We took your mother in Northern Dale the other Sunday. She did a bit of groaning getting over the walls and nettles. It just suited Alan – he did laugh at her.

Well Ernest, you said "keep smiling" and this we must all try to do. God bless you and bring you safely back to us soon, with love from us all.

Hannah.

Ernest Evan's grave in Alexandria, Egypt

On the 22nd June 1942, Mrs. Walker of St. Mary's View was looking from her bedroom window when she saw a telegram boy walking up the path from Cross Green School to Oker Road. When she saw him turn left onto Oker Road she knew straight away that it was Ernest Evans who had been killed. Peggy Wright, living at

'Thorntrees', on Oker Road, was a small child at the time, but remembers George Tomlinson from Oker Road arriving to tell her mother, Mary, about the news, and how it was the first time she had seen her mother cry.

Tom and Emily Evans were devastated and Emily never recovered properly from the tragedy. During the First World War she had lost her brother, Ernest Chell, and now her son had lost his life. Soon afterwards they left the parish, for Tom was drafted into the war effort to work at Rolls Royce, on Elton Road, Derby, and they went to live at 71 Wolfe Street.

A wooden cross with Ernest's name on, was placed in Hadra War Memorial Cemetery in Alexandria and later a stone plaque was erected. It brought some comfort to the family when Richard Hodgkinson, youngest son of the former South Darley butcher, who was serving in Cairo, Egypt later in the war, was able to take photographs of Ernest's grave and give them to his family.

PRIVATE ERNEST STAFFORD NO.4981966
14TH BATTALION SHERWOOD FORESTERS
(Died 14th March 1944 aged 31 years)

Ernest was the younger son of John Henry and Millicent Stafford of 8 Wilmot Street, Matlock and husband of Emily Harriet Stafford. Ernest had married a Stanton Lees girl, Emily Harriet Slack and lived with her parents in the small cottage next to Blind Billy Needham's post office at Darley Bridge.

Ernest entered service in the post office as an auxiliary postman on December 26th 1931 and was appointed postman on July 6th 1935. He was a quiet and conscientious worker and very popular with his colleagues.

The 14th Battalion Sherwood Foresters was raised at Markeaton Park in Derby on 14th October 1940 and Ernest Stafford enlisted in Matlock in early 1941. After training and Home Defence duties in Yorkshire, Berkshire and Surrey the Battalion was given orders on

March 19th 1942 for mobilisation for a tropical climate by 29th April. Embarkation leave was begun immediately and Ernest returned home to South Darley for sadly the last time.

On May 1st HM George VI inspected the Division drawn up on the village green at Cranleigh and on May 6th the Battalion entrained at Godalming for Gourock, Scotland. On May 10th 40 officers and 922 other ranks sailed on the United States ship Orizaba on what was to be a 16,000 mile voyage to the Port of Suez.

To avoid enemy action the route of the convoy was to be via South Africa and the Indian Ocean rather than through the Mediterranean Sea. It was not until June 9th that the Battalion could come ashore at Durban, South Africa. After marching through the city the Battalion spent five days in a bivouac area known as the Wool Sheds.

By June 19th the convoy was again on its way but on the 22nd, just when Aden was approaching, the USS Orizaba was ordered to detour to Bombay. The Indian port was reached on July 1st where the Orizaba was berthed for 5 days and shore leave granted. With no explanation forthcoming the Orizaba was then ordered to proceed to Suez, which was reached via Aden on Saturday 18th July. The 14th Foresters were finally in the Middle Eastern Theatre of War.

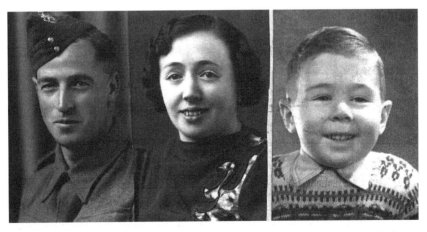

*Ernest Stafford, 14th Battalion Sherwood Foresters, died 1944 near Anzio, Italy.
Emily-Harriett Stafford (nee Slack) and son Gerald in 1946 aged 3½ years*

After much desert training with 8th Armoured Brigade the Battalion came under the command of 9th Armoured Brigade which eventually came under the command of 2nd New Zealand Division led by Lt. General Freyburg VC.

On October 23rd Montgomery's 8th Army attacked Rommel's Afrika Corps with four divisions, the Foresters' role being to support the Armoured Regiments in jeeps and trucks as and when required. After several days of desperate fighting and heavy casualties the German forces broke off the battle and retreated westward with 9th Brigade in hot pursuit.

On November 21st the Brigade was pulled out of the pursuit and returned to Cairo to reform and refit. On December 2nd the Foresters were informed they were to be moved to the Persia and Iraq force. The Battalion travelled 1000 miles overland to Baghdad where it spent five months as part of the 5th Indian Division.

By May 8th the Foresters were ordered back to North Africa, eventually arriving in Tunis and reverting to an English lorried infantry battalion. In October the Foresters moved on to Algiers and a period of training in preparation for the Italian campaign.

The Italian forces, with the loss of Sicily, had surrendered in September but German forces offered stiff resistance throughout the peninsula, eventually stopping the allied advance at the Gustav Line around Cassino. To overcome this desperate situation the U.S. 6th Corps was landed at Anzio, to the rear of the Germans. The landing was a complete surprise and a bridgehead 18 miles long and 9 miles deep was secured. The Americans failed to push on and allowed the Germans to counter attack and by January 1944 seal the bridgehead. Some 50,000 Allied troops were pinned down at Anzio in conditions akin to First World War trench fighting.

It was into this grim situation that the 14th Foresters entered in February. After a three day crossing to Naples from Algiers on the S.S. Champoilion the Battalion arrived at Anzio on February 24th to find the harbour under shellfire and a rapid disembarkation proved necessary. The role of the Foresters was as Corps reserve, counter attack force and mobile column against paratroop attack.

The Germans were pushing hard against the Beach head perimeter which was now only 6 miles from the harbour. Allied defence positions were located in a network of deep gullies, which were under continuous enemy observation and attack from their advantageous positions of higher ground.

The horrors of the Gallipoli Campaign in 1915 were not dissimilar to the next few weeks of fighting at Anzio. The Foresters sent out aggressive patrols to test the German positions, as did the Germans against the Allies. Heavy rain turned the terrain into a slimy mud bath but the fighting continued and casualties steadily mounted.

On the night of 13/14th March the Battalion tried to winkle the enemy out of a gulley called the 'Caronte'. All too soon the Battalion got into difficulties. 'B' Company was to have outflanked the objective but fierce Spandau machine-gun fire frustrated this course. In the dark the Foresters lost their way. The leading platoon came under heavy fire and the second one lost itself completely. To the right, 'A' Company had reached its objective but was immediately turned back by terrific fire.

Somewhere in this mayhem and confusion Ernest Stafford, South Darley's postman, was killed. A further 30 Officers and men of the 14th Foresters were killed or died of wounds during March in the Anzio beachhead and over 80 wounded.

Ernest is buried at the Beach Head War Cemetery, close to the site of a casualty clearing station. Ernest's older brother, Wilfred, who was a private in the 1st Battalion Welch Regiment, was also killed in the Italian campaign on the 9th September aged 36. Poignantly, Wilfred is also buried in Anzio's Beach Head Cemetery.

Ernest's widow and her infant son, Gerald, eventually moved to Keswick Cottage, Wensley, to live with her grandmother, the cottage being bought with the compensation Emily received from the army for her husband's death. Some twenty years later Emily married a widower, Bill Holmes, and they moved to Beeley to live.

GUNNER JAMES LESLIE RILEY, 44 BATTERY, 61ST LIGHT ANTI-AIRCRAFT REGIMENT, ROYAL ARTILLERY

(Died 26th January 1944, aged 36 years)

James was born in 1907, the son of Sam Riley the fishmonger, and his wife Lizzie of 'the Yard', Darley Bridge. His brother, Len, helped their father with the fish and green grocery round, whilst his eldest brother, Sam, had died at Ypres in 1916 when a German mine had been exploded under the trench he was defending.

Leaving school in 1922, James worked in a variety of jobs locally but after marrying a Darley Dale girl, Lillian Wood, he moved to Marple in Cheshire, where he helped run a general store and grocery shop. A daughter, Jeanne, was born in 1935 but they returned eventually to Derbyshire and settled in Buxton, where James worked as a grocer's assistant.

When war was declared, he joined the Buxton Home Guard for a year but was called up into the army on the 12th December 1940 and enlisted into the Royal Artillery. After initial training in an anti-aircraft drivers training regiment he progressed through various heavy anti-aircraft regiments until he was posted to a searchlight battalion for two months in 1941.

Gunner James Leslie Riley, 44/61st Light Anti-Aircraft Regiment, Royal artillery, died 26th January 1944

James's wife, Lillian, had meanwhile left Buxton with Jeanne and was living with her sister at Rotherwood Cottage, Dale Road South,

Darley Dale. On the 25th June 1941 James received his final posting when he joined the 44/61st Light Anti-Aircraft Regiment, one month before the birth of his son James Leslie, born in July 1941. By this time, Gunner Riley was stationed in the south of England and came home on leave to be at his sons' christening. It was the last time his family were to see him.

On the 25th August 1941, James began his overseas service in the North African desert campaign. During the first phase, December 1940 to February 1941, British and Empire troops had advanced 500 miles into Libya against Italian opposition, capturing 130,000 prisoners and large quantities of equipment in the process. However, on February 12th, the formidable German general, Erwin Rommel, arrived at Tripoli with the German Africa Corps and soon reorganised and revitalised the remaining Italian forces. By the time James' regiment arrived in North Africa, the easy British victories had come to an end as Rommel's forces forced the allies eastwards, with only Tobruk holding out.

In November 1941, James was involved with the British attempt to relieve Tobruk and eventually, in confused fighting during December, Rommel's forces did retreat. However, in late January 1942, Rommel made a surprise attack and by February 3rd was 375 miles from his starting base. During May and June the momentum was maintained and despite desperate fighting, the British Eighth Army withdrew to the Egyptian frontier, losing contact with Tobruk, where the 2nd South African Division was surrounded. On the 20th June Rommel launched his attack on Tobruk and by nightfall, the garrison had capitulated. Throughout these weeks of action, James' regiment was continually in action as they attempted to ward off the persistent air attacks on the Eighth Army by the Luftwaffe.

Rommel was promoted by Hitler to the rank of field marshal and he now kept up his advance and quickly regrouped his forces. The African Corps and Italian Mobile Corps were despatched towards the Egyptian frontier, where the British held only a delaying position. The British withdrew before this German advance in order to take up a more favourable position at the El Alamein line, a 40-mile gap between the

Sequence of photographs showing the military burial of Gunner James Riley at POW Camp Stalag 8B, in Poland, 1944

Mediterranean and the Qattara Depression. However, during this fighting retreat, Gunner James Leslie Riley was taken prisoner on June 27th 1942, one of 33,000 captured during the previous few weeks of battle. Only eleven days beforehand, another South Darley parishioner, Royal Marine Gunner, Ernest Evans, had lost his life when HMS Hermione had been torpedoed, only a few hundred miles away in the Mediterranean Sea.

As a POW, James was taken across that same Sea to an Italian prisoner of war camp in which he spent just over a year before the Italians capitulated to the Allies on September 3rd 1943. A long, tedious train journey then took place through Austria and Germany to its final destination, a German

POW camp in Southern Poland, between Krakow and Katowice. Before 1943 it had been known as Lamsdorf, Stalag VIII B, but was now known as Stalag 344, and James Riley became POW number 28097. Thirty thousand other POW's were interned in the camp.

The conditions were bleak and a hard East European winter lay ahead. Unfortunately for James, the prisoners were made to work for the German war effort. This area of Upper Silesia was of importance as an industrial area and the camp was in the Dabrowa coalfield, and so it was that Gunner Riley found himself being made to work deep underground in one of a number of coalmines, where conditions were grim and safety was often neglected.

Whilst a member of an underground working party, James was crushed by a runaway coal truck on Wednesday 26th January 1944, and died the same day, aged 36 years. The burial was carried out with full military honours at Milwitz Cemetery, near Sownowiec, on Sunday 30th January, comrades of the deceased being present. Two German soldiers led the procession and a volley of shots were fired over the grave, whilst the burial service was conducted by the Royal Artillery divisional Chaplain, Captain Kestell-Cornish.

By 1948 information came to his widow, Lillian, that James' body had been re-buried in a permanently maintained cemetery, Krakow British Military Cemetery, 160 miles S.S.W. of Warsaw. It is doubly sad to recall that James had escaped death on the battlefield, only to die through an accident, and that the Riley family from Darley Bridge had lost two sons, one in each of the two World Wars that plagued the 20th Century.

CORPORAL HERBERT PARKINSON GRIMSHAW, ROYAL AIR FORCE VOLUNTEER RESERVE
(Died 7.11.1944 aged 32 years)

Herbert was the eldest son of James and Florence Grimshaw of Farsley, near Leeds, Yorkshire, and was born on 5th June 1912. He was six years old when his mother died in childbirth, leaving baby sister Emily and three year old Nellie. His aunty had no family and so she adopted the two girls.

At the age of 12 years, Herbert and his father came to live at Winster and James, a fitter, began work at Mill Close Mine. One of his first jobs was to be involved with the demolition of the aerial flight, between what is now the car park/picnic site at Darley Cricket ground and the Mine. For almost two decades it had carried coal to the mine, high above the river in buckets, and gravel was transported on the return journey.

Herbert went to the Ernest Bailey Grammar School, but when he left the Matlock School he became a

Corporal Herbert Grimshaw, Royal Air Force Volunteer Reserve, died November 1944

turner on the lathes at Mill Close Mine. He was an extremely fine cricketer, excelling as a batsman and bowler, and often returned to Leeds to play for Farsley, but he eventually became one of the mainstays of the Darley Dale First Eleven during the mid and late 1930's.

His father, James, married a widow, Lucy Hardy (nee Sudbury), with children Ken and Joyce Hardy, and the family moved from Winster to live at one of the newly built houses on Flint Lane, Cross Green. Herbert, meanwhile, had met Marjorie Knowles from Matlock Green at a dance at the Whitworth Institute and in 1935 they were married at All Saints Church on Christmas Eve, making their home on the recently constructed Hooley's Estate. When Mill Close Mine was closed to most miners due to flooding in 1938/39, Herbert began work as an insurance agent.

In 1940, a daughter, Maureen, was born, but in that same year 28 year old Herbert was called up and joined the Royal Air Force. His

Darley Cricket Club First Eleven 1930's
Back row, l-r: X, Joe Wall, Reg Boden, Noel Jacques, X, X, X
Front row: Louis Jacques, Norman Lees, Herbert Grimshaw, Frank Unwin

*Herbert and Marjorie
Grimshaw*

initial training was at Blackpool, from where he travelled to Wadsworth to train as a rear air gunner in Bomber Command. Unfortunately, it was discovered that he suffered dreadfully from airsickness and it was decided that he should be posted instead to be trained in signals and radar.

After training as a technician in radar operations he found himself at RAF Hixon in Staffordshire for most of 1943 and part of 1944. His wife and child, now living at No. 2 Knowlestone Place, Matlock Green, travelled to stay with Herbert at Weston, a small village near Hixon, for the whole of

1943. The cottage had been condemned, having no gas or electricity and meals were cooked on top of the open fire. Yet at least she was close to her husband.

RAF Hixon had been constructed in 1942 and was the base for Number 30 Operational Training Unit. Wellington bomber crews did their initial training elsewhere and then came to Hixon to be formed into permanent crews that trained on daytime flying, then cross country flying, followed by night flying, before being sent to other squadrons to begin operational flying. By 1943, there were 3000 personnel connected with RAF Hixon.

Herbert was promoted to Corporal and Marjorie mistakenly sewed the stripes on upside down. By mid July 1943 news was received that his brother-in-law had been killed whilst taking part in the gigantic British bomber raid on Hamburg that began the horrific 'fire storm', destroying much of the German port.

However, after D-Day on June 6th 1944, signals and radar units were required on the Continent as the Allied forces broke out from the beachhead and forced the Germans out of France and through Belgium and Holland. Thirty two year old Corporal Herbert Grimshaw left Hixon in 1944 and went to the Base Signals and Radar unit at RAF Sawbridgeworth, Hertfordshire. Whilst there he played cricket for the base, but in late October, early November he travelled to the south coast, together with his unit and other RAF ground crew, to await the crossing of the English Channel. His last letter to Marjorie was to tell how they had made one attempt but had to turn back.

Three hundred RAF ground crew and seventy-eight naval crew were to embark on a landing craft, L.S.T. 420, for the crossing to Ostende. In previous weeks the craft had taken parties of army servicemen, but these were the first RAF personnel to be taken on board. The recent weather in the Channel had been atrocious and Herbert's party were kept in port for two days. They finally set off on the morning of Tuesday 7th November but during the journey to the Continent the weather deteriorated rapidly and a few miles from Ostende the captain of the vessel decided not to risk going into harbour and consequently turned around and made back for England.

The landing craft was being battered by the elements and, after steaming for about an hour on the return journey, a large explosion amidships occurred when a mine was struck, resulting in the vessel breaking in two and sinking quickly. A few rafts were floating in the heaving waters, with people swimming for their lives, but the bad storm prevailing at the time, the worst in local living memory, greatly hampered rescue operations and the greater part of the company, including the Commanding Officer, was reported missing.

On the following day a number of bodies were washed ashore from the wreckage, but none were identified as being Herbert. It was believed that a number of people on the boat must have been killed outright by the explosion whilst others were incapable of effecting their rescue through being injured.

News reached Marjorie by telegram on November 12th that her husband was missing but the Air Ministry were not prepared to presume death until the lapse of six months, or conclusive evidence was received. As a result, Marjorie Grimshaw was left wondering whether at any moment good news would be received about Herbert. A report appeared in the local newspaper that a Belper naval cook had been on board the stricken vessel and had been rescued. Marjorie wrote to his wife, who ran the Butts Bakery, Belper, and received some news of what had happened, but it was not until May 14th 1945 that she received news from the Air Ministry that death had now been presumed to have occurred on the 7th November 1944. During that period, not only did Marjorie have the heartache of not knowing whether her husband was alive or dead, but she had to provide for her family without the support of a pension.

Herbert's name is to be found on Panel 241 of the Royal Air Force Memorial, Runnymede, in Surrey, on South Darley's war memorial and also that of Matlock's.

Herbert Grimshaw would thankfully be the last South Darley parishioner to fall in the War.

Five names would have to be added to the twenty-two who had paid

Royal Air Force Memorial, Runnymede

the supreme sacrifice in the Great War. The two World Wars cast a long shadow over South Darley and twenty seven families had to face the future without a loved one.

We hope the brief biographies in this chapter go some way towards honouring the lives and sacrifice of the five of South Darley who died fighting fascism and securing Europe's freedom for democracy.

CHAPTER FOUR

LIFE ON THE HOME FRONT

We have already seen that throughout 1938, the nation had prepared for the possibility of war, with special emphasis placed on the probability of enemy air attacks and the need to combat this threat. Air Raid precaution measures had been taken, with a nationwide call for A.R.P. wardens and the provision of gas masks at the first sign of an emergency. The serious nature of the air threat can be gauged by the precaution taken in 1938 against aircraft landing on the 40 acre field known as the Cartledge, next to the Square and Compass Inn at Darley Bridge. Tall, sturdy wooden posts were hammered into the ground across the vast, flat surface as obstructions to enemy aircraft and remained there for the duration of the war (Mr. Gadsby, the farmer at Flatts Farm, asked for a few to be retained at the end of the war to act as 'rubbing posts' for his cattle).

On September 30th 1938, at the height of the Munich Crisis, the Infants classroom at South Darley School was used for assembling gas masks at the request of the A.R.P. and the Infants Department was closed at 10.15 a.m. for the day. The Munich Agreement brought a halt in the lurch towards conflict but most people believed war to be inevitable. When Germany invaded Poland on Friday, September 1st. 1939, the country awaited their Prime Minister's declaration of war.

As the might of Germany's armed forces swept across the Polish frontier on September 1st and Britain still remained at peace, the reality of the situation was brought home at midday to the people of South and North Darley with the arrival at Darley Dale Station of a special train, number M204, from Manchester. The evacuees had arrived, and with them the realisation that this time there was no 'turning back'.

Manchester's plans were to evacuate as many as possible of the 190,000 children from the city to places of safety and 70% agreed to be evacuated in the event of war. Allowance had been made for the housing of teachers and the billeting of helpers. The first contingents to leave Manchester, when the emergency was declared, should be school children travelling with their teachers, one adult to each group of ten children. Helpers would also travel with the children and then return home.

Schools had ensured that each child was given a small, turquoise, canvas rucksack for carrying clothes, whilst gas masks in boxes had been issued and food for 24 hours was to be carried. Parents were also told to put the children in their warmest clothes. As they arrived at school, a luggage label was tied to each child's coat with their name on it. Reception centres were organised at the children's destinations and in the case of Darley Dale, these were Darley Churchtown School, Darley Council School and South Darley School. To help out financially, the Government paid an allowance to the host family for unaccompanied children. For board and lodgings they received 10sh. 6d. for one child under 10 years of age, with a rising scale for older children.

Friday 1st September was a beautiful warm, sunny day in Darley Dale. The three billeting officers, headmasters Joseph Hancock (Council School), Mr. J.C. Bartram (Churchtown) and David Parsons (South Darley) waited anxiously on the station platform with their helpers, consisting of teachers, Women's Voluntary Service and special constables, whilst on Station Road several local buses were parked in readiness. The railings at the side of the platform had been removed and canvas screens erected to act as makeshift toilets.

The Manchester Schools involved with the evacuation to the Darley

Joe Hancock, headteacher and billeting officer. Darley Council School 1939. Bunting cup winners v Churchtown.
Back row, l-r: Ken Marsden, Dennis Brailsford, Harold Toplis, Dick Wagstaff, John Wilson. Middle row: Leslie Fearn (teacher), Gene Woodhouse, Ron Broome, Jim Charlesworth, Jim Hancock. Front row: Jack Hayes, Bill Smith, Brian Boam

MANCHESTER (1) School Ev/No. **Mcr.** 269

(2) LADYBARN School, Manchester

(3) NAME WILDMAN Mary
(Surname first, in block letters)

(4) Address 56 Ferndeane Rd, Withington.

(5) Age 10

(6) Time of Bus (if bus provided) 2.10 pm
(7) Name of Entraining Station CENTRAL
(8) Time of Train 3.10 pm
(9) No. of Train M 209
(10) Reception District W/x
(11) Reception Sub-District 8

area were Ladybarn Boys School and Ladybarn Girls School of Parrswood Road, Withington, with pupils ranging in ages from 5 years to almost 14 years. From Monday to Thursday of that last week in August the pupils had been practising the evacuation, with the assembly hall marked out as a railway station platform and

125

each class split up into small groups and made to assemble in a designated area. Each day, after completion of the exercise, the children were sent home, and the exercises became routine and monotonous. A relaxed, unsuspecting atmosphere prevailed which made Friday's events more dramatic.

On Friday 1st September the children were told they were going away for the weekend and filed outside to a road full of red Corporation double decker buses. Many parents were only to find out later that day that this time their children really had gone away. The buses delivered them to Central Station and at 10.30 a.m. the train departed. Later that day, at 3-10p.m, a second train would depart, carrying the remaining children from the school.

Most children remember how hot they were, dressed in their warmest clothing on a warm September morning. For many it was the first time they had been away from home, their first journey on a train and most had never been separated from their parents. Tense with anxiety as to where they were going, the children were hot and tired as they arrived at their unknown destination, for all the signs had been removed from the stations.

As they left Darley Station platform, the children were each handed a carrier bag, containing a packet of McVities biscuits, sweets, tea, sugar and other items. It was at this point that the children were separated into three distinct groups. 154 boys and twelve teachers, led by their headmaster Mr. Roberts and billeting officer Joe Hancock, formed a 'crocodile' and filed up Station Road to Darley Dale Council School. A number of lads grumbled to see that the parked Silver Service buses were for the convenience of Ladybarn girls, who were to travel to either Churchtown School or Cross Green.

One nine year old boy, Alan Pickstone, noted that they were amazed to see that all the orchards were full of fruit, as their only previous experience of fruit had been in city shops. At the school more volunteers provided tea and then split the boys into small groups, and took them to their billets. At this point, postcards were sent off to their parents to let them know where their children were located.

Meanwhile, Mr. Bartram, billeting officer at Churchtown School was receiving a large number of girls. The school was the hub of the main activities during the first fortnight of the war, for it was the A.R.P. Headquarters and ration book distribution centre.

During the summer of 1939 Mrs. Bartram had visited Hillside, Broadwalk and Northwood with a pad of billeting forms. Some householders had closed their doors on her but most people had been co-operative in accepting evacuees. In August the Bartram family had gone on their annual holiday to North Wales but a telegram was received recalling Mr. Bartram and the family packed their bags at once and returned to Darley.

Friday 1st September proved to be an exhausting day for the headmaster and teacher, Miss M. Briddon, helped by Reverend Martin of St. Helens Church and Eric Smith of James Smith's Nurseries, who both used their cars to transport children from the Station and then to their billets. Inside the school, the children were unusually quiet, as Mr. Bartram attempted to keep families together. One immediate problem was that the children had brought exercise and reading books with them and these had somehow to be stored in the school. The headmaster returned home to Whitworth Road at 8 p.m. that evening in a very tired state.

The post of billeting officer continued to be an exhausting and thankless task for people such as Mr. Bartram. Bed-wetting and head lice complaints from landladies or complaints from the parents of evacuee children had to be examined and passed to the district tribunals. On one occasion Mr. Bartram was informed that 50 pregnant women would be arriving at Darley Station from a city area. Arrangements were made for accommodation and prams were lined on the platform, but only three of the women stepped off the train. The whole process had been a waste of time and effort for the vast majority of the women had not appreciated the thought of spending time in the 'orrible bloomin quiet' of a rural area.

David Parsons was also kept busy that Friday, mustering a considerable party of Ladybarn girls in the Cross Green school

Evacuee children. Top left: Margaret Stevens and Pauline Dixon as young bridesmaids 1937. Top right: Muriel Owen. Bottom Left: Mary Wildman, Doris Wright and George Wright. Bottom right: Albert, one of the 'bombed babies' who stayed with the Wright family

playground and school rooms, ready for sending to their temporary homes throughout South Darley parish. Allan Wright of Oker used his car to transport some of these children and people still remember how bewildered and dazed many of the evacuees seemed as they arrived, clutching their rucksacks, gasmasks and carrierbags. At Oker a group arrived by car, crying as they stepped out onto the roadside and the general thought was that they were poor little souls. Oker folk gathered around to see who they were to have in their home. Two children went to live with Esther and Jack Boam, Sam Edge had one child, Allan Wright took in Mary Wildman and Joe Wilmott of Aston Farm received Brenda Scoular.

At nearby Wensley, more schoolchildren were being introduced to their new lodgings, including 13 year old Pauline Dixon and her cousin, Margaret Stevens (aged 12), at the Greystones home of Mrs. Fletcher. Twelve year old Muriel Owen stayed with Mr. and Mrs. Arthur Slack until 1941, whilst Joyce Tiller was billeted at Cecil Wright's home, 4 Eagle Terrace, and Nellie Carr at Keswick Cottage, the home of Mrs. Annie Wright. In passing, it is worth noting that Winster received 70 children and three teachers from Cavendish Road School, Withington, Manchester, and on Saturday over 40 mothers and babies arrived, being received at the Burton Institute, where teas were provided. Matlock schools were receiving a large influx of children from the Liverpool docklands area. It came as something of a rude shock.

For the first few weeks there was wonderment and just a hint of chaos as the new arrivals were assimilated. David Parsons writes in the school log book on 22nd September, "Since the 13th September there have been many callers who require billeting". However, the schools had remained closed from Monday 4th September until the 13th to allow the education authorities and teaching staff time to prepare a system that would accommodate the teaching of such a large influx of children.

Darley Council School opened on 13th September with a "shift system", whereby Ladybarn Boys School worked between 9.30 a.m. and 12.30 p.m. and Darley Council School children attended between

1.30 p.m. and 4.30 p.m., with the shifts to be reversed each week. Meanwhile, South Darley School also operated a 'shift system', but it was reversed each day.

This meant of course that half the day was spent away from school and the evacuee children had to be occupied somehow. Fortunately, the weather was lovely that autumn and the Ladybarn Boys would go with their teachers on long hikes over the moors and through the woods, with Alan Pickstone remarking that they went mad on the plentiful supply of fruit. "For one penny at a farm, they could eat as many 'windfalls' as one could manage, with disastrous results!" They went hay making on the farms and riding on the farm carts. For Alan it was a wonderful time.

The wide open spaces of the countryside could also spell danger for the youngsters from the city. On the evening of Tuesday 21st May 1940, a tragic report came in of a five year old boy falling into the River Derwent. Evacuee Alan Hall, son of Harry Hall of Withington, Manchester, was living at Rotherlea, Dale Road North, the home of Mrs. Taylor, together with his mother and elder brother. He was playing with a local boy, John Riggott, on the river bank. About 6 p.m. John went home and informed his father that Alan had fallen in the river and was clinging to the branch of a tree which overhung the river, opposite Darley House. The little boy had disappeared by the time rescuers arrived and dragging operations were mounted by the police. No trace of the missing boy was found until June 5th when his body was discovered near Cawdor Bridge, Matlock.

At Churchtown School, local pupil Lewis Jackson remembers that in those first few weeks, Churchtown pupils went with teacher Ernest Paulson on long nature walks, in which he passed on his love and knowledge of local history to the pupils. On other occasions, a great deal of gardening was undertaken in the school garden.

By the 3rd November 1939 the overcrowding situation at South Darley had eased a little, as a few evacuees had returned home, and one room had been made available at Oker Institute for school activities for the older, local pupils. The girls were allowed to use the only toilet in the hut, while Mr. Parsons had to take a file of boys to make use of a nearby hedgerow, a few fields away. On the 13th November the South Darley infants resumed their normal school hours, so allowing them to get away from the 'shift system', as their room was no longer required by the evacuee school. By the 27th November 1939, full time instruction was able to recommence for the whole school. South Darley pupils used the largest and smallest classrooms, whilst Ladybarn School used the middle-sized room.

The October meeting of South Darley W.I. at Oker Hut was the

An early photograph showing the Church and Sunday School, Two Dales (now Hayes Bakery). It became the 'Special Resources Centre' for woodwork and cookery lessons and during the Second World War it was used as school premises for Ladybarn Boys School, Manchester

occasion for a talk on the evacuees by a representative from Manchester Education Committee, whilst in December many Manchester parents took advantage of an excursion by motor buses to visit their children, billeted in the Matlock area. The majority of the evacuees returned to Manchester for the Christmas holiday, and a few of them did not return to South Darley.

At Darley Council School on January 26th 1940, Ladybarn Boys transferred to the 'Special Subjects Centre', Two Dales, formerly used in pre-war school days by all three local schools for woodwork and cookery lessons (today it houses Hayes Bakery).

'Digging for Victory' 1944. Harry and Jack Taylor of Wensley

This resulted in normal hours of teaching resuming for the local Darley children, though woodwork and cookery lessons ceased for the duration of the war years. All of the Manchester school's furniture was sent for. At South Darley, however, it was not until 12th April 1940 that the school reverted to its pre-war arrangements, with the evacuees, now reduced in numbers, to be found at the end of the Infant's room.

One consequence of the spare time resulting from the 'shift system' was Mr. Parson's decision to take over four old allotments on the Wenslees. Three were for the use of older local schoolboys whilst the fourth was to be tended by the Manchester girls and their teachers. This was an early foretaste of the 'Dig for victory' scheme. By December 1940 a report in the High Peak News says "Well done boys of South Darley Church of England School. At the beginning of the season they took over some old allotments and worked with such good will that up to a few weeks ago, they had grown and sold £8 worth of produce (1600 cabbages, 6 cwt. carrots, 3½ cwt. onions, 7 cwt. potatoes, 28 lb. haricot beans, 800 leeks, 2 cwt. parsnips and ½ cwt. marrows, as well as peas, beans and lettuce)". It should be added that David Parsons was not impressed by the use made of the allotment by the evacuees and eventually took it over. Gardening tools had to be collected from Mr. Parson's home at Darley Bridge and woe betide a dirty implement. The call would immediately go out, "Fetch me a willow from the river bank", and punishment would be meted out.

Manchester schoolgirl, Nellie Carr, aged 13 years in September 1939, recalls, "I stood in the playground with my mother, who was going with us to Derbyshire for a day or two. My brother, aged 11 years stood apart in the boys' school, for we were not together as a family. From Darley Station we girls were taken to Cross Green Schoolroom and told to wait until our names were called out. Everyone else had gone before the vicar was able to take us up to Keswick Cottage, the last cottage in Wensley, where Mrs. Wright, an elderly lady lived alone. She made us most welcome and after food I remember being so tired and was glad to go to bed, holding aloft a candlestick. This was a novelty as we had gas light at home. The cottage had no electricity, no running hot water and the earth closet was down the garden path. The latter was my real dread as I was terrified of all the creepy crawlies that may be lying in wait.

The third night there the siren started at 3.30 a.m. and it was a relief

Early February 1940 looking up Main Street from Wensley Square. Richard Hodgkinson of Wensley post office stands by Smith's coalwagon (note the hooded headlights due to blackout restrictions). This was a very severe winter with heavy snowstorms

February 1940. Richard Hodgkinson, Wensley post office, stands on the left and two evacuee schoolgirls from Ladybarn School, Manchester, are on the right

when the 'all clear' went. We heard later that it was a trial run. I was sad to see my mother leave but I loved the new experience of living in the countryside. I was in paradise and spent hours exploring and climbing the hills. The local children were quite friendly and didn't seem to resent the intrusion of we evacuees.

The winter of '39 was a very severe one, with deep falls of snow. For a few weeks transport in and out of Wensley was almost nil. The steep hill was just a sheet of ice and to my delight the local youngsters introduced me to the pleasure of sledging. These ice clad hills were a source of wonder and I had a great time. Many children, including my brother, billeted at Darley Dale, were homesick. They went home for Christmas and didn't return, but I was very happy indeed with 'Granny Wright', as she was so interesting to talk to and was always ready to lend me any of her collection of classical books. Mrs. Wright's son, daughter-in-law and little granddaughter, Peggy, who lived on Oker Road, became a second family for me and I became very attached to them.

Our headmistress, Miss Nesbitt, arranged a few outings for us in the spring of 1940 to see places of interest in Derbyshire and were greatly enjoyed by all. Many of the evacuees had gone home when I was informed by my father that my mother was ill and I would have to remain home after the summer holiday. The sadness at having to leave Wensley was softened when I learned that my mother was having another child.

I never lost touch with the family in Wensley and years later felt some guilt that the first year of the war had been one of the happiest times of my life".

13 year old evacuee Pauline Dixon, together with her cousin Margaret, had arrived with her mother acting as a helper, but she soon returned after completing her duties. Pauline remembers that many of the children on the train journey were very upset and also remembers the unusual mixture of food in the carrier bags, which included corned beef, cream crackers and chocolate biscuits. The Fletchers' house in which they were billeted was one of the few in Wensley with a

bathroom and other girls from the Manchester School, such as Nellie Carr, would arrive on bath night. Other memories are of gathering and eating watercress from the stream in Wensley Dale and of the Wensley countryside representing one big playground, albeit a green one. Throughout the years she felt fortunate in meeting a family who looked after them very well and the families remained friends for many years after the war.

Brenda Scoular was one of the children who had arrived on the second train, in the late afternoon. She arrived at Oker Hut by Silver Service bus and the children were placed at one end, whilst their carers waited at the other. At last, Brenda's name was read out, together with a fellow pupil, Sheila, and they found themselves in the kind and capable hands of Mr. and Mrs. Wilmot of Ashton Farm. Sheila, however, soon became homesick and returned to Manchester within three weeks. To Brenda, however, it was one big adventure.

She spent two and a half happy years with the Wilmots and was the last Ladybarn pupil at South Darley to return home, in late 1941. It was her father who arranged with a coach company at Longsight, Manchester, to bring parents on a number of visits to their children, but this fell by the wayside as less and less evacuee children remained in the parish.

The Wilmots gave Brenda the nickname of "Manch" and allowed her to prepare the hot mash for the poultry and to feed them. Every night Mrs Wilmot provided cocoa and home made buttered currant loaf and once a week the tin bath was brought out in front of the fire and everyone left the room, so that she could take a bath.

Eventually, only five Manchester children remained and so they were integrated with the village children when the last Manchester teacher departed. However, for the last twelve months of her stay, Brenda was the only child. She integrated well with the locals and became friendly with Hilary Duke at Robins Roost, Sitch Lane. It was with great sadness that she eventually returned to Manchester.

On the weekend that war was declared and the evacuees had arrived, Matlock Bath Venetian Fete and Matlock Carnival were cancelled and the two Matlock cinemas were closed, but only for one week. Quite a few accidents, involving broken bones, occurred in the Matlock district, due to the pitch darkness of the blackout. Pedestrians were taking to wearing white handkerchiefs round their arms at night, so that motorists might see them. In September the bus services were curtailed due to petrol rationing, with people being left standing during rush hour periods. Petrol rationing had begun on the 16th September 1939, when branded petrol was replaced by 'pool', a medium octane blend, and petrol for commercial vehicles was dyed red to prevent illicit use by civilians. A few of the Silver Service buses had their seats taken out

Nativity scene performed by scholars of Oker Methodist Chapel c1940.
Back row, l-r: Kathleen Shimwell, Peter Whittaker, Gladys Wood, Dawn ?, Mavis
Boam, Betty Farmer, Hazel Hendry, Sheila Dowling, George Wright, Ron Greatorex.
Front row: Barry Goodison, Joe Greatorex, Ron Slack, Brenda Petts, Dawn Wright,
Mary Farmer, Audrey Shimwell, Jean Peach

and re-arranged around the walls, facing inwards, so that more travellers could stand in the open space created.

From September 3rd to the beginning of December 1939 St. Mary's Church services were held in the afternoons but by December the blackout of the windows was successful and at the first night time service there was a large congregation This was partly due to the difficulty of blacking out the more numerous and larger windows of

Joe Marsh with one of his wedding cakes in the 1950's

St. Helen's Church, and thus Darley choir would travel across to South Darley. Minnie Potter (nee Pilkington) began to play the organ during the war years when regular organist George Buxton enlisted in the R.A.F. Between June and October 1940 the Church Sunday School did not meet because of the unsettled conditions.

South Darley W.I. Christmas Party was cancelled for Christmas time 1939 due to rationing. Instead there was to be a social and buffet supper on January 3rd 1940 in Oker Hut, to which all evacuee children were to be invited. Generally, it can be said that between September and December 1939 there was a standstill in social life but after this period it began to return.

Rationing of food arrived in January 1940, although the books had been ready ever since 1938. Butter, sugar, bacon and ham were first on the list but things did not get really difficult till 1942. Four ration books were eventually distributed; for food, petrol, clothing and furniture. Each family registered at a particular shop by giving the shopkeeper a slip from the ration book. He took the paper to the food officer to indicate now many customers he had and then the officer provided him with sufficient food. The housewife then took her coupon book to the shop, together with her money and a coupon was crossed off. By August 1942 sugar and fats rations were each down to 8 oz., whilst meat ration was 1 shilling and twopence a week and 2d. of this had to go on corned beef. Bread was never rationed until after the war.

The great wartime invention was points rationing, which widened the choice, for you could choose where to shop without being tied to the grocer where you had registered for basic rations. At May Lawman's wedding in 1944, Joe Marsh made her a small wedding cake and iced it, when only a few months before it would have been illegal. She was also fortunate that the parents of Ann Hall, an evacuee child living with the Lawmans, brought them a large ham and other items for the reception, almost certainly obtained on the London Black-market. Shortages resulted in the Government arranging for schools to collect rose hips to make into rose hip syrup (cough medicine) and Darley Churchtown pupils collected foxglove leaves to be 'bagged' and sent off to extract digitalis (medicine). During May, June and July 1942/43 and 1944, parties of children were taken to Hall Dale Wood by Mr Bartram to gather the leaves.

Chicken was seldom on the menu because hens were required for egg production and cattle for milk. Only pigs were in demand for bacon and pork, and Government sponsored 'pig clubs' were set up, allowing pig owners so much rationed pig meal. George Tomlinson at 1 Oker Road built a pig sty in his garden and built one for Dennis Wright at Thorntrees, Oker Road, whilst Mr. Shimwell of Toll Bar Cottage also kept two pigs. Mrs Tomlinson used the blood for making black pudding and sides of bacon covered in cloth were hug up in one of the bedrooms. Points rationing for clothes came in June 1941 and from now on it was points rather than money that counted. One main blow for children came in 1942 when sweets rationing was introduced. Phillip Bowler of Cross Green remembers how people went out to get fruit to make their own jam. They gave up their jam coupons in exchange for sugar coupons and all strange concoctions were made, including marrow jam and rhubarb and fig.

Besides the evacuee schoolchildren, other people arrived in Wensley. The outbreak of war did not prevent guests from coming to stay at the Hall. Many of Eric and Muriel Bowser's acquaintances from pre-war years lived in towns and cities where the strains of war began to tell, especially in relation to the menace of German air raids. They found a breathing space and respite from wartime stress in the relative peace and tranquility of Wensley Hall Guest House. The district appeared to be a peaceful backwater in comparison to Sheffield, Nottingham or Manchester, with the added bonus that fresh air and good food could still be obtained.

Eric was allowed petrol coupons to run his car, especially as it was often used to fill a social need, when people needed to visit or be rushed urgently to hospital. Muriel was not a natural cook but provided good meals, in spite of wartime rationing, due to great effort and attention to detail and managing to get the best out of what was available. A local addition to the weekly menu was rabbit, shot by Joe Hardy of Green Farm and displayed for sale, hanging from pegs, at a cost of 9 pennies each.

Ben Clay's wife, Florence, at Clifton House, took in boarders from Sheffield and the East Coast. She was kept extremely busy, for, whilst Ben was selling green groceries on Matlock Market, Florence was catering for the guests, whilst also selling green groceries and fish from her pantry and kitchen. Sometimes she used the Eagle Terrace home of Mrs. Beatrice Stone as an overflow, whenever she could not accommodate visitors. Also, during this period, soldiers were billeted above the Crown Inn, Wensley Square, and some would be allowed to take a bath at the Clay's house, for it was one of the few Wensley homes with such modern fitments.

At 3.30 a.m. on Monday 4th September 1939 air raid sirens went off

Matlock ARP with chief controller George Banks, 17th September 1942.
Back row, l-r: X, X, X, Dot Hill, Marion Turner, J Buckley, G Eastwood, X, J Gilbey
Third row: Jane Orme, Mrs Durham-Gee, Barbara Adams, X, X, X
Second row: Doug Twigg, Mat Bunting (junior), Ken Pursglove, Ken Booth, Gerald
Innes, John Cross, Peter Attwater, Peter Barks
Front row: A Drinkwater, X, Les Williams, BC Orme, G Banks, Frank Ford, Mat
Bunting (senior), H Wright, W Ridge
Photo from Peter Attwater

in the district and the Air Raid Warden system was tested in action. It was a false alarm but it revealed the need for a more adequate siren warning in this hilly and scattered area. During that first week of war A.R.P. officials in Darley had been very busy. The warden post was at the Grouse Inn and First Aid Dressing Station at the Stancliffe Works cabin. Sand bagging had been carried out to a large extent in many parts of the district, but gas masks were still being distributed.

140

Certificate No. D/ 14090

DERBYSHIRE COUNTY COUNCIL
AIR RAID PRECAUTIONS DEPARTMENT.

Certificate

This is to certify that *Mr John Fredk Taylor*
of *Yew Tree Cottage, Wensley, Matlock*
has completed a course of Anti-Gas Training under the auspices of the Derbyshire County Council, and has acquired sufficient knowledge of Anti-Gas Measures to act as a member of the Air Raid Precautions Services.

Name and qualification of Instructor *G. A. Banks*
L. A. R. P.

County Controller.

Date **MAR 14 1940**   Signed

County A.R.P. Organiser.

South Darley's A.R.P. headquarters was in the sandbagged Parish Room, underneath St. Mary's Church and during the first few months of the war and into 1940 was manned continually on a rota basis, night and day, during any alarm. This was very tiring for the majority of wardens who had jobs to go to during daylight hours. Amongst those who became A.R.P. wardens were Reg Boden, George Potter, Arthur Slack, Norman Taylor, Harry and Jack Taylor, Les Flint, Dennis Wright, George Shimwell, Tant Holmes, Tom Shimwell, Arthur Vardy and Les Walker. Another stalwart member was Miss Patty Potter of Toll Bar Hill, Wensley, who took her duties very seriously, and insisted most strongly that people should, "Put that light out!" Reg Boden remembered that most of the time spent on duty in the Parish Room seemed to involve playing cards. When A.R.P. Warden Arthur Slack left his house in Wensley, his daughter Edna and her mother went down into their neighbour's cellar for protection.

From early days wardens were issued with helmets and uniform, stirrup pumps, stretchers and partially shaded torches to prevent the upward glare of light. By November 1940 earplugs, issued by the Government to reduce the effect of air raid noises, had been distributed. Richard Hodgkinson remembers coming away from Church in October

1939 and being amused to see A.R.P. members practising decontamination drill, with gas masks affixed and stirrup pumps being used to spray the pavement near the plantation. A mobile gas van or shed was placed in the field by the side of the school so that A.R.P. wardens could practice crawling through the enclosed space with gas masks on, after smoke canisters had been tossed inside.

When the children went to school on September 13th 1939, they carried their gas masks in cardboard boxes and continued to do so on schooldays for the next few years. As the war progressed, all sorts of materials were used to cover these boxes and so make them more

Toll Bar Hill, Wensley. Paul Bowser and Frank Hardy off to Cross Green School with their gas masks, 1940. Sadly, Paul died in that same year, aged 5

Former air-raid shelter at South Darley School. Now a storeroom, in the year 2001

presentable. Woollen covers were knitted and plastic ones could be bought. Gas mask drill at school was a daily occurrence in those early months and air raid drill became second nature. Ron Greatorex remembers that on a number of occasions in the autumn of 1939 the class was led across to the plantation and told to lie down, two children to a tree, but in the majority of cases they would be expected to sit beneath the tables in their classrooms.

On the 26th September 1939, the vicar, Reverend Simmons, the Chairman of the managers, approved the air raid precautions taken. These were put to the test on the 21st August 1940 when the sirens sounded between 10.37a.m. and 10.47a.m. During the same air raid alert, Churchtown School teachers cleared the school of all children into St. Helen's Church in two minutes. An older child took responsibility for a younger child and all pupils were told to get under the pews for protection. Hymns were sung to calm the nerves of the children.

On the 17th January 1941, at Cross Green, only a few children arrived in the afternoon for the siren was said to have blown. Enquiries from the police confirmed that the hooter had blown a short blast, but that the alarm was false. There was another alert at 1.00p.m. on 31st January 1941, with the all clear at 1.15p.m. February 11th 1941 saw the sirens sounding at 3.00p.m. and the all clear at 3.55p.m, whilst on March 7th 1941 the sirens went just as the children left school at noon, with the all clear at 12.45p.m.

When the siren sounded at 2.15p.m. on Wednesday May 14th 1941, Mr. Parsons blew the whistle and for the first time the children filed out to the two newly built brick air raid shelters, one in the girls' playground at the back of the school and one in the boys' playground. The alert lasted just fifteen minutes. The last air raid alert recorded in the school logbook is on the 4th March 1943 when the siren sounded at 9.00a.m. and the all clear was given at 9.30a.m. Today, only the girls' air raid shelter remains and is used for storage space.

The schools' windows had been taped and fine mesh net fitted to them to prevent shattered shards of glass causing injuries. Families used a variety of materials to black out their own homes. Black hessian curtains were used and a thick, dark, blotting paper type of material could be pinned against the windows. Other people made wooden frames, covered with dark material, to slot into position.

The first large co-ordinated A.R.P. practice took place on Sunday 22nd October 1939. The peace of a beautiful autumn morning was broken at 9.00a.m. when air raid sirens sounded at Matlock, Tansley, Darley and Wirksworth. Wardens dashed off through the mist to their post. The "ghost raiders" arrived overhead, scattering high explosives, incendiary bombs and two types of poison gas. About 9.40a.m. the "Raiders passed" signal was given. The Wardens telephoned in their reports, including one of phosgene gas at Darley Bridge, high explosives at Two Dales and mustard gas at Church Lane, Darley. It was not until 11.30a.m. that the "All clear" was given.

By May of 1940 the Chief Warden said that an electric siren had now been authorised for Darley Dale and one would be shortly erected at Mill Close Mine. Another siren was fitted on top of a tall metal frame fixed to one of the buildings in the Council Depot Yard on Station

Road, Darley. On Friday evening 28th June 1940 a big A.R.P. demonstration was held on the Hall Leys, Matlock, to arouse public interest in precautionary measures. An imaginary air raid was staged with bombs being dropped, causing "casualties", some of which were buried under "wreckage" on the bandstand. Decontamination units cleared away mustard gas and stirrup pump demonstrations were given for the benefit of the public.

It is interesting to note that in mid December 1940 Enoch Smith of Lumb Cottage, Cross Green, was summoned for allowing a fire to burn in the open during the hours of darkness. The case was dismissed on payment of 9/-costs. It would be interesting to know which warden reported him.

During the 1940's Council Surveyor, John Wheeldon, organised exercises in the Depot yard, Station Road, Darley Dale, for Council employees who were also members of the A.R.P. One frightening exercise was to climb a swaying, vertical 30 foot ladder,

North Darley ARP man Wilfred Taylor 1942.
L-r: Wilfred, Maureen, Elsie

held upright by men holding retaining ropes, clamber over the top and descend on the other side. My father, Wilfred Taylor, was one of the many men who disliked intensely this particular training exercise.

By March 1942 a local newspaper reports that the A.R.P. had been reorganised and was in better shape than before, with the addition of a 'fireguard' or 'firewatchers' organisation. The report adds, "Much good work has been put in during the last few months and much training received and Darley Dale has a well-organised band of firequards who assemble on siren and watch over the welfare of their own particular areas. Number Five area is South Darley and each party of seven people

145

'A fine body of men'. Darley Dale's Special Constables in the County Council Depot Yard at Station Road c1940.
Back row, l-r: Sergeant Tansley, Eric Smith, Mr Tye, Mr Hanson, Police Constable Tooke.
Front row: Inspector JC Bartram, Mr Welsh (headmaster Stancliffe Hall), Mr White, Horace Turner

has one or two stirrup pumps, water containers and sandmats. The senior fireguard is Harold Hall, newsagent, of Wensley. Party leaders are W.Roose, H.Hall, H.Fawley, Joe Marsh and R. Walker and there are 105 fireguards enrolled." These included Esme (Bobby) Davison and Annie Pepper at Darley Bridge and Marion and Mabel Taylor at Wensley. Marion's daughter, Eileen, remembers that when the siren sounded and her mother went out into the night, she and her grandmother would lie behind the settee, with cushions for protection from enemy bombs. It is interesting to note that the stirrup pumps were also useful in other ways. George Shimwell of 4 Oker Road used his for spraying the pests on his apple blossom.

Helping the A.R.P. maintain the blackout were the Special Constables of Police, led by Special Inspector of Police, J.C. Bartram. He was a busy man for we have already seen that he was headmaster of Churchtown School and billeting officer. He had joined the 'Specials' during the General Strike of 1926, and in 1938 had been involved with his men in protecting Mill Close Mine at night during the height of the I.R.A. bombing scare. Their wartime 'mustering post' was the small Reading Room, then attached to William Deacon's Bank (now Royal Bank of Scotland) at the top of Station Road. They each received a boot allowance and Inspector Bartram was armed with a Luger pistol. If you were told to "Put out that light!", you didn't argue with a Luger pistol.

In actual fact, only two attacks by aircraft took place in the vicinity of Darley Dale, one at Rowsley Sidings in 1941 when incendiary bombs were dropped in nearby fields and the other on Sunday March 4th 1945, when, in the early hours a lone raider flew down the valley and fired several bursts of machine gun bullets at Matlock Town centre. Eldridge's (Outfitters) on Dale Road, the Ritz Cinema and Dakins hair-dressers were all hit, as well as a tree in the park.

However, the inhabitants of South Darley could often see from a distance the terrible pounding that Sheffield was taking in the 'Blitz'. During the blackout, the glow from the burning ruins of the city and the arc of tracer bullets were clearly visible and the sound of explosions was carried to their ears. This was especially the case on the nights of Thursday 12th December and Sunday 15th December 1940, when the German Luftwaffe mounted its severest raids of the war on the city of steel. It was during Thursday night's air raid that Ruth Walters of Eagle Terrace, Wensley, and Percy Wagstaffe, farmer of Two Dales found their wedding reception at Two Dales Café rudely interrupted when the sirens sounded and guests had to depart for their homes.

As a result of the Thursday night bombing, South Darley was to receive three more evacuee children. Mr. and Mrs. Brant and their three children, Doris (10), Dennis (7) and Ivy (4) lived at Shoreham Street,

Sheffield, between the Railway Station and the Tramcar depot. Bombing had taken place before and they had usually sheltered in the Tramcar depot shelter, but on the 12th December the sirens sounded and all three children and their mother went down into the cellar, instead, with a few provisions. Their father was out at work.

The trap door from the cellar into the street could be locked from either side and unfortunately they had forgotten to unlock the outside lock before sheltering. Cowering down below, they could hear the whistles of the bombs and the crumps as they hit their targets. The whole street of houses was flattened and unbeknown to them the tramcars had not been able to reach the depot in time. Later, when they emerged, they were to see the mangled wreckage of these trams.

They felt the shuddering jolt as their house was hit and thought that their cellar would collapse at any moment. It remained intact but they could not escape and were underground for three days. Rescuers eventually plucked them to safety as the second raid on the 15th December took place in another quarter of the city and they were taken to a rescue centre based in a school. Further trauma occurred when their mother was told mistakenly that their father had been killed and their father arrived in Shoreham Street to find the ruins of their home. Eventually they were reunited but they discovered that many friends and neighbours, including children, had been killed in the first raid, which resulted in over four hundred deaths. They witnessed the terrible sight of bodies being taken up off the streets and put into lorries.

In South Darley, many parishioners had stayed up late to witness the bombing of Sheffield. One of these was the children's aunty, Nellie Bishton, the second wife of John Charles Bishton, living next to Jobie Taylor at the bottom of Oker Hill, Cross Green. Nellie was quickly in touch with her sister and insisted that the children should come to the comparative safety of Cross Green and within a few days they were travelling by themselves on the bus to a new life in the countryside.

People in the parish were very good and Doris can remember Eunice Wright's mother providing some clothes, whilst Doris was told to visit the vicarage, the site of the Red Cross depot, where Reverend Simmons had a collection of clothing, including a nice coat that Doris thought was wonderful. This was their first real time spent in the countryside and they thought it was marvellous, although after the Christmas holiday, this was tempered by the fear inspired by headmaster Mr. Parsons and the threat of the willow cane.

It is worth noting that at Wensley, John Charles Bishton's son, Fred and his French born wife Leonie, had also taken in relatives as evacuees. Fred, a veteran of the Great War, had met his wife whilst serving in France and Belgium. Fred's nieces and nephews arrived in the Matlock district from Salford, Manchester. The three younger children lodged with their uncle, Bill Bishton in Matlock, but the two elder children, teenagers John and Margaret Potts, lodged with Fred and Leonie at Wensley. In late 1940 they returned to Salford, but it is ironic that when arriving at the railway station in Manchester, their train had to be diverted into a railway tunnel, as an air-raid was taking place over the city.

The Blitz on London also resulted in more evacuees arriving in September 1940. Margery Boden of 1, St.Mary's View, originated from Chapman Street in the East End of London, where she had been a neighbour and friend of the Wood family. Margery's friend, Florrie Hunter (nee Wood) was pregnant and her soldier husband wished to get her away from the dangers of the Blitz. In September it was arranged for Florrie to travel to South Darley with her sister Lou, who, shortly after arriving, left St. Mary's View to work at the New Bath Hotel.

However, a few days later, Florrie's sisters, Mrs Collins, with children Teresa and Veronica and Mrs. Peggy Henshaw and three children were put on the train bound for Derbyshire. Their husbands worked in the docks and as A.R.P. wardens had dragged children's bodies from the rubble. They too wished to get their families away from the danger areas.

In early October, Florrie gave birth to a baby girl at St. Mary's View, and she was named Margery. Her first cot was a wooden drawer pulled from the dresser. Meanwhile, the house was so crowded that the Collins family was sleeping on the landing floor.

*Top: 'Dale View', former home of Captain Ward and home to the 'bombed babies' of
evacuated London nursery, 1940-1945.
Bottom: Miss Silcock and young children from the nursery. This rustic summerhouse
was converted into a little 'church' with an altar*

When Mrs. Collin's sister-in-law, Nellie Collins, arrived at 1 St. Mary's View with her three children, things could not stay as they were. Florrie would stay with her baby at Margery's . Mrs Devaney, widow of the former Wensley cobbler, was very kind and enabled the two sister-in-laws and their families to live in the former cobbler's shop at Blindwell House, Wensley. Peggy Henshaw and her three children were placed with Margery's friends, Carol and Cyril Taylor, at Northwood Avenue, Broadwalk. The Collins children and the Henshaws went to South Darley School and the families stayed in the area till February of 1945.

Also arriving from the bomb shattered capital, but authorised by the London County Council, was a Ministry of Health Evacuation Nursery, consisting of 30 London children ranging in age from two years to five. They arrived in late 1940 at Dale View, Sitch Lane, Oker, the former house of Captain Charles Ward, and were known as the 'bombed babies'.

In charge was Miss Silcock, a teacher, and Miss Taylor, a handicraft teacher, both from Goldsmith College, together with Nurse Dunkley and Nurse Gretton and the cook, Mrs. Glen. A number of local girls lived in as part of their war work and looked after the children,

Ethel Corless with some of the 'bombed babies' at Dale View

including taking them for walks or out in push chairs. These helpers included Ethel Corless of Wensley, Kathleen Holmes from Oker, Patsy Morrissey from Snitterton and Marion Tomlinson from Oker Road. At the age of five the children had to leave the nursery, to return to their parents, although one or two went on to stay in South Darley homes, including five year old Albert, who was taken in by Mr and Mrs Allan Wright of Oker.

The Sunday School at St. Mary's had ceased activities for a while during 1940 but Miss Silcock and Miss Taylor helped to restart it as 'The Children's Church' and continued with it during the war years. In the grounds of Dale View, Miss Silcock and Miss Taylor converted a small wooden summer house into a 'makeshift' church, with tiny altar and seats inside, for the use of their small charges. Eventually, many years after the war, Miss Taylor married the former vicar of St. Mary's, Reverend Simmons, after he became a widower.

Throughout the War years music continued to play an important part in individual and community life.

Alan Pickstone, the Manchester evacuee photographed in Matlock, Christmas 1940

Ian Garrity as a young cornet player, around 1943, dressed in the uniform of Matlock Town Band. This photograph was originally incorporated into a Bakelite frame at the Darley Dale factory where his father worked

Horace Holmes, a fine comet player who had played the 'Last Post' at the first remembrance service at South Darley in 1919 now kept the Railway Inn, Matlock and tutored young musicians in the beer cellar. Matlock local, Ian Garrity recalls having lessons as a young boy, amongst the (to him) huge beer barrels in the cellar from Horace, who played in the Lea Mills Band. Horace would take no charge for the lessons but happily prepared Ian for 'Slow Melody' contests which still took place during the War years. These melodies usually consisted of sentimental Victorian airs and were immensely popular at the time. Ian went on to play cornet in the Darley Dale Band under Fred Slater's baton and as a National Serviceman played in the RAF Central Band before later becoming a semi-professional player in various dance bands.

Ian was one of many young lads to come under the wing of Fred Slater and receive tuition at Fred's house on Wellington Street. Another was the Manchester evacuee, Alan Pickstone. Alan's father had played the cornet and trumpet in his younger days and as War broke out had just started his son off on learning the cornet. The parents of the evacuees visited Darlely Dale just a week after War broke out and Alan's father arranged for his son to have lessons with Fred. The lessons would continue for four years, not without some difficulty.

Alan would catch the 5.45 pm North Western bus to Ashton's Corner (Smedley Street/Dimple), then walk up Smedley Street and Wellington Street, rather a frightening experience in winter months with the blackout and only a small torch for company. On one occasion Alan lost direction on his return and ended up walking down Bank Road into Matlock, unknown territory to the small evacuee, before finding his way back up the Dimple to Joe Ashton the baker who took Alan in to wait for the next bus.

Alan recalls Darley Band rehearsing in the Dukes Café in Two Dales, the little chapel near the Blacksmiths Arms and a barn on Oddford Lane. The Band was much in demand at Hall Leys Park bandstand as well as playing Christmas carols throughout the area.

Alan vividly recalls the band heading a Sunday morning Church parade from the Whitworth Institute to St Mary's, South Darley. It was early in the War and the two columns of men marched with rifles and large bayonets (in case of possible invasion!). Alan believes the Vicar insisted on the rifles being left outside for the Service. He happily recalls the easier route back down hill to the Whitworth and a welcome drink of pop in the Officers Mess.

The Darley Band were also present at the laying of Commemorative Stones around the Yew Tree at St. Helen's Church to mark allied action at Narvik (Norway), Dunkirk and Calais. A much needed boost to morale at a grim period of the War. The stones can still be seen today.

By strange coincidence Alan's first cornet was borrowed from Jack Waterfall, band member, who at the time lived on a farm above Two Dales. Many years later Jack would become the much loved and respected caretaker at Darley Dale Primary School, the very school to which the young Alan Pickstone was evacuated to.

If we now turn to farming, we find that war had brought changes to activities at Flatts Farm, Bridge Farm, Field Farm and Green Farm. The convoy system meant that priority had to be given to munitions and food for the fighting forces and the general public. Therefore, the War Agricultural Executive Committee (War Ag.) encouraged each of the South Darley farmers to plough up 10% of the grassland for the purpose of growing crops to feed their own animals. £2 per acre would be received if 10% was ploughed for producing oats, wheat, turnips, mangols and potatoes. In 1942, it was reported in the local press that Derbyshire had doubled the acreage of ploughed land compared to 1939.

Joe Hardy and his son Bill, at Green Farm, Wensley, ploughed a large, stony field near Brightgate on the Bonsall Road, to grow oats. Joe, a former cavalryman in the Great War, still worked with horses and contracted the Marshalls from Tansley and Bert Wheeldon on his green Fordson tractor from Winster to plough the land. At harvest time the army, based at the Whitworth Institute, agreed to transport the crop by road in their lorries but at the last moment could not fulfil their promise. Joseph and Bill made wooden sledges and transported the crop, instead, by horse and sledge down the hillside to Dalefield Barn. Mr, Upton, the thresher, then drove the threshing drum down into the dale and it was then winched up to Dalefield Barn, where the threshing was undertaken and the haystacks built. 'Old timers' such as 'Tiersa Bill' (William Taylor) and "Burley" Derbyshire helped out on the farm with hay making or the building of walls and so help from the newly formed wartime 'Land girls' organisation was not required.

It was during the Second World War that silage (second cut) was first introduced, instead of providing hay or corn. On Joe Greatorex's farm at Lobby, Oker Road, the crop was put into a crude pit to keep out the air and molasses were poured on top, at intervals, with a final topping of limestone dust, sheets and cow dirt to keep it airtight.

On Percy Mosely's farm at Snitterton, for a few months in 1942, a group of Italian prisoners of war were brought by lorry under armed guard each day to clear out the stream and make drainage ditches in Hall Pasture, in the dale just below Oker hamlet. There was no thought of escape in the minds of the prisoners and the guards were very relaxed, unless the farmer arrived on the scene. Ron Greatorex can remember a small group of POW's wandering by themselves through Lobby farmyard and even up into Northern Dale, chatting and joking. They wore brown boiler suits with a pale yellow star on the back. During their stay they made toys out of wood for some of the local children such as Pat Fox (nee Goodman) at the Wain's farm, Beech House, Oker. They would arrive at Beech House and Mrs. Lawman's to ask for boiling water to mash their tea. The Italians also resurfaced the road with stone and tar near Thorntrees and Lobby Farm. An Italian POW camp was at Buxton. George Easthope, a Sheffield coal merchant, had left the city with his family to escape the bombing and lived in Wensley Square. He brought with him his Morris Commercial lorry and used it to transport rations from Riber Castle Food Store to the Buxton POW camp. Bill Haynes, Silver Service bus driver, also transported the Italians at times.

In early 1940, John Lomas arrived with his family from Doveholes to take over from the Naylor family at Bridge Farm, Darley Bridge. They brought five horses and 50 cattle with them but three of the horses and the majority of the cattle died within the first few months, due they believed to the belland (lead poisoning) in the ground. George Abbott, knackerman from Brackenfield, was kept extremely busy.

With some compensation from Mill Close Lead Mine and a good wartime price for milk they were able to get a contract with an Irish dealer at Derby to replace some of the cattle. Mechanised milking was introduced because girls were being drafted into war work, but the biggest change was the ploughing of half the 80 acres of farmland. The Lomas's had decided to change from horses to tractors, but permission was needed in wartime. A tractor could only be bought if a certain acreage was ploughed, sown and harvested and this would only be possible if they contracted out their machines to other farmers. With their tractor, plough, drill and cultivator, John Lomas Junior worked the land belonging to the Tricketts, Hardy's, Clays and John Joseph Slack near Brightgate.

The family believed that the wheat they grew on the heavy yellow clay soil of Bridge Farm produced some of the best quality grain they had seen. A large number of potatoes were also grown and at harvest time a number of women were employed to gather them. An 'Eat more potatoes' campaign started in 1940, to save grain, and potato consumption rose by 60% during the war. Joe Hardy remembers as a schoolboy during the war years being sent with other lads by Mr. Parsons to help out at Bridge Farm in weeding and thinning the turnip crop and getting paid a small amount for doing so. Phillip Bowler of Cross Green walked with his brother Alf and sister Margaret plus wheelbarrow to collect potatoes from farmer Charles Wildgoose's field on Old Road, opposite the Red House Stables.

Whilst the farmers were doing 'their bit' for the war effort, the general public in the Matlock area were also being asked to make extra efforts. In August 1940, the Matlock district took part in a "Spitfire fund", to attempt to raise £5000 for the building of a warplane. In January 1941 the committee arranged for an exhibition of a

Darley House Estate residents potato picking 1942 in Charles Wildgoose's field near Red House, Old Road, Darley Dale.
Back row, l-r: Nellie Hayes, Mrs White, Sam Hayes, Mrs Marsden, Joan Dudbury, Mrs Wheeldon, Sydney Wildgoose, Mrs Andrews, Fred Wildgoose, Mrs Marriott, Charles Wildgoose, Mr Bradbury, Mrs Smith, Mrs Oldfield, Gordon Winder, Mrs Gregory, Roy Smith, Mrs Robinson, Billy Smith, Mrs Wood, Mrs Harris.
Front row: Rose Winder, Joan Moore, Jean Wood, Audrey Marsden, Margaret Wildgoose, Rita Marsden, Joan Smith, Ann Winder, John Cook, Derek Marsden, Ann Rhodes, X, Owen Moore

Messerschmitt 109, brought down in action, to be held in William Twigg's loading bay on Bakewell Road to raise money, but the fund was closed at £1350 in March 1941 when it was announced that Matlock was to host a "War Weapons Week," to be held from Friday 9th May to 17th May, with the target being £75,000.

Friday 9th May was Children's Day, with a film shown in a Matlock cinema at 2.30p.m. whilst South Darley and Darley Dale Senior school-children should have attended the film at Churchtown School. However, owing to the siren being sounded at Darley, the film show did not take place. Instead the children were shown Churchtown's War Weapons Exhibition. South Darley School closed at 3.40p.m. to allow the children to reach Causeway Lane Sports ground at Matlock, where buns and teas were served and the children participated in sports events.

Saturday the 10th saw the official opening by the Duke of Devonshire at a massed meeting on the Hall Leys, where an armoured car and searchlight unit was on display and a football match took place between the R.A.S.C. (3) and Chesterfield Town (2). The day ended with a bowls competition, band concert and a dance in the Town Hall.

At 3.15p.m. on Sunday, a drumhead service was held on the Hall Leys, attended by 700 people, preceded by a large procession. Monday should have been Refugees Day but owing to a lack of response from evacuees etc., a babyshow was put on at the Town Hall, instead. Wednesday 14th May was Forces Day, including a ceremonial changing of the guard with military band in attendance, a physical training display by the A.T.S., a forces swimming gala at the Lido and an open air forces boxing tournament near the bandstand.

The week ended with Civil Defence Day on Saturday 17th. A gas hut was provided at Park Head for locals to test their respirators'

Darley Dale Council School.

WAR WEAPONS WEEK. 9th. to 16th May 1941.

This School is taking part in the Darley Dale special effort and this appeal is addressed to all parents with the hope that they will their strongest support to the following inducements to save.

1. Every scholar is urged to become a member of the National Savings scheme so if your child is not already a member will you allow him to join the Darley Dale Council School Savings Group?
2. Group members are also urged to increase their contributions during War Weapons Week - by doubling or trebling their loans.
3. All children will be allowed to bring their savings each day to their Teachers who will save the money until it is transferred to National Savings stamps or certificates during War Weapons Week.
4. The older children have undertaken to make special efforts to earn more money before 9th May which they have promised to put into National Savings.
5. Total effort- there are 275 scholars in the school - will you support the the effort to reach a total of £300 loaned through National Savings.

Similar appeals will be received but we are confident that the thrifty habits formed by the children through the School Savings Group will be to their benefit in later life - will you help them?

By joining the Savings Group money is LOANED to the Government for the further prosecution of the war - a Savings Certificate costs 15/- and in 10 years time will be worth £1.- 0.- 6. Sixpenny or half - crown stamps may be purchased until 15/ is saved

LEND TO DEFEND YOUR CHILDREN AND YOUR COUNTRY FROM THE PERILS OF NAZI DOMINATION.

April 1941.   J. HANCOCK. (Headmaster.)

A copy of the information given regarding the National Savings Scheme for War Weapons Week. Alan Pickstone cashed his in 1955 for his wedding

NATIONAL SALVAGE CAMPAIGN

This is to Certify that

George Wrig ?? Baker

has been appointed a

SALVAGE STEWARD

By the Matlock Urban District Council

Signed E.L. Wright ..... *Date* 6/8/42

Acting Clerk S.P.36

WASTE INTO WEAPONS

proficiency. A football match between Youlgreave and the R.A.S.C. was contested and a dance was held at night. A schools slogan competition had been organised for the week and the winning choice was "Britain's Might needs Matlock's Mite" and a large wooden target barometer was placed during the week at Park Head. The British Legion had got hold of a 'dud' German bomb and wheeled it round the streets to collect money in it. The target of £75,000 was sufficient to equip a squadron of fighter planes but the splendid news was that Matlock and district had raised £212,026.

The following year, between 21st and 28th February 1942, another effort was mounted to raise £210,000 but this time £154,000 was raised. During May to June of the same year a National Salvage campaign was carried out with special emphasis on collecting paper and rubber. At Darley Council School, a competition was organised by Joe Hancock, for collecting old books from neighbours. For 50 books a child received a Captain's badge, rising to the possibility of gaining a General's badge and the books went towards the Salvage campaign.

Meanwhile, Saturday June 3rd 1944 saw the opening of Matlock's "Salute the Soldier Week" with the aim being to raise £150,000 to run a base hospital for a year. The fund raising week coincided with the Normandy landings (D-Day) on Tuesday 6th June and the total was surpassed, with well over £200,000 being raised. Saturday's opening ceremony saw a display of Highland dancing and music provided by the Band of the King's Royal Rifles and an impressive drumhead ceremony was held on Sunday.

The closing day, Saturday June 10th, saw a gymnastic display by the A.T.S. and a battle scene recreated by 'C' Company of the 1st Battalion Derbyshire Home Guard. Some members wore enemy uniforms and were well and truly "wiped out". Paratroopers then demonstrated, showing manoeuvres after a landing and the use of the new folding motor cycle. Some children were given rides on these machines. There followed a skilful performance by dispatch riders of the Home Guard. Finally, a comic football match by the Mobile Platoon of 'C' Company, Derbyshire Home Guard brought proceedings to a close.

The winter of 1939/40 was the worst on record for 45 years, with snow, burst pipes and fuel shortages. The RAF was grounded and troops were called in to keep the trains running. In Derbyshire there was very severe weather starting on January 26th, when great blizzards swept the Peak. In January the Whitworth Institute had still not been taken over by the army and a large number of people took advantage of the frozen conditions of the boating lake and enjoyed a good spell of skating. However, in early January 1940 the Trustees announced that the Institute would be closed to the public from the end of January.

As in the rest of the country, St. Mary's Church was banned in June 1940 from ringing the Church bells for the duration of the war except as a warning of invasion by parachutists. This government declaration silencing the sound of bells throughout the nation also nullified the content of Reverend Simmon's letter in South Darley parish magazine of June 1940. He wrote, "What we need at this time of danger is the grace to keep our spirits strong. We owe this to all our men who are labouring, and maybe dieing to keep alight the torch of Justice, Freedom and Truth. I have a suggestion to make which I believe will help us all to keep in touch with the Eternal. I announced in Church that

I intend each day at 12 noon, when I am at home, to ring the Church bell for a minute. We will call it the Prayer Bell. The idea is that all who hear it should join with me in breathing a short prayer, as we are at our work, and wherever we may be. At this hour of the day, you will remember, our Saviour stretched forth His arms upon the Cross. By this means we shall be doing something of great value. Anything said with the intention of praying for our cause, our Country and our victory, will be of everlasting value." Unfortunately the sudden movement of events in Holland, Belgium and France during May/June 1940 prevented this idea from reaching fruition. It was the surest sign of "the end of the beginning" when the bell was allowed to ring out again on 15th November 1942 to celebrate Montgomery's victory at El Alamein, in North Africa.

All roadside signposts and station signs were taken down or blotted out in the Darley area from June 1940 in order to confuse any German invasion force, although it probably caused more difficulties for the 'rooky' army drivers who eventually came to do their initial training at the Royal Army Service Corps base at the Whitworth Institute. One such sign that was 'blotted out' was the wording 'Darley Dale Cricket Club' etched into the stone wall at the entrance to the present day car park. A metal plate was fastened over it.

Although Matlock Cricket Club decided not to play during the coming 1940 summer season, Darley Dale made the decision to carry on at the annual general meeting held in April at Two Dales Café. Unlike in the wartime years 1914-1918, the committee decided that morale would be bolstered if they continued playing but to have one team only and a modified fixture list of 17 matches. The results for 1940 were 9 matches won, one lost and seven drawn. Cricket continued at the Darley ground throughout the war years, with the army teams able to play on Saturdays that were vacant. It is interesting to see that First Team wicket keeper, Reg Boden, was chosen to play four times for Derbyshire during the 1943 season, including the match against Nottinghamshire at Trent Bridge on July 17th.

As the war was threatening to break out in 1938/39, Darley Bridge

Formerly the shop belonging to Albert Fawley, Darley Bridge, it was taken over by Mary Neville. In the early war years the iron railings were removed for wartime salvage. (The shop is now Derwent House.)

welcomed another shopkeeper at the former residence of Joe Marsh and Charles Bower. Vincent and Mary Bell arrived and set up a general provisions store, whilst in 1940, Joe Marsh's wife Annie died at Oker and his niece Kathleen arrived to help him out in the shop throughout the war years, although she also had to do munitions work in Matlock.

During the month of July 1940, South Darley responded to the call by Lord Beaverbrook, "Women of Britain, give us your aluminium. We will turn your pots and pans into Spitfires and Hurricanes, Blenheims and Wellingtons". One of the first items to disappear for use as scrap metal was the First World War Artillery Field Gun which had stood for years in the grounds of the Whitworth Institute. The authorities also came round with saws to cut off metal railings and collect metal gates. One can see the results of their work if we look at the photograph of the shop front at Derwent House, Darley Bridge. These railings were removed, whilst outside Jasmine Cottage, Wensley, one can see the stubs of former railings protruding from the wall. However, as David Petts relates, they did not disappear from outside the houses on Kirby Lane, one of which belonged to his father, Councillor Daniel Petts, and greengrocer Ben Clay made sure that his fine metal field gate was hidden away for the duration of the war, ready to re-appear soon after armistice day. This was probably quite sensible considering that much of what was collected was never made use of.

In 1939 the Government had issued the message "Let dig for victory be the motto of everyone with a garden" and by 1945 Britain was importing one third of its food instead of two thirds as before the war. We can certainly see that the South Darley School lads were taking it seriously, for on the 10th February 1942, the Senior Class attended a cinema film on gardening at Churchtown School in the afternoon. The following month, the gardening boys met at the school garden on the Wenslees and not at school, in order to save half an hour per day.

Late August 1940 saw South Darley Red Cross Depot move from Ivanbrook to the vicarage. Mrs. Simmons, the vicar's wife was the leader and Mrs. Petts her assistant. The depot was open on Thursdays from 2.30p.m. to 4.00p.m. and in view of the urgent need for warm clothing for the forces during the coming winter, additional knitters were required. In response to the 'Overseas League' appeal, a collection was made in the district on May 24th 1940, to provide cigarettes for the servicemen of the British Commonwealth. On September 6th, a whist drive and dance took place in the schoolroom, Cross Green, arranged by the Air Raid Wardens in aid of the 'Comfort Fund' for men in the services, whilst on Friday November 22nd a social and dance in the school realised £17 2sh 2d for the same cause. John Potter Marsden and S. Wood played for the dancing. Each local boy serving in the forces would receive for Christmas 10 shillings, one pair of socks and handkerchiefs.

In all parts of the Matlock District similar voluntary efforts were being made to raise money to help provide comforts for their own particular menfolk. In 1941 the schoolgirls from Darley House Estate were organised by local resident, Mrs. Wheeldon, to put on a pageant representing the Allied nations drawn into the war. Darley Council School teacher, Leslie Fearn, who months later would leave to join the R.A.F., acted as compere and a collection was raised from the appreciative audience that viewed the proceedings taking place on the terrace of Darley House. In June 1943, the Girls Friendly Society, which had been started two years earlier, entertained their mothers at Cross Green schoolroom. Ann Marsden and Brenda Petts gave recitations and Florence Taylor sang 'Kerry Dance'.

Tableau of countries involved in the Second World War 1942. Darley House Estate children performing on the steps of Darley House to raise money for the war effort.
X, Margaret Smith, Una Wheeldon, Joan Moore
Jean Wood
X, Margaret Wildgoose
X, Barbara Marsden
Audrey Marsden,
X, X, Rita Marsden, X

By 1944, events were still being organised to raise money in aid of the South Darley parishioners serving in the forces. During that year a comic football match between opposing men and womens' teams took place in the field upon which Gold Close is now sited. The men, including Len Riley and 'Little Roger', were dressed as women and the opposition were kitted out in the blue strip of the old Mill Close Mine team. The men obviously took the game a little too seriously, for they eventually ran out the winners. In December 1944 South Darley Women's Institute and other organisations were still holding whist drives, dances etc., but now it was to raise money for 'The Forces Welcome Home Fund'. The war was being won and South Darley folk

Comic football match at Darley Bridge in 1945 (Three Stags Head Inn) to raise money for the servicemen of South Darley.
Back row, l-r: Mr Grubb (later Rogers), Joe McNeville, Len Riley, Billy Silverwood, Allan Wright, Mr Chandler, Roy Furniss, Mr Shepherd, Mr Webster, X, Iris Pepper, Vincent Bell.
Second row: ? Woodhouse, ? Chandler, Esme Roose, Kathleen Shepherd, Little Roger, Ada Marsden, Mabel Stevenson, Betty Woosnam, Edna Roland
Front row: ? Robinson, Barbara Silverwood

were beginning to think that it might not be too long before their men folk would return.

Back in the dark days of 1940, however, South and North Darley had rallied to the cause, when, on May 14th, Anthony Eden broadcast to the nation that volunteers were required for a new force called the Local Defence Volunteers ('Look, Duck and Vanish'). People were asked to give in their names to the local police station. Eventually the organisation would be renamed the Home Guard.

The 1st Battalion, Derbyshire Home Guard consisted of three Companies; Matlock Company, Darley Dale ('B' Company) and Bakewell Company, under the overall command of such officers as Captain Douglas, a crack shot at Bisley. South Darley's contribution included such men as Bill Hardy, Harold Blood, Frank Hodgkinson, Dick Slack, John Lomas, George Woodhouse, Horace Woodhouse and Ben Walker. 'B' Company, Darley Dale, consisted of 4 platoons of 40 men each (Darley provided 2 platoons, South Darley one and Elton one).

One of the officers was Eddie Cauldwell of Rowsley Flour Mill and one day he called on Ben Walker of St. Mary's View to ask that he become the Company Sergeant Major. Ben had served

Left, Corporal George Woodhouse, right, Sergeant Horace Woodhouse, of Darley Home Guard, standing with Horace's two sons by the ruins of Watt's engine house in Clough Wood, South Darley

with distinction in the 16th Battalion Sherwood Foresters (Chatsworth Rifles) during four years of the Great War, rising to the rank of Regimental Sergeant Major and being awarded the Military Medal and Bar. Nationwide, four out of ten volunteers were people who had taken part in the Great War. Rank of course, was often based on class rather than military experience. In those first few weeks of May/June 1940 the L.D.V. could be seen drilling in civilian clothing, armed with broomstick handles on such improbable parade grounds as the yard of the Three Stags Head public house, Darley Bridge. Uniforms eventually arrived, as did 1st. World War Lee Enfields and bayonets, packed in grease. The Quarter masters stores were in the Club Room of the

Square and Compass Inn. Members of 'B' Company remember how skilful Ben Walker was in teaching manoeuvres and demonstrating a movement.

In command of the Company was Major Charlie Lymn, Solicitor and stalwart of Darley Dale Cricket Club, whilst other officers were Captain Peter Gregory of Victoria Saw Mill and Eddie Cauldwell. Mr. Cauldwell was well over 6 feet in height, whilst Charlie Lymn was very short in stature and this caused all sorts of problems on ceremonial occasions when marching in step was required. The officers met at the Square and Compass Inn once a month to discuss Company matters whilst South Darley Platoon met at the Three Stags Head.

The headquarters was in the Stancliffe Quarry Yard. Rifle firing practice took place on the second floor of the stone saw cutting building, within the yard, nowadays used by Molyneux Engineering Works. It was a long building but the space only allowed members to practice with .22 calibre rifles. Practice with Lee Enfield, Sten guns and mortars took place on the outdoor firing range at Cuckoostone, Matlock Moor. Unarmed combat was taught by army regulars, including R.A.S.C. instructors from the Whitworth Institute, whilst Sunday training sessions and parades were held on Stancliffe Hall playing fields.

The night time headquarters and communications centre was in two rooms in Judge Newall's home at Darley Hall (now an old people's residential home), where a number of telephones were installed, and Home Guard members went on nightly duty on a rota basis. Farmer Bill Hardy from Green Farm, Wensley, remembers walking down Toll Bar Hill to go on guard duty, when the siren sounded. Eccentric ARP warden Patty Potter dashed outside clutching her helmet and gasped, "Willy! Willy! Do get inside!" Different posts situated at Masson, Beeley Moor and Stanton Moor would phone in to the Hall to report on matters. The main post for Darley Home Guards was near Gladwin Mark, on Beeley Moor. Roadblocks were in operation and the men's job was to look out for possible German parachutists. A small wooden hut provided some shelter from the elements. During the summer

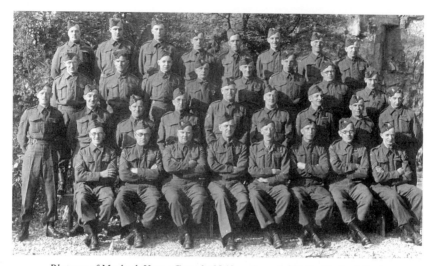

Platoon of Matlock Home Guard c1943 on Lover's Walk, Matlock Park
Back row, l-r: Stan Hawley, Horace Hopkinson, X, X, X, X, Les Crowder
Third row: X, Cliff Beech, Billy de Ville, Richard Harris, S Tyrell, X, Jeff Birkett, Bill
Smith
Second row: X, Cyril Fletcher, Frank Salmonds, X, Tom Spencer, Percy Olive, Jim
Fearn, David Maskery, X
Front row: X, Albert Slater, Colin Wheeldon, Sam Fawkes, Percy Statham, Jack Allen,
X, X

months of 1940 and 1941 an important job was to beat out the moorland fires that broke out occasionally. Such a fiery glow might otherwise have persuaded enemy planes approaching Sheffield to have dropped their bomb loads.

Bill Hardy recounts of one Sunday going on training manoeuvres to defend Rowsley marshalling yard against supposed German paratroops dropping over Beeley Moor. The Company marched up the Rowsley Bar Road to where it levelled out and lined up with bayonets fixed, whilst regular army soldiers acted as the German paratroopers. The regulars began throwing smoke bombs and the Home Guard members retreated down the hillside, through the East Lodge grounds, before their officers ordered them to stop and attempt to drive the enemy back. The 'Germans' came off the better on that particular day.

Councillor Tom Spencer of Snitterton was in Matlock Company of the Home Guard, as was Jack Allen. Jack was born in the same Snitterton cottage as his uncle, Guardsman William Allen, who had been killed in Belgium in November 1914, aged 18 years, and whose name is on the South Darley war memorial (see 'A Derbyshire Parish at War – South Darley and the Great War 1914 – 1919).

In 1938, whilst living in Matlock, he started a coal business, and during the Second World War his lorry was used in Home Guard exercises by the Matlock Company. It played the role of a German tank and the sacks of coal became German soldiers. After awhile, Jack became less enamoured with this situation, as the bayoneting of the sacks resulted in holes appearing and the coal escaping whilst being delivered around the district.

Matlock Home Guard spent many jittery hours during the anxious months of 1940, awaiting the arrival of enemy paratroopers near their post in the vicinity of Jug Holes, near Masson, Bonsall. On one such occasion a noise was heard and no reply was received when the challenge rang out. Jack Allen fired low and it resulted in the deep displeasure of Masson farmer, Mr. Gratton, when it was discovered that one of his cows had received a bullet wound to the leg.

During the months of 1940, when invasion threats seemed very real, twelve inch girders from William Twiggs were welded together to from 'dragons teeth' or tank obstacles. A series of holes, covered by metal plates, were dug in the road on the Dale Road side of Matlock Bridge, between the present riverside restaurant and the collonaded Bank entrance. At the first sign of enemy action, the plates could be removed and the tank trap slotted into position to form a bulwark against approaching vehicles. The metal 'dragon teeth' were stored in the yard next to the station entrance and on certain Sundays during the year, Matlock Home Guard would take part in exercises to practice the erection of these devices. Unwary passers by could be commandeered into assisting with this task.

John Lomas, son of the farmer at Bridge Farm, Darley Bridge, was a

Matlock Air Training Corps, Remembrance Sunday 1941, Lime Grove Walk.
Kneeling: 1st left Ralph Fisher, 4th left Billy Clay, 5th left Gill Evans, 7th left Fred
Harrison
Photo from Peter Attwater

2nd Lieutenant in Darley Home Guard. Eventually he moved to 'B' Platoon at Elton, when it was decided to transform it into the Mobile Unit for 'B' Company. Elton village had three lorry drivers and their haulage company agreed that use could be made of the three lorries. The whole unit consisted of lorries, a car and a motor cycle dispatch rider and if anything was reported amiss, it was the unit's responsibility to get to the scene first. On board the vehicles they carried a Sten gun and a rather cumbersome mortar.

At one meeting of Company officers at the Square and Compass pub a Colonel from the regular army arrived to test and assess the readiness of the Mobile Unit. It was agreed that the Colonel and staff should set off 15 minutes ahead of the Unit and take up defensive positions in the grounds of Sydnope Hall. However, embarrassment occurred when the Colonel arrived at Darley Station, for the gates were closed to allow an enormously long freight train to pass through. The Mobile Unit diverted along Old Road and arrived at Sydnope Hall well ahead of the army party and took over the grounds unopposed.

When Darley Dale 'B' Company, under the command of Major C.R. Lymn, gave a demonstration to the public in the grounds of Stancliffe Hall School on Sunday 16th May, 1943, the contrast with the equipment at the time of Dunkirk, exactly three years earlier, could not have been more stark. In May 1940, bowler hats and civilian clothes had been worn and broomsticks, sporting guns and pikes carried, whilst on the lawns of Stancliffe Hall, drill, bayonet fighting, mortar and Sten gun firing were proudly presented to the watching crowd.

By December 1944, with the Germans on the retreat in Europe, the purpose of the Home Guard was no longer relevant and on Sunday 3rd December 1944 the 1st, 2nd, 3rd and 15th Battalions of the Derbyshire Home Guard paraded for the last time, when they were stood down at an impressive ceremony at Buxton. They had gathered by the cemetery on the Buxton to Ashbourne Road and over 2,200 men took part in the parade, marching past the saluting base in the Crescent. Motor cyclists rode at the head, followed by the regimental ram of the Sherwood Foresters. Afterwards, the Battalions proceeded to the Royal Opera House, where speeches were made by local dignitaries.

It was usually men in reserved occupations who opted for war work in the ARP or Home Guard. Most South Darley women served their

Group of munition workers 1941 at Lammon, Archer and Lane, who took over Paton and Baldwins factory during the war. Eunice Wright of Wensley is first right, on front row. Clifford Jackson is on back row, fifth from the left.

country by taking up those jobs vacated by men who entered the armed services. Wensley girls Eunice Wright, Mary Concannon, Gwen Taylor, Margaret Bonsall and Edna Slack all opted to work in munitions at Matlock when, in 1941, they went on Smedley Street to Lammon, Archer and Lane, a London firm

South Darley girls' wartime night out 1941.
Back row, l-r: Esme Roose (Davison), Edna Slack (Wood), Eunice Wright (Blaydon), Edith Tomlinson (Cook)
Front row: Mary Concannon, Gwen Taylor, Marion Tomlinson (Price)

that had taken over the premises of Paton and Baldwins wool factory and had installed machinery to make taps and dies (screw threads) for the military. It was very hard work, for twelve hour shifts were worked, with one month on nights and the next on days. Ann Walker of St. Mary's View, also went to work at Lammons, but in the offices.

Bus drivers Bill Haynes, David Lowe, Vic Carter, George and Wilf Woodhouse, Harry Yates, Harry Bailey and Fred Phillips continued to operate the Silver Service buses during the war years but this period saw the introduction of the female bus conductor. Lucy Wain, farmer's daughter from Beech House, Oker, and May Haynes (nee Wayne) from Oker Terrace, Wensley were the first 'on the buses', with May starting in the spring of 1940. In 1940 Ethel Hendry (nee Turner), born on the Wenslees, South Darley, had married her soldier husband Malcolm, and with him away at war, fighting in the East African campaign, she found herself directed into war work in 1941, when asked to join the Silver Service as a conductor. She remained in the job until 1945. Joan Evans of Wensley and Kath Fielding joined the Company and just after the war, Lucy's sister Ethel and Joyce Pennington of Wensley made up the contingent of conductors. May's husband, Bill Haynes, a member of

Darley Home Guard, drove the bus whenever the Company needed transporting to various destinations.

Petrol rationing certainly meant fewer buses running but the conductors made sure that as many passengers as possible travelled on each journey, especially with the late night schedules. Buses running from Matlock to Winster after the last showing at the cinema were bulging 'at the seams' and it was common practice for the Bakewell to Birchover 39 seater to be carrying as many as 80 passengers. On a number of occasions the Elton policeman pushed them on then held on tightly himself to the door, as he was himself the last passenger. The lighting allowed inside the bus was very dim, due to blackout regulations, and clipped onto the strap of the conductor's ticket punching machine was a small torch, used to illuminate her task.

Other men and women were drafted into munitions war work further afield, at Derby. My uncle, Cyril Taylor, travelled each day by rail to

Women replace the men. Thelma Boden, goods porter at Matlock Station and Mrs Lomas, LMS lorry driver. Sugar and dried fruit were taken to the food store at Riber Castle.

the Qualcast lawnmower factory, now converted into the production of tank caterpillar tracks, whilst Tom Evans and George Shimwell of Oker Road and Jack Boden of Cross Green worked at the Rolls Royce works and Herbert Chell, former chauffeur of Captain Ward of Dale View, was drafted to the ground staff at Burnaston aerodrome, near Derby. Tom and Herbert eventually found the travelling too much and moved with their families to live at Derby.

For those still travelling by rail, conditions were difficult. The railways were a weapon of war and civilian passengers were reminded that "food, shells and fuel must come first". By 1944 the number of miles covered by passenger trains had fallen to a third of the pre-war figure, but every train was carrying twice as many people as in 1939. Travel by train had never been so uncomfortable nor so expensive, with fares tripling over the war years. When air raid sirens sounded the trains had to stop at the next station to give passengers the choice of getting off to take shelter or of continuing the journey at snail's pace. The speed limit during raids was 15 m.p.h. until November 1940, when it was raised to 25 m.p.h. During 1940 and 1941 those passengers travelling home from war work at Derby would arrive at Darley station far later than the scheduled times.

In Chapter Two we saw how the Bakelite Plastics Company returned from Birmingham to Old Road, Darley Dale, during the war years. Plans were prepared for creating an industrial site on the nearby 40 acre Cartledge Field, with the possibility of a tyre factory being built, but fortunately nothing came of the scheme. However, other industry did come to the area, with the building of a wartime 'shadow factory' alongside the A6 at Darley Dale.

Firth Derihon were drop forgers and stampers specialising in forgings for the motor and aircraft trade. In 1919 premises were obtained in the Tinsley area of Sheffield. The Company had made great progress in the years from 1934 and in 1939 the firm could claim that it held a unique position amongst the many suppliers of drop forging to the Aircraft, Automobile and Allied industries, with special emphasis on gear boxes and back axles. The Company, by supplying special forgings had contributed extensively to the success of many record breaking achievements, including the winning of the Schneider Trophy in 1929 with the Rolls Royce and Napier engines and the land and water speed records of Sir Henry Seagrave, Sir Malcolm Campbell and Captain Eyston. During the war years the Sheffield factory was instrumental in solving the jet engine blade problem, consequent on the invention of the jet aircraft engine by Sir Frank Whittle.

The heavy bombing of Sheffield caused the Ministry of Supply to be afraid that the Sheffield factory would be badly damaged. The Company was asked to look for a suitable site for a 'Shadow factory' in

Derbyshire. The managing director, Mr, Julian, made a survey of three possible sites and chose Darley Dale because (i) the A6 trunk road made for easy access to Rolls Royce at Derby, the main place for components (ii) the nearby river Derwent could be used to provide water for cooling purposes during drop forging operations and (iii) the site had its own sidings and branch line onto the main Manchester – London railway line.

The site for the factory was the L.M.S. Sports field and the buildings housed a number of heavy forge hammers which required deep and massive foundations insulated with hardwood packings to minimise the transmissions of vibrations into the surrounding ground. The construction began in 1942, undertaken by Irish Navvies, and was completed very quickly. Communal air raid shelters were also provided. Many of the people working at the 'shadow factory' were women, including Jack Flint's future wife, Mary, and Edna Roland from Darley, who drove a small mechanised crane, and was later to marry railway-man Ron Allen of Eversleigh Rise. Women were also highly visible in

In the First World War the RASC also had a camp at Darley Dale, It was located in the fields now housing the telephone exchange, Parkway and John Turner housing developments.

Rowsley Sidings in wartime.
Top: Loco cleaners (young lads) c1943
Back row, l-r: Tommy Thorpe, Charlie Kemp (Wensley), Jack Boden (Cross Green), Ike Belfield.
Front row: Doug Goodall, Ken Lill, Sam Briddon, Gerald Thompson, Jock Brassington.

Bottom: Lady loco cleaners

Boating lake in the Whitworth Institute grounds 1930's

Boating lake, Whitworth Institute. The boathouse is shown in the background. RASC motor cycles were stored there during the Second World War

177

'Tea Rooms' Whitworth Park, during happier times in the 1930's. It catered for weekend and bank holiday visitors. During the war it became the RASC cook-house and trainees mess

Tea Rooms' Whitworth Park, in happier times. Silver Jubilee Celebrations for George V and Queen Mary, 6th May 1935. Committee members ready to distribute silver spoons to schoolchildren, after a children's tea.
Back row, l-r: Mrs Wyles, Joseph Alsopp, X, Mrs Howse, X, X, X, Fred Smith, Councillor Hibbs, X, Joseph Hancock, Mr Shaw
Front row: Mrs Newell, Judge Newell, George Thompson, X, X, PC Wallace

the operational running of the nearby Rowsley sidings during these years, especially in the task of cleaning the locomotives.

Possibly the most obvious physical change to the Darley area, brought about by the war was the requisitioning of the Whitworth Institute and grounds as an army base by the Royal Army Service Corps in the Spring of 1940, with the resulting influx of soldiers and army vehicles. Between February and May 1940, very little changed, except that the grounds were barred to the public, but preparations were already being made as the swimming pool room was emptied of water and a wooden floor put in.

In June 1940 local people were amazed to see how the Allied military situation had reached such a low ebb when remnants of the British forces evacuated from Dunkirk arrived by train at Darley Station and also by lorry. For people instilled at school with the invincibility of the British nation, it came as a great shock to the locals to see soldiers of the British army lying on the grass at the top of Station Road and alongside the A6 in a filthy condition, without uniforms in many cases and certainly without weapons. Fortunately the weather was glorious and some soldiers could still raise smiles and throw French coins to the children who gathered to watch. Large Bell Tents were quickly erected in the fields alongside the A6 between the Whitworth Hotel and Broadwalk, and a number of Broadwalk residents invited soldiers into their homes to bathe away the filth and grime. Similar scenes were occurring at Matlock and it was a sorry spectacle to see British Expeditionary Force soldiers having to wash themselves in the waters of the paddling pool and boating lake on the Hall Leys. It became normal to invite these soldiers, and later the R.A.S.C. personnel, home for a meal. Locals coined a name for them – "Uphomers" – as in "would you like to come up home for a cup of tea and a chat?"

A few of the Darley based soldiers were in the Sherwood Foresters and borrowed bicycles from local lads to visit their homes. However the authorities were keen to get the soldiers back to their units and within a fortnight the Dunkirk soldiers had gone. Preparations could continue to equip the Whitworth Institute as a training base for the R.A.S.C. (or Royal Army Scrounging Corps as they called themselves). We should remember that during the whole of the Great War period the R.A.S.C. were also stationed at Darley Dale, in the same fields and maybe even the same Bell tents as the Dunkirk evacuees had found themselves in June 1940.

Four Companies were in the area. In 1940 and early 1941 the Bakewell Company trained soldiers to be drivers, Wirksworth Company trained in transport and drill, Matlock Drill Hall was the headquarters and, at first, the Whitworth Institute Company trained men at drill. Eight squads, 30 men to a squad, would stay at the base for a six week period.

In the early days, conditions were more primitive. One soldier, Donald Rhodes, arrived in August to do his initial training at Cromford Meadows and then spent September – October 1940 at the Darley base. They were billeted in First World War bell tents inside the grounds. The toilet facilities were basic and they washed and shaved in cold water at outside taps. Occasionally you could 'scrounge' a cup of hot water from the cookhouse and mess hall, based in the Tea Rooms (demolished early 1960's) next to the football field. The food at that time was instantly forgettable. As the nights grew colder some lucky ones were billeted over the stable block at the Grouse Inn.

As time passed, conditions improved. The hotel housed the officers and their mess was in the upstairs room of Laura Dukes, Two Dales café. Thirty mechanics and personnel were accommodated in a series of two tier bunks in the old swimming bath room. Four large Nissan huts were constructed to accommodate the trainees in the area where the swings are now situated, next to the cemetery, and the Tea Room became their mess. The leftovers from the cook house were collected by a vehicle from Frank Toplis's haulage company, Two Dales, and transported to Hazel House, Chesterfield Road, where it was used as pigs swill for a large number of animals kept in outbuildings by Frank's father, Fred Toplis. The Sergeant's mess was at the back of the hotel and the Corporal's mess was in the room adjoining the William

Deacons Bank (now part of the Royal Bank of Scotland). The Museum (now the Terrace Room) became the NAFFI.

Mary Johnson remembers coming to Darley Dale in her khaki uniform to serve in the Navy, Army, Airforce Institute in 1944. She was billeted with five other women in 'Avoca', a house on Station Road, next to the Council Depot yard. Local women such as Mrs. Hannah Haynes of Wensley helped serve in the NAFFI, which provided the men with hot scones, doughnuts and sausage and chips. It was here that Mary met her future husband, Owen Lewis, who was an instructor at the base in 1944.

Sergeant Patrick Pritty, RASC, instructor at the Whitworth Institute

During February 1941, Corporal Patrick (Pat) Pritty came from London to the Whitworth Institute as a drill instructor and weapons

Officers and men of the RASC and Army Training Service (ATS) women, inside the Institute c1942. Sergeant Jim Boyack is third from the left on the front row. The ATS members were billeted at the Red House

trainer in the 8th Training Battalion, RASC. The base was still solely training the men in drill. This was performed on the terrace, next to the NAFFI, and on the roadways leading through the grounds towards the lake and boathouse. His loud voice allowed him to send the squad marching to the lake and back, whilst he remained standing on the terrace. Unfortunately, the locals also got the full force of his voice. Bayonet practice was against straw dollys on stands and recruits had to pass through the gas chamber.

Corporals and sergeants were billeted in premises outside the confines of the Institute and South Darley provided quarters for a large number of RASC personnel. Mayfield, on Eversleigh Rise, was requisitioned, as was Oakleigh on Kirby Lane, whilst the Clubroom above the Crown Inn was converted into sleeping quarters. From the middle of 1941 the Oker Hut was also used by RASC soldiers. Corporal (later Sergeant) Pritty and others slept at Oakleigh on the floor on pallets and each morning they marched three abreast for breakfast in the mess.

By autumn of 1941 the RASC Company at Darley Dale had doubled up as a trainee driving school. The roads inside the grounds were widened to allow two lorries to pass abreast. The first transports were impressed vehicles such as furniture vans and haulage lorries. Three out of ten were out of service when they were brought in but eventually they obtained better quality vehicles. Approximately sixty vehicles and staff cars and 20 motor bikes were used, with the bikes stored in the boathouse and the lorries parked in rows within the grounds. A small office was positioned at the bottom Station Road gate and vehicles departed at this entrance, but only with the issue of a chitty. A number of the early driving instructors were London bus drivers who had been drafted into war work, with the promise that they would not see overseas action.

The trainee drivers always drove in convoys of approximately 20 vehicles, nose to tail and practised both day and night time driving. Many of the walls in the area received their fair share of knocks, especially during night operations. In the blackout, lead vehicles drove on sidelights, as did the rear vehicle, whilst the others had none showing, except a small spotlight fitted underneath, shining onto the rear white axle casing. The convoys often drove through Wensley, Winster, Pikehall and Stanton. Instructors sat in the lorries with their trainees, whilst sergeants such as Pat Pritty rode ahead on motor cycles. During one foggy night, Pat remembers his convoy heading towards Buxton, where it was to turn round in the square, but many vehicles went missing in the swirling fog and the next day was spent in 'rounding them up'.

Sergeant Pritty, who by late 1941 had married Joyce Hardy of Cross Green, was also involved in training the 'rooky' soldiers in rifle shooting at the Oker Hill firing range. Lorries would bring the men and ammunitions to Kirby Lane, which would be closed off below the hill. The range was on the far side, overlooking the Derwent Valley and consisted of a concrete base to stand or lie on (still in existence), a shed and targets consisting of small cardboard rectangles with the bull and 'outers' painted on. These were sited against the steep bank of the hillside, into which the bullets would lodge. Five shots were fired form a standing position and five lying down. Some soldiers were frightened of the rifles and occasionally fired over the top of the hill, resulting in bullets zipping high in the air in the direction of Wensley. To pass the test they had to hit five times out of ten shots, but Pat Pritty often helped out by pushing a pencil through the card. Whenever the range was in use a red flag flew from near the white triangulation point and guards with red flags were stationed at either sides of the hill. Pat also brought motor cycle despatch riders to test them on the slopes of the hill. After the red flags were retrieved, local lads would search the steep bank of the range for spent bullets.

Though the Whitworth Institute and grounds were out of bounds to the public, the RASC held popular dances in the ballroom, with army bands serenading the dancers, whilst Cross Green School was used by them on other occasions. Many local girls and women attended these dances. It is not surprising that with this influx of servicemen into the area and many local lads away at the war, that relationships developed which led to marriage, as we have seen with our drill instructor.

Although the R.A.S.C. soldiers may have damaged numerous walls during training exercises, no serious incidents occurred that resulted in serious casualties. However, two events involving the armed forces did result in death and destruction,

Australian crew of Wellington bomber W3941 at their Lichfield area base 1942.
L-r: Rear-gunner Tom Easton, Sergeant Ken Killeen (died), Pilot Officer Neil Trayden, Sergeant Bill Catron (died), S ergeant Neil Craigie

although reports of them never appeared in the local press at the time.

During the first years of the war, two R.A.F. training aircraft had crash landed in the South Darley area, one near Snitterton and the other a 2 seater Miles Magister, between Bridge Farm and Enthovens. These incidents paled into insignificance, however, compared with the horrific crash of Wellington bomber W/3941 on Darley Moor, in the early hours of the 30th January, 1943.

The Wellington, with an all Australian crew on board, had been returning to base in the Litchfield area, after a night time simulated bombing raid on London Bridge. At around 1.30 am, as the navigator became unsure of the plane's exact location, the crew members spotted a line of lights, similar to a flare path, through the clouds. Going down to investigate, the plane clipped the top of a line of trees and crashed on the moor, a short distance from the isolated Moor Farm home of Hubert and Marion Mills. The devastation was immense. Evacuee schoolboy Alan Pickstone, visiting the scene a few days later remembers a 'trail' of thousands of fragments stretched like a paper chase across both fields. The engines had left their mountings and carried on for a number of yards before burying themselves in the ground.

Tom Easton, the rear gunner, though badly injured, regained his senses and found two colleagues alive, but in a bad way. Two other crew members were dead. Tom staggered and crawled for help through the pouring rain, and after a desperate journey across boggy terrain, saw the outline of Moor Farm's roof. Hubert and Marion heard his screams from afar and when he knocked on the door, Mr. Mills challenged him with his shotgun, for they believed he may have been a German airman or paratrooper. However, Tom had passed out with pain by this stage.

Hubert Mills alerted the emergency services but by 5.30 am no trace of the bomber had been found and the searchers returned to the farm. Tom then remembered a haystack near the crash scene and from his description Mr. Mills was able to lead the rescuers to the aircraft. The

South Darley Church fete at Eversleigh House, Midsummer Day June 1944, to raise money for a carillon of 8 bells.
Kathleen and Barbara Shimwell, Eileen Taylor and Teresa Daniels, Noreen Wain and Betty Shimwell, X, X, X, X
X and Joy Flint, X and Ann Marsden

Fancy dress at Eversleigh House, June 1944
Top: Kathleen Shepherd, X, Alan Marsden, Edna Shimwell, Eileen Wain, Zoe Bark,
Terry Shepherd, Vivienne Shepherd, Bessie Pocock, Annie Pepper, Maurice Dowling,
Peggy Wright, Florence Briggs, X
Bottom: Norah Bark, Kathleen Shepherd, X, Mrs Dutton, Mary Harrison, Mrs
Marshall, Edna Shimwell, Doris Wright, X, Miss Walker, Bessie Pocock, Florence
Taylor, Teresa Daniels, Mary Gull, Zoe Bark, Florence Briggs, Noreen Wain
Ann Shimwell, X, Alan Marsden, Eileen Wain, Terry Shepherd, Vivienne Shepherd, Ann
Marsden, Peggy Wright, X, X, Molly Grimshaw, Jean Wood, Audrey Shimwell

survivors were taken to the Whitworth Hospital, with Tom transported in Hubert's old van, and the hospital ward was sealed off to the general public. Next day, when Mrs. Mills went to the hospital with eggs and cakes, she was refused admission and told she could not see the airmen.

The second tragic accident occurred only a short distance away and involved the British Army. A convoy of six quad vehicles, each quad towing an artillery 2516 field gun, arrived on the moorland roads from the direction of Chesterfield. Three vehicles took the turning for the steeply descending Rowsley Bar Road, whilst three attempted the descent of Sydnope Hill. The quads were not designed to deal with such a steep descent and near 'Top o' the Hill' they got into difficulties and began to career down the hill. Two vehicles crashed near the top but the lead vehicle crashed into the coppice at Starr Cottage, on the notorious bend near the bottom of the hill. The driver was taken to the Whitworth Hospital but his back was broken and he died shortly afterwards. Other soldiers were also treated for injuries received. The vehicles and guns attempting the descent into Rowsley fared no better, for they too crashed on the steep hill and were 'written off'.

In comparison, a social event in 1944 seemed to bring an air of normality to the parish when, on mid-summer day in June, St. Mary's Garden Fete was held. More than 400 people attended the event in the grounds of Eversleigh House by kind permission of Mr. Trickett and this was to be the first effort to build up a centenary fund to mark the 100th anniversary of the Church in the the following year, 1945. An iced cake, made in the shape of the Church by Joe Marsh, was raffled by Misses Florence and Eileen Taylor, producing nearly £10.

Members of the Girls Friendly Society were responsible for the jumble sale and pound stall, whilst hundreds of teas were served. Led by Mrs. Marshall, the Women's Institute gave a fancy dress parade and Minnie Potter arranged one for the youngsters. A country dancing competition was given on the lawn, with the girls trained by Mrs Potter, who had made the girls' dresses out of blackout material.

Maypole dance, South Darley Church fete, Eversleigh House, c1943.
X, X, Hilary Duke, X, Barbara Devereux, Florence Taylor
Edna Shimwell, Mary Clay, Margaret Bowler
Joy Flint, X, X, Betty Shimwell, Zoe Bark, Audrey Shimwell, Kathleen Shimwell

Mr. J. Taylor gave chariot rides in a nearby field and Miss Duke organised pony rides, whilst Phillip Bowler and Ken Fletcher organised the sideshows. A splendid total of £255 was raised.

Almost a year later, the war ended in Europe with the defeat of Germany and Victory in Europe (VE) Day was celebrated on Tuesday May 8th. In Matlock the news on Monday evening resulted in people rushing to put out bunting. Flags of the Big Four powers flew from the Town Hall and coloured lights were fixed on the Hall Leys entrance, the Promenade and Fishpond at Matlock Bath. Crowds stood on the hillsides at dusk to see their reappearance after years of blackout. There was no real celebration on Monday evening though, for everyone obeyed the call to 'wait for it' to hear the official announcement by Winston Churchill on Tuesday afternoon.

Rain fell on Tuesday morning and early afternoon but the skies cleared later and the streets of Matlock filled with crowds. Bands

Victory in Europe Day (VE) celebrations in Wensley Square for South Darley schoolchildren, Tuesday 8th May 1945

played in the park and in the evening there was a 'free for all' dance at the Town Hall. Soon after the Prime Minister's announcement, short services were held in all churches and the bells rang out. VE Day came at an unfortunate time for some licensees whose stocks were low at the beginning of the week. Some 200 people gathered in Crown Square at midnight to sing community songs. In the hills there were the glows from bonfires and the singing was interspersed with loud explosives as military units let off practice 'bombs' and some townsfolk let off fireworks stored away for the occasion.

School was closed for two days holiday and in Wensley Square, VE Day was celebrated by a street party for all the schoolchildren within the parish. Bunting and flags were strung from the buildings, trestle tables were obtained from the public houses and the mothers did a wonderful job in preparing sandwiches, cakes, buns and jellies, despite wartime rationing. Bus trips were also organised in the Darley area to see the lights shining in the Matlock district after years of enforced darkness.

A few months later, in August 1945, Japan also surrendered after the dropping of atomic bombs on Hiroshima and Nagasaki, and the war was finally over. There was a collective sigh of relief, but although in Matlock, similar activities took place on VJ day as had occurred on VE Day, we have come across no evidence that the day was celebrated collectively within the parish of South Darley.

And so came to an end South Darley's participation in the second global conflict to shatter the peace of the 20th Century. The closeness of war, even in a 'backwater' such as South Darley had seemed tangible, especially in the aftermath of Dunkirk and the Fall of France, the perilously fine line between victory and defeat in the Battle of Britain, the real threat of invasion by German forces in 1940 and the continuous pounding of cities and industrial targets during the Blitz.

At the forefront of everyone's mind had been the knowledge of actual involvement by a family member or friend in the fight against Nazi aggression or Japanese Imperialism. It is to the stories of these people that we now turn.

CHAPTER FIVE

THE SURVIVORS

For those inhabitants of Britain who remained at home during the six years of war, austerity, resulting from the early introduction of rationing, and the realisation that the enemy could strike at the heart of their country by means of modern technology, meant that they were often at the forefront of the conflict. South Darley would escape the ravages of the Blitz, though Sheffield was close enough for them to understand the attendant dangers.

People could not escape, however, the worry and despair experienced when members of their family were 'called up' and posted for service overseas. As in the Great War, few people in South Darley were protected from such emotions. Whether serving on land, sea or in the air, the South Darley service personnel were exposed to great danger and fortunately the vast majority returned safely to their homes. We have attempted to cover the wartime stories of a number of these people on the following pages.

ROY TAYLOR, 714TH GENERAL CONSTRUCTION COMPANY, ROYAL ENGINEERS

Roy's grandparents, William and Martha Taylor lived at Cowley Hall,

South Darley, between 1900 and the early 1920's, where William was the farm bailiff.

In January 1914, Roy was born at Church Lane, Darley Dale, to John and Alice Taylor but after Roy's father came back from the First World War, the family moved to Bakewell.

By the early 1930's Roy was employed as a council workman on the Urban District Council, based at the depot on Station Road, Darley Dale and passed his driving test on a 15 ton steam roller at Rowsley. By mid 1939, with war threatening, he found himself involved in filling

Roy Taylor, Royal Engineers

sandbags with silt obtained from the river and placing them against prominent buildings in the area, as part of the air raid defences.

In early 1940 he volunteered for the services at Bakewell, where the Council wished to form a company of Royal Engineers from 260 local council employees, with a civilian surveyor acting as major. They were actually called up on 12 March 1940 at Boythorpe Barracks, Chesterfield, and then reported to Chatham Barracks, where they formed part of 714 General Construction Company of the Royal Engineers. Roy's specialist job was as a steel bender, helping in reinforcing concrete constructions.

The company embarked for France at Southampton and travelled by train to Paris, where lorries were waiting to transport them by road to just north of Verdun, arriving on 20 April at the small village of Marcheville, behind the Maginot Line. With just five weeks training behind them they were now in the fighting zone.

Their destination was a forward fighter airbase, but within three weeks they were being bombed night and day as the Germans launched their attack on France through Holland and Belgium on 10 May. Roy and his comrades spent their time filling up the bomb craters on the runway with stone and concrete obtained from the old ruined bunkers of the First World War Hindenburg Line that ran nearby, enabling the Hurricane and Spit fire pilots to continue operations.

The work was difficult at these aerodromes, with enemy fighters and bombers constantly overhead and soon the order arrived for them to retreat. For the next few weeks they were continually on the retreat, stopping and consolidating, but never stopping long enough to do anything worthwhile.

Travelling by train, often in cattle trucks and attacked by German planes whilst in the sidings, they eventually arrived at Brest on the Brittany coast. By this time their lorries had caught up with them and orders were given to smash the cylinder heads with heavy hammers and burn the lorries.

Roy came across the Channel on the 'Lithland', an old coal barge, but fortunately the weather was reasonably calm and leaving Brest at tea-time, they arrived at Falmouth at lunch time on the following day. Eventually, after home leave, Roy's detachment of Royal Engineers was attached to the Royal Marines at Plymouth, and after being issued with tropical kit and receiving training, they embarked from Liverpool in September 1940 in a task force destined for the French port of Dakar on the West African coast. An ill-judged landing here by General de Gaulle's Free French forces, supported by the Royal Navy, was repelled by the Vichy French forces defending the port, and a few weeks later Roy's company found itself in Scotland.

Whilst in Paisley, Roy met his future wife Jenny, who was working in a Clyde Munitions factory, but in 1942, after intensive training on assault courses, forty members of the company travelled by ship from Liverpool to Scapa Flow. The convoy of ships they joined journeyed round the Cape of Good Hope, putting into Durban for four days, before arriving at Ismailiya in Egypt, where they were to join Montgomery's 8th Army.

Roy and his comrades were quickly trained in mine lifting operations and sent to the front line in readiness for the Battle of Alamein. Tanks could be seen as far as the eye could view and after the initial bombardments of the German positions, the Royal Engineers began seeking ways through the vast minefields. Once a mine was located, a second person followed with a metal plate to place on top of the mine and a third member of the team picked it up. For the next few weeks they pushed forward as part of the 8th Army's successful advance against Rommel's Africa Corps.

Though held up at Mersah Matruh, they eventually reached Tunisia and arrived at a captured German aerodrome near Misurata. The area proved to be a death trap as the Germans had started to booby trap the actual mines. Whilst riding on an armoured carrier along a wadi, one man next to Roy was killed when a mine exploded, whilst a corporal was badly wounded by a booby trapped mine.

After Rommel's defeat, the 714th General Construction Company returned to Cairo for recuperation but soon found themselves being transported westwards again towards Algiers, but at Tripoli, 30 members, including Roy, were separated from their mates and posted to the American 5th Army. They had to quickly learn to swim because they were to be involved in the Salerno landings in Italy, the so-called soft under belly of Europe.

Off the Salerno beachhead, on 9 September 1943, the old battleships Warspite and Nelson used their formidable guns against the entrenched defenders, whilst German bombers attacked the landing parties. The beach-head was extended and as they fought further inland they at last reached the River Volturno, a German defence line, in early October. Roy's' company was ordered to place a bridge across the river but whilst constructing it, Roy was wounded in the upper arm and chest by a German sniper, firing from the opposite bank.

Taken to a field hospital and then the 90th General Hospital in Naples, he found himself transferred to Malta for four months, before returning home for lengthy treatment at the Alder Hay Hospital in Liverpool.

The final months of Roy Taylor's war were spent quietly in the Orkney Islands before being demobbed and returning home. After marrying Jenny, his wartime girlfriend from Paisley, they settled down to married life at Stanton Lees. Roy returned to his work on the Council as a lorry driver but soon began work for haulage contractors such as George Siddall of Darley Bridge.

COLIN HADFIELD 5TH BATTALION, NORTHAMPTONSHIRE REGIMENT

Colin was born at Lobby House, Oker Road, before moving at 5 years of age to Greenstile Cottage, Wensley. After working for Jack Masters, delivering newspapers on his push bike, he began working at Mill Close Lead Mine on the flotation plant and waste heaps, before being called up to serve in the war.

Colin Hadfield, 5th Battalion, Northamptonshire Regiment and prisoner of war

Conscripted at 18 years of age, in April 1942, he travelled to Norwich for 16 weeks infantry training and then joined the 5th Battalion Northamptonshire Infantry Regiment. After travelling to Glasgow the battalion boarded a Dutch vessel, and, whilst anchored on the Clyde, they practiced landing exercises on the banks of the river.

The following day they sailed to join other ships forming a convoy in the Atlantic and were told they were to be part of the Operation Torch landings in North Africa, led by the Americans. Having entered the Mediterranean Sea, they landed unopposed on the beach near Algiers on the 8 November 1942. The following day they marched into the outskirts of Algiers and took positions on the flat roof of a hospital overlooking a fort manned by the Vichy French, who were collaborating with the Germans. Fortunately the French surrendered after a cruiser in Algiers Bay sent forward a party with the terms of surrender.

The battalion was now pushed forwards towards the Tunisian frontier by way of Bone and Phillipeville but they were very exposed, for they only had a small amount of transport available and had to leave small parties behind every now and again to protect such targets as captured airfields, against the threat of German paratroops being dropped.

On the four-day journey to the Tunisian border, they raided orange groves to supplement their meagre rations. At Tabarka, they rested amongst the trees on a hillside but the next morning were attacked by a Stuka dive bomber and a platoon commander was killed.

By now their strength was only 100 men and they were in unknown territory. At 4am, in dim light, they took cover under bushes, whilst their transport was stationed on the main track some way back. The officer decided to make a reconnaissance at daybreak and a party went down into the valley where the single track railway led towards Tunis. With a major in charge, Colin led a section of 8 men up the railway line but after three miles they heard a rumbling sound and leapt into the concrete cutting that was nearby. The major scrambled up the concrete wall and spied a German armoured column with seven tanks heading it, followed by lorries filled with infantry.

Colin and his fellow soldiers hid themselves beneath camouflage netting whilst the major reported to them what was happening. The armoured column destroyed the lorries they had left behind and German infantry began searching for them along the railway track. They were soon spotted, despite their camouflage, and the firing started. They loosed off rounds from the Lee-Enfields in response but the Germans began throwing 'potato master' grenades into the cutting and began to encircle it. Realising that their position was hopeless, Colin's commanding officer gave the order to put down their weapons and they were ordered out onto the road and into trucks.

On arrival at Bizerta they were interrogated and then taken to the aerodrome, where a three engined Junkers 52 was waiting to take them across the Mediterranean to Palermo in Sicily, where they stayed the night in cells. Another Junkers 52 then flew them to Naples, and for several weeks they were in a POW camp at Capua, where the conditions were terrible because many of the prisoners from the desert campaign were suffering from dysentery.

Colin was then transferred by rail to a POW camp containing eight and a half thousand prisoners set in a former jam factory at Fermo, just inland from the Adriatic coast. Conditions improved when Red Cross parcels began arriving containing 2oz packets of tea and 4oz packets of coffee. To prevent the prisoners hoarding food for future escape purposes, the Italian guards used a spiked hammer on the food parcels and so punctured the contents. The boxes containing the parcels were used to build an open-air stage where concert parties entertained and boxing tournaments were held.

POW Camp at Fermo, Italy. The stage is constructed from Red Cross packing cases

On 3rd September 1943, the Italian forces surrendered to the Allies and the sentries seemed to 'melt away'. However, the British officer in command told the prisoners to remain in the camp, although one hundred did attempt to escape into the hills, but five days later the Germans arrived to take over the camp.

The prisoners were loaded into cattle trucks and travelled by rail northwards through the Brenner Pass into Austria and on to a camp at Oschatz, near Leipzig in Saxony, Germany. They slept on slatted boards and a 'No Mans Land' of barbed wire separated them from the Russian prisoners of war, who were being treated far more inhumanely, with no luxury of Red Cross parcels for them. The British prisoners would throw bars of chocolate across the 30-yard gap because it had been reported that, on average, seven Russians a day were dying of malnutrition.

Finally, Colin was moved with other prisoners to a paper making factory at Döben, between Leipzig and Dresden in Saxony, where they were made to put bales of waste into sieving machines and this material went into the mill below, where brown paper was the end product of the process.

With the Russians advancing from the East into Germany in 1945, an old German guard, known to the prisoners as 'Pop', led twenty-four of them south-westwards on a long march of 20 miles a day towards the

River Elbe and over it, to escape from the Russians. Travelling from farmhouse to farmhouse and feeding on potatoes, they eventually lost their guard and met an advanced party of American soldiers near Freiburg. A captured German truck, with German driver, was handed over to the British POW's and after numerous incidents they arrived at a large camp at Erfurt, where white bread and better food proved most welcome!

Colin's party was flown from Erfurt to the French city of Rheims, where they began to feel almost normal again after bathing and passing through the delousing procedures. A Lancaster bomber then flew them over the Channel to a camp in Buckinghamshire, with the bonus of a months pass on home leave, with further extensions until Christmas 1945.

It was not until Christmas 1946, however that Colin was eventually demobbed and he returned to work at Enthovens as a plant operative in the chemical side of the operations.

NEVILLE SIDDALL, ROYAL NAVY

Neville was born at Manchester, the son of Jack and Lucy Siddall. Jack was an engineer and in 1920 the family arrived at Darley Bridge from where Jack started work on the surface at Mill Close Lead Mine and Neville went to South Darley School. When Tom Wright had Cross Green Cottages built in 1929 the Siddalls were the first to move in.

Neville had a fine singing voice and sang in the choir at St Mary's Church as a boy. His mother was proud of his ability and took him around the county and further afield to compete at different choral events and competitions.

However, he was determined to enter the navy

Neville Siddall of Cross Green, Royal Navy

and in 1935 he began his naval career at HMS Ganges on the River Medway and was then posted to HMS Pembroke at Chatham. Neville had always been a dare-devil and had no fear of heights, so it was no surprise that he excelled in the mast exercises that formed part of the training for all seamen. At both bases there were tall masts on which the ratings practiced and Neville received the highest accolade by being made the 'button boy' who climbed to the very top point of the mast and stood aloft on the "button". In 1938 he proudly represented the Royal Navy as 'button boy' at the Earls Court Show in London.

In April 1936 Neville joined the newly commissioned destroyer, HMS Grenade, and sailed from Chatham for the Mediterranean, to join the First Destroyer Flotilla of the Mediterranean Fleet, consisting of 9 destroyers, based at Malta and helping in trying to keep in place oil sanctions against Musssolini's Italy, which was involved in its war against Ethiopia.

On reaching Malta, news was received of the outbreak of the Spanish Civil War on 18 July 1936 and the Flotilla was ordered to proceed to Spanish waters to protect British interests. Between September 1936 and January 1937 the First Flotilla was mainly employed carrying refugees from Spain, but in April 1937 it was selected to attend the Coronation Naval Review by King George VI in May 1937, after which it split to its home ports where seven days leave was granted.

By June 1937 it was back in Spanish waters. Later in the year HM S Grenade was involved in anti-piracy patrols in the Eastern Mediterranean but on 24 May 1938 the Grenade arrived at its home port of Chatham, after its two-year tour of duty.

Between May 1938 and the start of the Second World War Neville was engaged in training on the new Asdic echo-sounding equipment that would later be used in anti-submarine detection, for he was blessed with a very good sense of hearing. However, this did not prevent him returning to South Darley School as a well-respected 'old boy' on Empire Day, 24 May, 1939, to give a talk on 'A Two Year Voyage on HMS Grenade'. In the afternoon the school closed because of Empire Day.

By this period, he was part of the crew of the 10,000-ton County Class Cruiser HM. Cumberland, armed with eight 8-inch guns mounted on four turrets. Shortly before the outbreak of war, the ship was ordered to the South Atlantic where she joined Exeter and

Neville Siddall's ship, HMS Cumberland

Ajax to form the South American Division (Force G), sailing out of Freetown to meet the threat of German surface raiders.

On 11 September 1939 the German battleship Graf Spee's aircraft sighted the Cumberland, only 30 miles away on passage from Freetown to Rio de Janeiro. The Graf Spee slipped away to the east.

At the beginning of December 1939, Exeter and Cumberland were both in Port Stanley on the Falklands. Achilles, who had joined the Division, was off Rio de Janeiro, and Ajax on passage from Port Stanley to the River Plate, South America.

On 5 December, Ajax and Cumberland intercepted the German merchantman, Ussukama, which succeeded in scuttling herself. It was believed that Graf Spee would next be off the River Plate by 12 December. Ajax, Achilles and Exeter concentrated in the area, whilst Cumberland returned to Port Stanley for boiler cleaning and re-fuelling.

The Graf Spee was engaged by Force G on 13 December. The Cumberland was ordered to leave Port Stanley and made very quick passage from the Falklands. In company with Ajax and Achilles, Cumberland steamed past the blazing wreck of the scuttled Graf Spee and entered Montevideo harbour on the evening of the 17 December.

At the end of June 1940, the Cumberland escorted convoys to the Middle East and by the end of July sailed from Simonstown naval base to sweep the oceans once more for enemy raiders, without success. She also took part in Operation Menace, the unsuccessful attempt to capture the Vichy French controlled port of Dakar in West Africa in September 1940.

After leaving the Cumberland, Neville was told to report as a member of the crew of HMS Hood, 46,300 tons, the flagship of the battle cruiser squadron of the Atlantic Fleet, but he missed the sailing due to him being taken ashore ill and diagnosed as possibly having diphtheria. Instead, he later boarded HMS Relentless and was saddened to hear that the Hood was sunk off the Greenland coast, 24 May 1941, in action against the German battleship Bismarck, which scored a direct hit on the Hood's main magazine at a range of 13 miles. There were fewer than a dozen survivors from the crew of 1,418.

On one occasion Nevillle's ship was on Arctic convoy duty to Russia and he disliked the voyage intensely, mainly because of the extremely cold conditions that resulted in thick ice covering all the superstructure.On another voyage his ship was torpedoed and casualties occurred, including the death of Neville's best friend, Andy.

By December 1944, with the war in Europe drawing to a conclusion, Neville's ship was anchored in Pireous harbour, Athens, during the start of the murderous Greek Civil war. Left wing guerrillas of the ELAS were operating and taking hostages, including British personnel, for the British Government was opposed to the aims of the ELAS guerrillas. A group of sailors, including Neville, went on port leave and, neglecting to take the required precautions, were captured by guerrillas and forced to go on a 450 mile trek into the Greek mountains of Thessalia, to Thebes and Lamia. After protracted negotiations, the Greek hostages and British personnel were released in exchange for captured ELAS guerrillas on 25 January 1945 and taken from Volos harbour by landing craft to a waiting ship.

At the end of the war, Neville was eventually demobbed and married Betty Woosnam of Broadwalk, Darley Dale, before beginning married life at Eagle Terrace, Wensley. However, on 25 June 1950, North Korean troops invaded South Korea without warning and the Korean War began, lasting till 1953. Neville was recalled into the navy and was based at Sheerness, from where they operated Motor Torpedo Boats out to the Irish Sea area in an attempt to intercept cargo boats that might have illegal immigrants on board.

JOHN POTTER MARSDEN (ROYAL NAVY)

John's father, George Potter Marsden, was a younger brother of John Potter Marsden, who had been killed during the First World War whilst serving in France in 1916. George, who had worked at Mill Close Mine from 1910, helping to keep the steam engines running, took his family to Chesterfield in 1920, where he began work at a power station.

John Potter Marsden was born in 1922, the sixth child in the family but his mother died shortly afterwards and the baby was brought to Wensley to be raised by his grandparents at Hillcrest Cottage, Wensley Square. When

John Potter Marsden of Wensley, Royal Navy

John left South Darley School in 1936 he began work as a gardener for Mrs Marshall, the owner of Wensley Hall, who promised him that she would match the wages paid at Mill Close Mine. When war was declared on 3 September 1939 John acted as messenger boy for the newly formed South Darley ARP, before becoming a fully fledged member.

In June 1941 John Potter Marsden volunteered to serve in the Royal Navy because one of his brothers from Chesterfield was already serving in that branch of the armed forces. John was posted to HMS Duke at Malvern, Worcestershire, where stokers and engineers were trained, before being sent to a patrol service depot at Lowestoft for further training.

His first draft in late 1941 was to Scapa Flow in the Orkney Islands, where his ship was a converted drifter (herring boat) which acted as a rescue boat. Hatson airfield, near Kirkwall, was a large Fleet Air Arm base at which new naval pilots were trained. Many accidents occurred during flight training and pilots and aircraft often ditched into the water.

John's ship patrolled the harbour and further out to sea, with a diver in full diving gear on board, ready to rescue any pilot who may have crashed, or sailors from ships that may have been hit. However, in 1943 he was posted back to Lowestoft and further training ensued.

By the early months of 1944 John found himself at Plymouth on a purpose built mine-sweeper of American construction named HMS Pyramus, made of wood and sailing from Gosport to sweep the English Channel. Five mine sweepers were in the Flotilla, under escort of a French destroyer, 'La Combatant'. The sweeping for mines took place as near as possible to the French coast in preparation for the D-Day landings in Normandy on 6 June 1944. The British and French sailors got on well with each other, swapping rum for wine, but sadly German E-boats attacked under cover of dark and sank the French ship with loss of life.

Prior to D-Day the Flotilla was pulled out of mine sweeping operations and instead their duty was to run ammunition supplies to the big ships involved in supporting the landings. This enabled them to continue using their powerful guns to smash away at the German shore defences and also prevent enemy aircraft attacking the vast armada. Danger was always present, for whilst supplying the ammunition to the larger ships after D-Days, another flotilla of mine sweepers in a different sector was decimated during an E-boat pack attack.

Returning to the Lowestoft depot, John soon found himself sent abroad on a troopship to the Far East, and after patrolling near the Burmese border, a large number of naval personnel were pulled back to HMS Maynea, the naval depot at Colombo, Ceylon (Sri Lanka). Preparations were being made for the invasion of Malaya and Singapore and the authorities attempted to turn these sailors into soldiers so that they could go into Malaya on D-Day plus one, and look after the port installations, after the Japanese had been 'ejected'.

Just prior to the invasion the atomic bombs were dropped on Japanese cities, but the operation still went ahead, although with few casualties. Shortly afterwards, however, John returned to Colombo and was posted to another mine sweeper that crossed the Indian Ocean and began sweeping operations in the Bay of Siam, close to Bangkok.

At long last John's demob notice arrived and he joined the crew of

HMS Suffolk, the ship on which the Armistice had been signed by the Japanese, in the presence of Admiral Mountbatton, and he made his way back to England and home.

HERBERT POTTER MARSDEN
(ROYAL ARMY MEDICAL CORPS)

John's Uncle, Herbert Potter Marsden, also served in the Second World War. When he was called up in 1940, Herbert was 38 years of age and he joined the Royal Army Medical Corps. We have already seen that his older brother, John Potter, had been killed in 1916 whilst serving in the Great War.

Born at Wensley in 1902, Herbert lived at Hillcrest Cottage and in 1925 married a Winster

Left: Private Herbert Potter Marsden, 1941
Right: Herbert's son, Warrant Officer Geoffrey Marsden, 1945, Royal Army Educational Corps. Both father and son served in the Forces during the Second World War

girl, Edna Bateman. They moved eventually across the valley to live near the Whitworth Hospital and Herbert worked as a traveller for Marsdens, the grocers, at Matlock Green, collecting and delivering the orders. Although a member of the Anglican church, he also acted as a lay preacher on the local Methodist circuit.

Training with the R.A.M.C. at Aldershot, he was posted eventually to Elgin, in Scotland. In 1942 he was seriously injured when in collision with a motor cycle dispatch rider, receiving amongst other injuries a broken pelvis, and for the next fourteen months was confined to a hospital bed at Elgin.

Whilst in hospital he was fitted with a calliper, which he wore for the rest of his life, and for a considerable period walked with the aid of two sticks. He remained in the army, however, first with the P.A.Y.E.Corps and then in the Royal Army Catering Corps at Inverary, Scotland. Having always been interested in cooking, he enjoyed his time with the Corps and was commended by his officers for the fine quality and taste of his soup on one occasion. He did not care or dare enlighten them that one of the ingredients he discovered later at the bottom of the large army soup cauldron was a 'black leading rag'. which had been used to black lead the cooking range.

When Herbert was demobbed in 1947 he could not return to his former job, for he could no longer drive a vehicle, and so he began his studies at Hinckley College and passed his Civil Service exam, enabling him to go to work in the offices at Derbyshire Stone Limited.

TOM FLETCHER (ROYAL NAVY) AND GEORGE FLETCHER (ROYAL ELECTRICAL MECHANICAL ENGINEERS)

They and their younger brother Kenneth were brought up at Greystones, Wensley, from where their father Fred went to work as a stone cutter at a Stanton quarry. Amongst other jobs, he helped to cut the stones used in facing the wall of Ladybower Reservoir when it was constructed during the 1930's.

Tom Fletcher was working as a laboratory assistant at Derbyshire Stone when he volunteered for service in the Royal Navy at the end of 1942. The Royal Navy had taken over many of the Butlin's holiday camps for use as training bases and Tom spent his basic six weeks seamanship course at the Skegness Butlin's camp (HMS Royal Arthur). This was followed by a telegraphist training course (as a wireless operator) at the Marconi College, Holloway Road, London, where

Morse procedures were gone through and his final training was undertaken at HMS Mercury, in Hampshire.

Passing from general service to patrol service, Tom found himself stationed at Leith/Granton, near Edinburgh, for the next eight months, sailing on board an armed coal burning trawler called HMS Stoke City. She was a deep-sea trawler,

George Fletcher (Royal Electrical Mechanical Engineers) and brother Tom Fletcher (radio operator and radar, Royal Navy), from Wensley

requisitioned from 'Consolidated Fisheries' of Grimsby and could accommodate thirty crew members. A number of guns were fitted to the superstructure and a depth charge ejector placed on board.

The front fish-hold had been converted into a mess deck with fold up bunks instead of hammocks but Tom was fortunate. As senior wireless operator on the trawler he had a nicely fitted bunk in the cabin. There was extra pay of 1/- a day, called 'hard lying' money and neat rum instead of the usual watered down version. Rats were a menace, for they got on board in port, and ran around the channels above the mess. It was necessary for the rat catcher to come on board before departure and put down bait.

Convoys were escorted at the mouth of the Firth of Forth and taken through the northerly Pentland Firth to the west coast anchorage in Loch Ewe, where Russian bound convoys were being gathered. Trawlers such as Stoke City were sent out on duty in very rough weather when the corvettes could not manage the task. The journey was always worst in the passage through the Pentland Firth but Tom was fortunate that his stomach was not too badly affected by the stormy seas. Enemy activity, especially from the threat of German U-boats, was often worst when they rounded the northerly coast of Scotland, onto the western coastal area. On a number of occasions the trawler escorted the convoys as far as Iceland.

After a period on general service, Tom was posted to HMS Belfast and they sailed to the Far East via the Red Sea and Sydney, Australia and then into the Pacific Ocean. However, further action was curtailed with the dropping of atomic bombs on Hiroshima and Nagasaki and VJ Day was celebrated at Freemantle with a 24-hour pass.

Travelling on to Formosa, they helped in the liberation of Allied prisoners of war who were placed onto hospital ships that had been converted from fleet carriers. These then made their way back to Sydney, but HMS Belfast continued her journey to Shanghai, via the Yangtse River and Hwang-Ho (Yellow River). The Belfast stayed in the Yellow River till February 1946, with occasional shots being fired by certain Japanese soldiers who had not surrendered.

Eventually the Belfast arrived back at Sydney and Tom Fletcher left it there to return to England and his demob on board an American troopship. Fortune again favoured Tom, for a crewman aboard the troopship was Joe Gregory, a Bonsall man, whose job it was to serve out meal coupons and Tom was favoured during meal times.

Meanwhile, Tom's younger brother, George Fletcher, had gone from South Darley School to work for Hothesalls Garage at Darley Bridge and then to George Siddall, haulage contractor at Stanton. In May of 1944 he joined the Army and was attached to the Royal Electrical Mechanical Engineers. Posted to the Anti-Aircraft Command on the East Coast of England, he travelled from one base to another, servicing the diesel generators that provided power to the radar screens and guns.

As the war in Europe progressed towards likely victory, George began a retraining programme, which resulted in him being sent out to the Far East for the final advance against the Japanese. He had arrived in India when news came through that the Japanese had surrendered after the dropping of atomic bombs on the Japanese mainland.

George's war was over but it took some while before he arrived safely home in Wensley. Trouble had flared up in Palestine and terrorist activity was rife as organisations such as Irgun and the ever more extremist Stern Gang attempted to wrest power from the British occupying force and forge a homeland for the Jewish people. Assassinations of British diplomats, soldiers and policemen increased and George Fletcher found himself in Palestine at the height of these troubles. It was only relatively safe to travel the streets in groups of four, with sten guns at the ready, and for most of the time the servicemen stayed inside the barracks.

However, at long last, George was demobbed and travelled home to return to civilian life in the haulage business.

ABLE SEAMAN BILL RICHARDSON GUNNER IN THE ROYAL NAVY

Hector and Carrie Richardson moved with their son Bill from Elton to 7 Eversleigh Rise in 1936. Bill and Hector both worked at Mill Close Mine. When war broke out in 1939, Bill was 17, and without telling his mother he travelled to Chesterfield and volunteered for the Royal Navy. They kept his name on their records and in November 1941 he became an Ordinary Seaman at HMS Raleigh in Plymouth, where he trained as a naval gunner.

Bill Richardson of Eversleigh Rise, Gunner in the Royal Navy

During his stay in Plymouth he witnessed the terrible pounding the town received from the German Luftwaffe. Eventually, in May 1942, Bill was posted to Glasgow and boarded an American freighter of 6000 tons, the USS 'Monargo' on which he was to be one of the gunners as it returned in convoy to Boston.

Time was spent in New York and Rhode Island before crossing the continent by rail to San Francisco, where Christmas 1943 was spent. In the docks an aircraft carrier, HMS Stalker, was being commissioned in the American 'Lend-Lease' programme and eventually it was ready and Bill went on board as a gunner. He was to stay with this ship to the end of the war.

Sailing through the Panama Canal, they arrived eventually near New York and found themselves attached to an invasion convoy set for North Africa and the American led attack on Algeria and Tunisia, code named 'Operation Torch'. After unloading supplies and aircraft parts at Casablanca, HMS Stalker set off for Liverpool and a refit.

At Belfast they took on board a Fleet Air Arm crew with twelve Seafires and four Swordfish aircraft and became part of the 24th Aircraft Carrier Squadron. From Scapa Flow in the Orkneys, the squadron sailed south for Gibraltar where aircraft landing trials took place, with the loss of a number of aircraft and pilot lives.

Eventually a convoy set off for Malta, protected by the Squadron, and were attacked three or four times by Focke Wolf Condor aircraft, before arriving safely at Valetta Harbour. From there, HMS Stalker and her sister ships helped in the Salerno landings on the Italian mainland, assaulting the German positions with their aircraft and naval guns from a range of 15 miles off-shore. More aircraft were lost through faulty landings on the carrier's deck than by enemy action.

On 6 June 1944 the Squadron sailed from Alexandria for the southern coast of France, taking up position between Marseilles and Toulon, in order to provide support from the south for the main invasion of Europe in Normandy. Day after day, during August, Stalkers' aircraft blew up anything and everything that moved, destroying bun batteries, lighters near Marseilles, nine locomotives, ten rail cars, 118 motor vehicles, ten barges and 100 vehicles in the Rhone Valley.

During September 1944, HMS Stalker transferred to the Eastern Mediterranean, where it operated round the Dodekanese Islands, which were being evacuated by the Germans. The Stalker's aircraft helped to protect British mine-sweepers operating off the coast of Crete and Rhodes, and attacking ships and airfields. By October, she was part of the escort carrier squadron helping in the Greek landing operation on 15 October 1944, before returning to Alexandria.

In March 1945, Bill departed Alexandria en route to Colombo, Sri Lanka, ready to take part in Operation 'Dracula', the invasion and capture of Rangoon, Burma. The troops went in and soon secured the port, whilst HMS Stalker and the other ships turned south, where its aircraft attacked Port Victoria.

The Japanese surrendered after the dropping of the atomic bombs on their cities and HMS Stalker was ordered to Singapore to take on board prisoners of war. With 300 of these poor souls on board they sailed for Colombo, where they could spend time recuperating in hospital. Bill then sailed with HMS Stalker to England, where in 1945, 23 year old Bill married Mona Spencer.

After his discharge from the Royal Navy in May 1946, Bill began work at Firth Derihon and settled down to married life, first at Eversleigh Rise and finally at St Mary's View. A fine footballer, he became Captain of Wensley Red Stars and can be found on a number of football photographs contained in the chapter on the 1950's.

PRIVATE LEWIS WEBSTER, 2/5TH BATTALION SHERWOOD FORESTERS AND POW

Lewis Webster lived in Wensley Square together with his parents, brother Bert and sister, Rosie. A member of St Mary's Church choir, he worked with his brother, Bert, at Mill Close Mine and was a player with Mill Close Football Team.

With the flooding of the mine in 1938/39, Bert was persuaded by Consolidated Goldfields, owners of the mine, to take up a job at another of their mines in West Africa, on the Gold Coast. Lewis remained in Wensley and at the start of the Second World War he joined the 2/6th Battalion of the Sherwood Foresters.

Lewis Webster of Wensley, POW from 1940

After eight months of training and guard duties in England it went to France and disembarked at Cherbourg on 27 April 1940, with the aim being to train and be employed in airfield construction. By 10 May they were located in the Rennes area when notice came of the German invasion of the Low Countries and were moved forward to the Franco-Belgian frontier. By 17 May the Battalion had taken up defensive positions on a canal to the south of Lille in support of French troops.

On 25 May, these French troops began to fall back and small parties of Germans, who had been attacking vigorously in the vicinity, started crossing the two canal bridges. The Battalion, supported by Durham Light Infantry and some tanks, advanced to re-establish their old line. They came to close grips with the enemy, with the loss of seven officers and 49 other ranks. A withdrawal took place.

The prolonged defence of this area greatly helped the withdrawal of other troops to Dunkirk. On 27 May the Battalion marched to Avein and from there went by motor transport to Steenvoorde and moved into the Dunkirk perimeter, just south of the port, to cover six bridges. For the next three days their defences were not heavily pressed by the enemy, apart from some shelling and German patrols.

The 2/5th Battalion went to Malo les Bains, just east of Dunkirk on 1 June and embarked on a variety of craft for England on the following day. Armed with little more than rifles, on a low scale of transport and lacking artillery, they had displayed a staunchness customary in their Regiment.

Lewis Webster did not escape from Dunkirk with his colleagues. Whilst soldiers waited on the beach, a plea went out for volunteer drivers and helpers to take ambulances inland from the beach head to collect more wounded. Lewis volunteered but was captured by the Germans on this journey and was to remain a prisoner of war for the following five years.

Arriving in Germany as prisoner Number 6336, he was to suffer privation in a number of POW camps, but in many ways he was 'lucky' to be allowed to live and work on a nearby farm for a number of years. He was treated well by the family and on many weekends the farmer supplied him with civilian clothes and took him to the local beer house or inn.

By late 1944, however, the Allies were encroaching on German territory from both east and west and Lewis Webster found himself being taken on a series of marches to escape the clutches of the victorious allies. Eventually he arrived at Stalag 20A, a camp at Thorn Podgorz in Poland, but in 1945 he was released and faced the joy of repatriation to England and the welcome from his family in Wensley.

A story about Lewis encapsulates his resolute spirit that kept him going through those dark, difficult years. He arrived one day at Matlock bus station, having bought a large dustbin, with the intention of boarding a Silver Service bus with Wensley born conductress May Wayne in charge. Refused entry with such an object, he still boarded the bus and then ordered two fares to Wensley Square.

JOE DEVEREUX,
ARMOURER IN THE ROYAL AIR FORCE

At the end of the First World War, Arthur Devereux arrived from the Luton area to live at Bumper Castle and work as a shot firer at Mill Close Mine. In 1920 he married Mary Webster from Portico House, Wensley, and the couple lived there with her parents. A son, Joe, was born in 1921 and later a daughter, Barbara, was born.

Joe Devereux, first on left, in front of Spitfire in Canada. Joe was an armourer in the RAF

Joe Devereux, who started working life as an apprentice mechanic to George Cooper at Darley Bridge, was determined to join the RAF and to do so he supplemented his schooling by travelling with Mill Close lead miner, Eric Fisher from Winster, in his car, to Technical College at Chesterfield. In 1938 Joe became an armourer in the RAF and was therefore a regular when war broke out in September 1939.

He embarked for France in the early days of 1940 with a Spitfire

212

Squadron and they found themselves in desperate action when the Germans invaded the Low Countries on 10 May. The airfield had to be vacated after enemy air strikes and a temporary one found further behind the lines. Churchill had decided that the terrible loss of aircraft in France could not be sustained if Britain was to resist invasion and he ordered RAF squadrons to return to the relative safety of British airfields. The pilots were able to fly across the Channel, but ground crew personnel such as Joe Devereux had to make their way as best they could overland to the French coastal ports.

Joe and a RAF colleague were the last people to leave the airstrip, for as armourer to the squadron, it was Joe's job to blow up the ammunition dump before it could fall into enemy hands. The two only just escaped, for they blew up the last traces of ammunition as the German advance party arrived at the far end of the runway. The RAF ground crew did not escape across the Channel through the port of Dunkirk, but instead sailed from a French harbour on board a small French fishing vessel.

After a spell of leave, Joe returned to his squadron in the South of England. During the beautiful, late summer days of August and September 1940, they were involved in one of the key battles of the Second World War, the Battle of Britain, set high in the blue skies above the southern counties of England.

During desperate days of fighting, in which many of the squadron's pilots and aircraft were lost, it became clear that Hitler's invasion plans were dashed. As the Germans turned to the night time Blitz of London and the provincial cities, Joe Devereux was withdrawn from action as an armourer and travelled to Nova Scotia in Canada, where for many months, he helped in the training of RAF and Canadian Air Force personnel.

Returning from Canada he spent some time near Thirsk, Yorkshire, but soon was posted to a Lancaster bomber base near Ridgewell in Suffolk, where his task as armourer was to attend to the guns and load the bombs onto the aircraft. It was whilst attending a dance close to the base that he met his future wife, Maureen.

Joe remained in the RAF until 1950, when he returned to Wensley with Maureen and began work for a while at Bennett's Quarry, Grangemilll, with other former Wensley servicemen, George Fletcher, Jimmy Taylor and John Potter Marsden.

WALTER BOWLER, GUNNER IN THE ROYAL MARINES

Walter Bowler was born at Rowsley in 1898. During the Great War, he enlisted at Nottingham in 1915 at the age of 17 years 2 months 18 days, signing on for 12 years. He joined the Royal Marines as a gunner and joined the battleship HMS Barham, serving in the war during 1917 and 1918, although not coming into contact with the enemy. He was fortunate to be at Scapa Flow in the Orkneys in late 1918 to witness the scuttling of their Grand Fleet by the defeated German Navy.

Gunner Walter Bowler, Royal Marines, first left, on board 'Duffield'

He continued to serve on HMS Barham after the war ended, until his discharge in 1928. He had married an Ashford-in-the-Water girl in 1924 and lived there, travelling to work each day at Mill Close Lead Mine after 1928. However, in 1932 he moved to Darley Bridge to be closer to his work and in 1934 finally settled down in the recently built Cross Green Cottages.

Since his discharge from the Senior Service, he had been in the Royal Marine Volunteer Reserve, and at regular intervals during the inter-war years he would go for two weeks training. On 15 August 1939, nineteen days before war was declared, he was taking part in training exercise on the 'Calypso', a civilian tanker armed with one naval gun. He was the military man on board the civilian ship.

Between January 1940 and February 1941 he sailed in convoys round the Cape of Good Hope to Aden and the Red Sea area a number of times. On each occasion he sailed on a civilian tanker or freighter and acted as a gunner on the lone naval gun attached to each craft.

In April 1941 Walter found himself on the Newcastle based tanker 'Duffield' as a gunner. Northwest of the Canary Island, North Atlantic, the London steamer 'Harpathian' was torpedoed by a German submarine, whilst the 'Duffield' was hit by three torpedoes. The survivors scrambled into the lifeboats and Walter Bowler discarded the remnants of his uniform, for, as one of the few military men on board he did not want to be interned when he reached a foreign country.

With little water on board and the temperature extremely high, conditions were dreadful. Survivors resorted to sucking buttons and a number of men died and were pushed overboard. After journeying for 9 days they were sighted and rescued by a neutral Spanish vessel. She picked up 48 survivors, 27 of them from the 'Duffield' and they were landed at Santa Cruz de Tenerife in the Canary Islands on 29 April. Seventeen were injured and were placed in hospital.

The survivors, including Walter Bowler, eventually left Tenerife on a neutral steamer for Gibraltar and from there they were brought home on a British ship.

After returning home to Cross Green on leave, Walter was never to go back to sea again. Instead he spent his time at Western Approaches; a land based establishment near Liverpool.

From there he was 'demobbed' in 1947 and, with Mill Close Mine no longer operating, he went to work at Firth Derihon before eventually going on to Enthovens.

CORPORAL GEORGE WAYNE, ROYAL AIR FORCE VOLUNTEER RESERVE

We have already met George's sister, May, who was a conductor on the Silver Service buses. George, the son of John and Sylvia Wayne, was born at Oker Terrace, Wensley in 1923.

In 1939 he was living with his grand-mother and uncle on a farm near Chinley, from where he went to Manchester before he was 18 to sign on with the RAF. He was trained to drive at RAF Weeton at Blackpool in July 1941 and stationed on a Wellington bomber station north of Grimsby. From there he volunteered to go overseas as a driver and arrived at Greenock in November to join a convoy bound for South Africa and Alexandria in Egypt, via Freetown and Durban.

In Alexandria, vehicles and equipment were ready to allow them to form a unit capable of making and maintaining forward airstrips for the RAF. They set off

George Wayne of Wensley, Royal Engineers in North Africa. His crane is in the background

through the desert and arrived at Sidi Barani landing ground LG 105, where scrapers were attached to the vehicles to enable them to construct a landing strip of hard sand. However, they had to retreat as Rommel's Africa Corps advanced once again.

George's unit was stationed twenty miles behind the front line at El Alamein and its job was to salvage and repair aircraft that came down in the desert (Repair and Salvage Unit). They formed an advance party that went out to retrieve aircraft and their vehicles consisted of a crane (operated by George), articulated high loader and a low loader. The fuselage was placed on one vehicle and the wings on the other. A Ford Chevrolet carried the fitters and armourers. Whilst on operations they would be out in the desert for ten days. Eventually three advance parties joined together to become Advance Salvage Unit, Western Desert. The logo on their vehicles was a spitfire and the words 'Down but not out'.

At the Battle of El Alamein they advanced behind the attacking 8th Army force and followed through with them to Benghazi and Tunis, where they met the American and British forces who had fought through Algeria and Tunisia in Operation Torch. The two allied forces did not get on with each other and there was fighting between 1st Army and 8th Army soldiers in the Kasbah.

Eventually, George's unit went by Tank Landing Craft to Corsica and Sardinia, onto former Italian airfields, but eventually they followed in behind the advancing Allied forces on mainland Italy and finally arrived in Naples in 1945. There they helped to service Lancaster bombers that were flying service personnel back to England.

The war was over and the Salvage and Repair Unit found themselves travelling home by rail. George Wayne came home on leave, travelling on the milk train from Derby to Darley at Christmas 1945. Finally he was posted to the bomb dump at RAF Harpur Hill, near Buxton, from where he was demobbed in 1946. In all his travels through North Africa, Corsica and Italy, George had kept the same crane throughout, and it had become a second home for him.

With his wartime driving experience, George was accepted by haulage contractor George Hothesall of Darley Bridge to work for him, before he joined Toft and Tomlinsons as a driver.

GUNNER GEOFFREY ALLEN, 42 BATTERY, 2ND FIELD REGIMENT, ROYAL ARTILLERY

Geoffrey's father, Ernest Allen, had been born at Lumb Cottage, Cross Green, and during the Great War had served with distinction in the 15th Battalion, Sherwood Foresters. On 12 June 1918 he had won the Military Medal, when, although receiving a shrapnel wound down his shoulder and back, he went into the open to drag and fetch his wounded comrades to safety.

After the war Ernest, worked at James Smiths Nurseries and married Laura Turner from Brook Bottom, Two Dales. Two sons, Ronald and Geoffrey were born in Two Dales, but the family then moved to Bank House Cottages, South Darley, where sisters Joan and Evelyne were born.

Geoffrey was called up in late 1940 and entered the Royal Artillery, completing his initial training at Caernarvon Castle, whilst many further months were spent training in Norfolk. On 9 March 1943, the Regiment went to Algiers and then to Bone as part of the Operation Torch landings in North Africa.

On 14 April they were in action at Medfes-el-Bab. Whilst lying low in forward positions ready for the big attack on Tunis, the regiment was unexpectedly attacked by the enemy at 10pm. Their position was

Left: Geoffrey Allen of Eversleigh Rise, Royal Artillery
Right: His father, Ernest Allen, 15th Battalion Sherwood Foresters (Military Medal), First World War

overrun but was retrieved and they took part in the main attack a few days later and were still in action when the cease-fire sounded.

However, during this action, a shell had exploded nearby, and the gun crew received many casualties, including Geoffrey, who was blinded temporarily. He spent many months in hospital and was not

Gun crews in North Africa (Western Desert) 1942. Geoffrey Allen is third from the right on the back row. Most of the crew were wounded or killed at the time of Geoff's injury

with his Battery when they landed in Sicily. Geoffrey had rejoined them by 27 January 1944, when the 42nd Battery went into Anzio beach-head five days after the initial landing.

They occupied their positions for 105 days, receiving

numerous casualties, before breaking out at the end of May and crossing the River Tiber. Geoff's Battery fired the last rounds, knocking out an enemy battery on 6 June. By 9 June the Regiment was in a rest area between Rome and Ostia and was visited by H.M. the King who shared tea with them. The River Arno was crossed just east of Florence on 31 August and, fighting north through Borgo San Lorenzo, the Sieve River was crossed on 11 September. At Palazzudo the Regiment was engaged in one of the most critical operations of the war, the support of the 3rd Infantry Brigade in the attack on Mount Cece in October. The Regiment arrived south-east of Bologna and they stayed there from 10th November until firing its last rounds at the enemy on 15th January 1945.

DRIVER BEN EDGE, ROYAL ARMY SERVICE CORPS AND POW NUMBER 140575

Benjamin Edge was born in December 1917, the son of Oker wheelwright, Sam Edge. The family, strongly Methodist, lived next to Oker Chapel at 'The Yews'. Ben joined the firm of John William Wildgoose, Matlock, as a joiner. He enlisted at Chesterfield in the RASC in December 1939 and became a driver in that Regiment.

Left: Driver Ben Edge, RASC
Right: POW Ben Edge on left, with a friend

Having been evacuated from Dunkirk in early June 1940, training took place in England before his Company departed by convoy to take part in the North African campaign in late 1941. Ben found himself involved in Field Marshall Rommel's Second Offensive against the Allied forces between January and June 1942, when he was part of the garrison holding Tobruk, a supposedly impregnable Allied fortress on Rommel's flank.

At dawn on 20 June, Rommel attacked Tobruk with his two Panzer divisions and the Italian 20th Corps, supported by JU87 'Stuka' dive bombers. Progress was rapid. By 8am the forward troops had bridged the anti-tank ditch so that the armour could immediately exploit the breach, and by mid-day the ships at anchor in the harbour were being pounded by heavy artillery. By nightfall the forts at Solaro and Pilastrino had fallen and the next morning Major General Klopper surrendered the garrison of Tobruk. Thirty-three thousand men, including Ben Edge, and many vehicles fell into Axis hands, but the greatest windfall for Rommel was the huge quantity of fuel for which the German armour was desperate.

The fall of Tobruk in a single day was entirely unexpected by the British Army, by Churchill and also the general public and sent shock waves throughout the nation back home.

The story of what happened to POW Ben Edge was reported three years later in a May 1945 edition of the local paper 'The High Peak News':-

'Flags are out in Wensley and Oker this week to celebrate VE Day and the return of the men who have been prisoners of war in Germany. Driver Benjamin Edge, aged 27 years, told a reporter that his native countryside looked like a fairyland after being a prisoner since June 1942. He arrived home about 10pm last Thursday, the day after his mother had received a telegram stating he was safe and well.

Driver Edge was taken prisoner at Tobruk and was handed over to the Italians, proceeding via Benghazi to Naples, where he was in hospital for a time with diptheria. Later he went to Campo No. 53, a new camp which was not well organised at first, but fortunately the Red Cross parcels were awaiting them.

Driver Edge was with a working party on a farm in 1943 when Italy capitulated, but he and his party were removed to Venice, where the Germans took them into custody. He had a nightmare journey into Germany with a party of 50 British prisoners as well as many New Zealanders, South Africans and Indians. They were packed into trucks, and during the three day journey had only two meals. A camp near

Munich was their destination. "We had a good view of an RAF raid on Munich," said Driver Edge, "but we had to be careful as the Germans loosed dogs in the compound in order to keep us inside during an air-raid."

From Munich he was transferred to Stalag II a, near Magdeburg, under poor conditions, both as regards food and clothing. Then came another transfer to a camp near Hanover, where Driver Edge was put to work in a mine. "We did 12 hour shifts," he told us "and some of the lads on the surface did 14 hours, all on one meal during the day." It was while working in the mine in November 1944 that Driver Edge lost a little finger from his right hand, through an accident with a machine saw.

Last month came deliverance. "For some time we knew our lads were getting close, and one day when the Germans were trying to transfer some NCO's from our camp they had to return as they were unable to get through our lines. We then knew we were pretty safe and we raided the camp store and had a good feed. I got some oats, and plenty of sugar on them. On 16 April we saw some tanks coming across the fields. We thought at first they were Jerries on the retreat, but then we saw they were ours and the whole camp went mad. Some men climbed on the roofs, others cried with happiness and some just stood and stared." Driver Edge came back to England by plane, and is now enjoying a seven weeks leave.'

Ben returned to Wildgoose's and in 1946 married a Nottingham born girl, Dorothy Harrison.

NUMBER 1760920, ROWLAND BAILEY
'D' COMPANY 2ND BATTALION CAMERONIANS, SCOTTISH RIFLES

Rowland was the son of Roland George Bailey, Royal Garrison Artillery, who was killed on 13th October 1917 in the Battle of Passchaendale, Ypres.

For a further account of George Bailey see 'A Derbyshire Parish at

War, South Darley and the Great War 1914-19'.

Rowland's mother, Millicent, never remarried and brought up her son and his sister, Marjorie at Oker Terrace, Wensley. He eventually became employed at Mill Close mine.

Rowland was posted to the 2nd Battalion, Cameronians on its return from Dunkirk where it had suffered heavy casualties. After a lengthy period of training the Battalion left for India but was diverted to take part in the invasion of Madagascar, to prevent its occupation by the Japanese. This was the first large-scale operation involving air, sea and land forces under a single command.

After eventually landing in Egypt the Cameronians were sent to Persia (Iran) as part of the occupying force, safeguarding oil resources. This was the first time that the Allies had occupied a neutral country.

Rifleman Rowland Bailey of Wensley, 2nd Battalion Cameronians (Scottish Rifles)

Rowland visited Baghdad and went onto the Lebanon for rest and retraining, near to Beirut.

In 1943 the Cameronians took part in the assault of Sicily, as the first stage in the invasion of Italy, and later was involved in the Battle of Anzio. Eventually by June 1944 the Cameronians were the first British troops to reach the River Tiber, near the Italian capital.

By 1945 the Battalion was involved in fighting in the Rhineland, Germany and Rowland, by April 1945, was at Wismar, Lusbeck and Stendal in North Germany; "having the satisfaction", as Battalion records state, "of being in at the kill," as Germany surrendered.

Rowland Bailey was awarded the North Africa Star, Italy Star, and France and Germany Star; these medals remaining with the family.

After the War, Rowland married Hilda Allsopp of Tansley and they lived at Brick Cottages, Wensley; Rowland working where Permanite are now, making pre-cast concrete.

Jim, Bill and Frank Taylor, the three sons of Godfrey (Gof) and Sarah Taylor of Tiersall View, Wensley Square, all served in His Majesty's Services during the Second World War. Their father had volunteered for duty in the First World War, in early 1915, and served throughout the conflict in Gallipoli, France and Belgium.

DRIVER JIMMY TAYLOR, 262 FIELD COMPANY, ROYAL ENGINEERS

Jim was the youngest son, and after working for newsagent Jack Masters for a short while, he was employed underground at Mill Close Mine from 1930 to 1939. By the time war was declared, Jim had settled down to married life with wife Daisy and two young sons Roy and Geoffrey.

Brothers Bill and Frank were already serving when Jim enlisted in early 1941 and was posted into the Royal Engineers, where his

Left: Jim Taylor of Wensley, Royal Engineers, with sons Roy and Geoffrey
Right: Bill (Goff) Taylor of the Welsh Guards

company, 262 Field Company, specialised in bridge building. Time was spent in training at Wrexham, Leyburn and Maidstone before they arrived at Hayling Island, near Portsmouth, in early 1944, in preparation for the invasion of Europe in June.

For three weeks the Company trained at nearby Brackelsham Bay for their job of landing on the beaches and clearing the girder obstacles with explosives. They were to be under the command of 3rd Canadian Division, which was to spearhead the advance of the British Corps on Juno Beach.

262 Field Company RE constructed this Class 40 Bailey Bridge near the Zuid Willens Canal at Nederweert, Holland, in November 1944

On the 2nd June they moved to Southampton Docks, ready to embark for the invasion of Europe. However, Jimmy Taylor was in No. 3 Platoon and was to go onto the beaches on D-Day plus one.

The other platoons of 262 Company landed on Green Beach, twenty minutes into D-Day, with the job of clearing 200 yards of beach of girders and mines in readiness for the arrival of tanks. By the time that Jimmy and No. 3 Platoon arrived, on the 8th June, 262 Field Company was in the village of Graye sur Mer, three quarters of a mile from the beach. They started to bridge a couple of small ditches with trees etc. and felt quite happy at the way the advance had gone, although they were visited a couple of times during the day by the Luftwaffe.

As the Germans destroyed the bridging points of rivers and canals during their long retreat, 262 Company members were in constant action, often under enemy fire, as they attempted to provide alternative crossing points for the advancing Allied forces. Throughout the remainder of 1944 and well into 1945 Jim's Company was involved in the actions around Caen and Falaise, the crossing of the River Seine, entry into Antwerp, the crossings of the Albert Canal and Rivers Maas and Waal. An example of a bridge constructed by two platoons of 262

Field Company was the 130 foot Bailey Bridge at Nederweert (Holland), near Maesyck, over the Zuid Willems Vaart Canal on the 14th /15th November 1944.

As the advance continued to the German border, an incident occurred when the lorry Jimmy was travelling in left the road and crashed into a tree, resulting in injuries to his jaw. He was transferred across the Channel to a hospital in Leeds for treatment, but eventually he returned to his unit as they crossed the Rhine, into the heartland of Germany.

By 29 April 1945 they were crossing the River Elbe in Germany and at the end of the war in Europe found themselves part of the British Army of the Rhine, stationed near Bielefeld.

When Jim Taylor ended his service with the Army he returned to civilian life at Wensley and made use of his driving skills in the employment of Darley Bridge haulage contractor, George Siddall.

GUARDSMAN BILL (GOFF) TAYLOR, WELSH GUARDS

Bill Taylor was a regular soldier who had joined the Welsh Guards in 1927, serving for three years and then nine years on the reserve. During his three years in service he spent time in Egypt and later, whilst on reserve, he worked for some years at Mill Close Mine and then at Cawdor Quarry, Matlock.

After marrying Ida Wood and starting a family, they eventually lived at the White House, Wensley. When war was declared in 1939, Bill was still on Reserve and was automatically called up into the Guards Regiment. However, he was not to face action overseas, for during his time at Cawdor Quarry a fall of rock had resulted in the loss of a finger and restricted mobility of the remaining fingers of the hand.

As a result of this problem, he spent the war years serving at Pirbright, Caterham and the Guards Depot at Wellington Barracks, on Birdcage Walk. For a great deal of this time he served as batman to a series of officers at Esher.

FRANK TAYLOR

Little is known of Frank's war time service record. Married to Emma Wigley and living at Tiersall View, Wensley, he worked at Mill Close Mine in pre-war years. After joining the Army in 1940 he was posted eventually to India and the Far East and saw much action against the Japanese forces in the Burma campaign.

As with so many servicemen participating in this theatre of war, he suffered many deprivations, not least from the jungle terrain in which they fought, the climate and the attendant insects and pests that preyed upon them.

When Frank eventually returned to his native Wensley, he was one of the handful of men who worked in post war years for Hopton Mining Company in retrieving spar and barytes from former lead mine spoil heaps in nearby Cambridge Wood.

GUNNER TOM EVANS, ROYAL ARTILLERY

Tom Evans, son of Tom and Emily Evans of 'Leafield' 3, Oker Road, was the elder brother of Ernest Evans, Royal Marines, who had died due to enemy action whilst on board the cruiser HMS Hermione in the Mediterranean Sea in June 1942. Tom had worked as a lead miner at Mill Close and enlisted in the Royal Artillery during 1940.

In 1941 he was posted to No.133 Coastal Battery, 533 Coast Regiment, on the tiny Island of Flotta, in the Orkney Islands. On that lonely, windy, rain swept post, the large coastal guns protected the vital Home Fleet base of Scapa Flow. Any journey to the larger islands meant facing the prospect of sea-sickness on the lurching deck of a boat.

Tom Evans of Oker Road, Anti-Aircraft Regiment, Royal Artillery

Whilst on Flotta he received the tragic news of the death of his brother Ernest and was granted compassionate leave for the long journey to Derbyshire, in order to visit his father, mother and sister Phyllis, and take part in a memorial service for Ernest at St Mary's Church.

On the return journey to rejoin his battery he was to meet his future wife, Lillian, who lived at Duffield. Whilst travelling with his father on the overcrowded train to Derby, she entered their carriage and was soon in conversation. On his next leave they became engaged.

Tom was eventually posted to a coastal battery of massive guns at Dungeness in Kent, covering the approaches to the Straits of Dover. It was whilst on his next leave, from Dungeness, that Tom and Lillian were married on 19 June 1943. On their wedding day he received a telegram to say that he was to join a different coastal battery, this time in Suffolk, where he was stationed until 1944.

It was then that he joined the field artillery and found himself making the long journey by convoy to join the Reserve Mobile Anti-Aircraft Regiment of the India Command. Time was spent in Ceylon (Sri Lanka) and, as with many others, he was ready to form part of the planned invasion of Rangoon and Malaya. The dropping of the Atomic bombs intervened and the battles fortunately did not occur, but eventually Tom's Regiment was stationed in Singapore after the Japanese surrender.

In 1946 he returned home to England for demobilisation. His sad regret was that on both outward and homebound routes he had been unable to spend time in Alexandria and visit the graveside of his younger brother, Ernest.

On arrival in England he rejoined Lillian and they resumed married life at Depot Street, Derby, where Tom became a postman and remained in that job for the rest of his working life. Telling reminders of his time spent in the Far East were the recurring bouts of malaria Tom suffered during the early years of his return to civilian life.

RON ALLEN, RAILWAY FIREMAN

Fifteen years old Ron Allen from Eversleigh Rise was employed at Rowsley Sidings as a "knocker upper" on both night and day shifts. Armed with pockets full of gravel to throw against bedroom windows, he travelled on his bicycle to make sure that railwaymen were awake and to give them tickets as to where they would be going with their locomotive on that shift. Ron graduated to cleaning locomotive before finally becoming a fireman, just prior to the start of the Second World War. Two other South Darley men working at Rowsley were Syd Gladwin from Eversleigh Rise and Tommy Simcock, who worked in the offices.

Ron Allen of Eversleigh Rise, seated. Fireman on the railway during the war years.

When war was declared, Ron Allen was fireman on the Manchester/ Liverpool and Birmingham/London runs, often serving with driver James Jackson. From 1940 onwards all locomotives had to have tarpaulins or sheeting covering all parts of the open cab to prevent the possibility of enemy aircraft spotting the glare when a fire-box door was opened. This was a necessary precaution during the blackout but it did result in very uncomfortable, hot working conditions being experienced by driver and firemen, especially on warm summer nights.

If air raids were expected on Derby, or other towns or cities on the journey, the loco driver was stopped at the signal box and given the air raid red signal, and would proceed with caution until given the air raid clear signal. On the night that Coventry was devastated on 14 November 1940, Ron was proceeding slowly to Birmingham, with the air raid red alert in action all the way, and the glow in the night sky could be seen from the locomotive cab for much of the journey. The air raid had introduced a new standard of concentrated severity with the dropping within a limited area, by all-night relays of raiders, of 500 tons of high explosive bombs, 30,000 incendiaries, and 50 parachute mines.

On wartime runs into London, Ron and his driver would lodge overnight in the Railway barracks in Kentish Town, and here they would experience first hand the conditions of the London Blitz, endured by Londoners day after day from 7th September to 2nd November 1940 and thereafter more intermittently, though individually more severe.

Ron continued working as a railway fireman until 1947, when, having already married Edna Roland of Darley Dale, he left and began working at Enthoven's lead smelter.

MARION WALKER,
WOMENS' ROYAL NAVAL SERVICES (WRENS)

Marion Walker, daughter of Ben Walker, the Company Sergeant Major in Darley Home Guard, of St Mary's View, was born at Stanton Lees in 1921. In May 1941 she joined the WRNS as a stewardess and did initial training at Hampstead and Greenwich, London.

Isabelle and Marion Walker of St Mary's View, during the war years. Marion served in the Wrens as an armourer

Her first station was at HMS Glendower (Butlins Holiday Camp) before she volunteered as an armourer and eventually arrived at HMS Merlin in Fife, Scotland. This was an operational Royal Naval Air Station for the Fleet Air Arm and Marion was kept busy stripping, cleaning and assembling the different weapons used on the planes. In 1943 she moved to a smaller, nearby station called HMS Waxwing.

During early 1944 she travelled to Portsmouth for a three month course at Whale Island RN Gunnery Establishment and was billeted on the sea front at Southsea. Preparations were well advanced for the invasion of Normandy and the seafront at Southsea was boarded off to prevent people seeing the activity taking place. Marion returned in 1944 to Waxwing and then Merlin in 1945 before finally being posted to HMS Vulture Operational Air Station at St Merryn in Cornwall. She looked forward to visiting the place her great grandfather engineer, Stephen Thomas, had left to come up to Mill Close Mine to erect the mighty steam engine known as 'Jumbo'.

LEADING AIRCRAFT WOMAN OLIVE BOWLER, WOMENS AUXILLARY AIR FORCE (WAAF)

Born in 1925, Olive was the eldest daughter of Walter Bowler of Cross Green Cottages, himself serving in the Royal Marines as a gunner.

She joined the Royal Air Force on 4 February 1943 and, after early training, became a Medical Equipment Assistant, serving for most of her wartime duty at Cleveleys, near Blackpool. Olive spent a good deal of time in the stores, supervising the provision of bedding and equipment for the Royal Air Force hospital.

Olive Bowler of Cross Green, serving in the Waafs during the war

By 1945 she had returned to complete her duty at Rockside RAF Hospital in Matlock, where many bomber crews came to recuperate after their traumatic experiences on bombing raids over Europe. It was from here that she was finally released from service in February 1947.

SERGEANT BERNARD DEVANEY, ROYAL ARTILLERY

Bernard Devaney was born in 1925 and lived with his mother Mary and grandparents John and Phoebe Devaney on Main Street, Wensley, at Blindwell House. John was the Wensley cobbler.

Bernard was working at Cawdor Quarry Yard, Matlock, when, at the age of 17 he volunteered at Derby recruiting base for twelve years service. On the 2 September 1943 he enlisted into the Royal Artillery and eventually found himself on a gunnery course at Larkhill on Salisbury Plain.

In August 1944 his unit found itself in Normandy, helping in the attempt to trap large number of German soldiers and armoured vehicles at Falaise by sealing the Falaise Gap. Though some escaped, large number of men and equipment were captured or destroyed.

Bernard Devaney, Royal Artillery

The British and Canadian forces now pursued the retreating German forces northwards, attempting to prevent the German use of the Channel and Belgian ports. Bernard's artillery unit was posted to liaise with the Canadian forces at this stage. After the isolation and capture of Antwerp they moved inland in order to occupy the territory in Belgium and Holland being used to launch V2 rockets, not only on London but also on Antwerp and the ports being used by the advancing Allied armies.

As the advance continued into the Schelde Estuary and flat polder lands of Holland, the Germans breached the dykes and water flooded the lowland. The frantic order was received to get into their vehicles and move out. Bernard survived, but out of 450 men, only 18 made it to safety. The rest were either taken prisoner or drowned.

The survivors reached the famous town of Menin, where the locals provided them with four days of hospitality before they were reassigned to a medium artillery unit based with an airborne regiment. During the severe winter of 1944/45 the Germans launched their last desperate offensive in the west, the 'Battle of the Bulge' against the Americans in the Ardennes Forest. To help to ease the pressure and retrieve the position, Bernard's unit was involved in action in the area of Arnhem and the Germans fortunately began to retreat towards their 'Westwall' and Rhine defences.

During the attempted crossing of the Rhine, 200 artillery pieces were massed to bombard the German positions, day and night for the five days, under the continuous cover of a smokescreen. The conditions were most unpleasant.

Once across the River Rhine, armoured attacking units were formed, consisting of a few tanks, armoured carriers and artillery pieces, that would attempt to push their way into enemy territory ahead of the advancing allied army. It was dangerous work for they were exposed and did not know what to expect around the next corner.

Eventually they arrived on the bank of the River Elbe on the outskirts of Hamburg. Instead of crossing the river and incurring heavy casualties, the artillery began shelling the German food supplies, so forcing Hamburg's defenders to surrender.

At long last Bernard received two weeks leave in England, but on 4 June 1945 he embarked for India and finally arrived in Bombay. There the men were posted to various artillery units and he found himself on a train bound for Burma, and the attempted capture of Rangoon from the Japanese. Two days into the journey they were relieved to see a man walking along the track bearing a placard saying 'Japanese surrender!'".

Whilst in India, Bernard Devaney rose from Private to Sergeant and as a regular soldier remained there till 1947, when he returned to England to attend a gunnery course at Larkshill. Eventually he was to be posted to a gunnery school in Korea, but as he had met his future wife, he decided to resign from the army and took up a job in the London Docks. Finally he joined the National Provincial Bank and settled down to married life in London.

SERGEANT JOSEPH WILMOT, ROYAL ELECTRICAL MECHANICAL ENGINEERS (REME)

Joseph was the son of John and Helen Wilmot, of Ashton Farm, Aston Lane, Oker. John worked in the quarry of Constable Hart, Matlock, whilst Joseph worked for awhile at Bakelite on Old Road, before beginning work in 1933 for Tom Smith, driving one of his milk lorries. The family had an interest in poultry and Joe was closely involved in developing a smallholding on the site.

In June 1940 Joe married Frances Tomlinson from Ashover and they went to live at Oker. By August 1940, 29 years old Joe Wilmot had been

Sergeant Joe Wilmot
REME

called up and joined the Royal Army Service Corps. As a young married woman with no family, Frances shared in the war effort by working in the communications room at Matlock fire station.

During April 1941, Joe sailed from England, bound for Egypt and

Sergeant Joe Wilmot REME on extreme right

233

was on the last convoy to attempt the journey via the Mediterranean Sea. The journey was fraught with danger, especially from enemy aircraft attacks, and from that point onwards, other convoys always sailed around Africa and through the Red sea to reach Alexandria. When Joe arrived in Egypt he was posted to a REME unit.

From 1941 till August 1945 he was mainly based in the Nile Delta, with the unit's main purpose being to recover and repair damaged tanks. This entailed moving up behind any Allied advance and either dealing with emergency repairs or taking the vehicle back to base. He therefore found himself involved in the Allied retreat of 1942, the Battle of Alamein and the Allied advance towards Tunisia.

When the Allies invaded Sicily and the mainland of Italy, Joe's colleagues became involved, but Joe had contracted Malaria and so did not participate in the Italian Campaign. He remained in Egypt until the end of the war and in August 1945 travelled home to England and demobilisation, by boat across the Mediterranean to Toulon and then by rail to the Channel ports.

ACTING STAFF SERGEANT RICHARD HODGKINSON, RASC AND RAOC

Richard was the youngest son of Darley Bridge master butcher, Frank Hodgkinson. In 1940 he left his Eversleigh Rise home to enlist in the Northamptonshire Infantry Regiment and was visited by Alfred Lawman in his barracks before Alfred sailed with the British Expeditionary Force for France, and his eventual death near Dunkirk.

After a few weeks initial training, Richard went into the Company Office, an environment he was familiar with, due to having worked as a clerk in the offices at Mill Close Mine in pre-war years and having a mastery of

Acting Staff Sergeant Richard Hodgkinson in Cairo c1944

shorthand. He changed regiments to the Royal Army Services Corps and in 1941, Richard sailed by convoy en route to the Persian Gulf, via Durban and Bombay.

Eventually he arrived at Basra in Iraq, where he was to join 'Paiforce' (Persia and Iraq Command). He was to remain with the Force for the next two years. 'Paiforce' had been created in April 1941 at about the time of the Iraq rebellion. Political disturbance, with attacks on British property, led to the occupation of the strategically important oil rich area of Mosul by British forces.

The purpose of 'Paiforce' was to check a possible move by the Nazis to conquer the Middle East. After Syria had been occupied by the Allies, Paiforce prepared to meet a German attack either through Turkey or via the Caucasus, or both. When that threat had vanished it became responsible for the deliveries of war material to the Soviet forces. This 'lift' of war materials proved to be its greatest achievement. The force consisted of both British and Indian Army units, mainly the latter.

The flat, stony, dusty desert, combined with the tremendous heat and discomfort from sandflies, made conditions very uncomfortable. Occasional relief came when leave was granted to visit Baghdad and the cooler hills of Northern Persia.

After two years service in 'Paiforce', during which he changed regiments again to the Royal Army Ordnance Corps, Richard was posted to GHQ Middle East Forces, Cairo, Egypt. He visited the Lebanon, including the ancient temple of Baalbek, near Damascus, on leave entitlement, as well as Upper Egypt and the Holy Land.

The war in North Africa had come to an end by now and during his service at GHQ, Richard was able to visit the grave of South Darley serviceman, Gunner Ernest Evans, Royal Marines, in Alexandria. An Arab gardener provided a vase of flowers for the occasion and photographs were taken. These photographs brought some comfort to Tom and Emily Evans in Derbyshire.

Eventually, after being away from home for four years, Richard was repatriated at the end of 1945 and demobilised in May 1946 and was able to return safely to his family in South Darley. Within a few weeks of demobilisation, Richard entered employment in the offices of H J Enthoven and Sons Ltd.

PRIVATE RONALD STEVENSON, 9TH BATTALION NORTHUMBERLAND FUSILIERS AND P.O.W.

Ron had been born in South Darley but the family moved later to live at 13 Stancliffe Avenue, Broadwalk. His mother was the daughter of Sammy "Fishy" Riley and sister of Len. Ron, a single man, was a member of the Territorial Army and when war was

Left: Ronald Stevenson, 9th Battalion, Northumberland Fusiliers

Right: Sergeant Sam Stevenson, Royal Electrical and Mechanical Engineers, with his wife, Mabel

declared he was called up and eventually joined the 9th Battalion Northumberland Fusiliers, together with Tansley colleagues Lewis Ryder and brothers Jack and Bill Taylor.

During the latter part of 1941 the 9th Battalion was sent out to the Far East as reinforcements for Singapore, at the tip of the Malayan Peninsula, in readiness for a possible entry by the Japanese into the world conflict. Events moved quickly after the Japanese attack on Pearl Harbour on 7th December, 1941.

Singapore was a protected naval base from which a powerful fleet could operate and was defended against attack from the sea by fixed coastal defences. Unfortunately, these guns could not be turned to combat a Japanese attack on the city from the Malayan Peninsula. When Japan launched its invasion of Malaya on 8th December 1941, a British naval force, consisting of the Battleship Prince of Wales and

Battle Cruiser Repulse plus four destroyers, left that evening to intercept Japanese transports. With no fighter cover, both capital ships were sunk the next day.

By the end of January 1942 British forces had been pressed back to the southern tip of the Malayan Peninsula and onto Singapore Island. A Japanese landing was effected in early February and on the 15th the British Commander surrendered after the Japanese captured the main water supplies for the island.

The Malayan campaign cost the Japanese 3507 dead and 6150 wounded. The Allies lost 9000 dead and 130,000 as prisoners of war, most of whom were treated with appalling cruelty and inhumanity by their captors, who regarded the Allied troops as unworthy of honourable treatment because they had chosen surrender rather than death.

Ron Stevenson and his three colleagues from the Matlock area were amongst the P.O.W.'s who were set to work on constructing the dreaded Burma Railway that linked Burma with the Siamese rail network.

In October 1942 the Japanese conquerors of Burma decided to reconstruct the line for military reasons, using labour of mainly Dutch and British P.O.W.s and conscript Asian labourers. They worked in appalling conditions, were treated with great brutality and lacked adequate food and medical attention. The railway, over 280 miles long, was completed in November 1943 at the cost of over 63,000 lives (13,000 Allied prisoners and 50,000 Asians) out of a total labour force of 150,000.

Ron suffered dreadfully at the hands of his Japanese and Korean guards. On one occasion he cursed one of his captors who responded by hitting him over the head with both his rifle butt and steel helmet. Ron was fortunate that another prison colleague was able to stitch the wound successfully.

At the end of the war, Ron returned to his mother's home at Broadwalk, but he was a changed man as a result of his horrendous experiences. For a number of years he worked as a driver for the Silver Service bus company, with Lucy Wain often acting as the conductor, and eventually he began driving lorries for Darley Bridge haulage contractor, George Siddall.

However, for many months after his return, he would eat his food with his bare hands, as he had done in the camps, and when returning from work would often sit for hours staring at the wall. Eventually the state of his health and mind improved, but he was never able to rid himself of those terrible wartime experiences. In 1963 he and his mother returned to South Darley to live at 21 Eversleigh Rise.

SERGEANT SAM STEVENSON, R.E.M.E.

Before the Second World War, Ronald's brother Sam was employed as a mechanic at the haulage company of Frank Toplis, (now Loggins Supermarket and petrol station). He was married to Mabel Wilson and they started married life down the Fold (Yard), by the side of the Three Stags Head at Darley Bridge.

Sam enlisted in the Royal Electrical and Mechanical Engineers (R.E.M.E.) and in 1941 found himself on the island of Crete in the Mediterranean Sea. British troops had occupied the island at the request of the Greek government in November 1940 and in the last days of April 1941 some 27,000 British and Imperial troops were evacuated to Crete from Greece, which had been overrun by the Germans.

The German units, constantly reinforced, attacked the island on May 20th 1941. A sea-borne landing was prevented by the Royal Navy, but German airforce, airborne and parachute units attacked the island. After prolonged resistance, the British, including Sam Stevenson, were compelled to evacuate the island, the navy suffering serious casualties during the operation (completed June 1st). The only airborne division of the German army received such crippling losses during the action that the Germans refrained from forming further similar units.

Sam's unit was evacuated to North Africa, where he took part in the remainder of the Western Desert campaign, including the Battle of Alamein, and in operations through Libya to the Tunisian border.

In January 1944, he was again in action when he landed on the beaches of Anzio, in Italy. Fierce fighting continued through February, March and April. On May 25th 1944, Anzio troops established contact with the advancing 5th Army, thereby establishing an Allied front across Italy.

On the 23rd May 1946, by the King's Order, the name of Sergeant Sam Stevenson was published in the London Gazette as mentioned in a Despatch for Distinguished Service during the war.

When Sam was demobbed in 1946 he returned to Darley Bridge and when he walked down the Fold, the bunting was out and a large Union Jack pinned to the house door.

SERGEANT PATRICK PRITTY, RASC

We last met Pat Pritty at the Whitworth Institute RASC base, instructing trainees on drill and driving. However, in early 1943 he left Darley Dale and his wife in South Darley and joined a General Transport Company in the South of England.

From there the company went to North Africa to join the 8th Army, in order to participate in Operation "Husky", the Allied amphibious invasion of Sicily on 10th July 1943. Pat was in charge of transport in 'A' Company and their landing craft went in six hours after D-Day. Unfortunately the craft sank but the men escaped through the windows. By the evening of 11th July, 80,000 troops and 8,000 vehicles were ashore, virtually unopposed. However, as Montgomery's forces advanced across the Eastern plain of Sicily, things became progressively more difficult, but by 17 August the campaign ended with the capture of the whole island.

'A' Company returned to North Africa to refit but were soon sailing for the port of Taranto, on the heel of Italy, which the British forces occupied on 10 September 1943. The 8th Army took Bari on the Adriatic coast, fought a three day battle for Termoli and crossed the Sangro River against strong resistance and in vile weather. Patrick's

Company was sent back to the port of Bari to clear the debris of war from the harbour.

They moved on to Naples on the west coast where they were attached to the American 5th Army and used their transport to deliver supplies and ammunition. The Allies decided to outflank the main German defensive line, the Gustav Line, and open the road to Rome. The site for the landing was Anzio on 22 January 1944. Two of 'A' Company's platoons were sent to take part at Anzio but Pat's platoon was fortunate to be left out. The conditions were grim as 6 tons of food and ammunition were loaded onto each lorry that occupied specially constructed two tier landing crafts, which continuously operated from ship to Anzio beach head.

By 5 June 1944 Rome had been occupied and Pat Pritty transferred from the General Transport Company to a Forward Field Dressing Station. Its job was to take in the first wounded before sending them onto hospital. He remained with this unit until he was demobbed in November 1945.

Finally, we arrive at a group of South Darley servicemen for whom we have little detailed information about their wartime activities.

CORPORAL JACK FLINT

He was the first son of First World War veteran Harry Flint and his wife Polly, and together with his parents and sister Freda, he lived at Wensley.

In 1939 he was one of the first men to join up and went into the Sherwood Foresters. Unlike his colleague, Lewis Webster, he was rescued at Dunkirk and returned for a few days leave to Wensley in June 1949,

John Potter Marsden remembers that Jack, sister Freda, Tommy Concannon, George Farnell and himself walked to Youlgreave Wakes and well dressings and back, to celebrate Jack's safe return.

Corporal Jack Flint of Wensley

Shortly, afterwards, he joined another regiment and for a considerable period he served in Iceland, helping to guard the Atlantic Approaches. When Denmark had been occupied by the Germans in April 1940, British naval and army forces had occupied the island to prevent a possible invasion by German forces.

Returning to England, Jack went with his regiment into Europe after the Normandy landings of 6 June 1944 and took part in many of the operations throughout Belgium and Holland, including the dash towards Arnhem, before entering Germany across the Rhine.

STAN BLAYDON, ROYAL ARMY SERVICE CORPS

Stan originated from a village near Mildenhall in Suffolk. He was called up into the RASC and in 1941 arrived first in Bakewell, then the Whitworth Institute base for six weeks training as a driver. Finally he finished his training at Tansley. During this period he met Eunice

Left: Stan Blaydon, RASC. Met and married a Wensley girl, Eunice Wright.
Right: David Devaney of Wensley, in Anti-Aircraft Regiment, Royal Artillery

Wright from Eagle Terrace, Wensley, and though by now training in Kent, they became engaged in 1942.

Overseas service in North Africa then followed, including involvement with the follow up to the Alamein campaign. Eventually, Stan's platoon was involved with the invasion of Italy. Their lorries and other vehicles were used to transport supplies and ammunition to the front line. By January 1944 the Allies had reached the Gustav Line, the main German defensive position covering Rome and Stan's platoon took part when the Allies opened their assault on its key point, the town and monastery of Monte Cassino, on 30 January 1944.

The battle was desperate and bitter and in the fighting that ended with the capture of the hill on 8 May 1944, the monastery was razed to the ground. It was heavily bombed from the air in the belief that the Germans used it as an observation post.

On 22 December 1945, Eunice and Stan were married, though he was not demobbed until 1946. He started work for a short time at Rowsley Sidings. However, in June 1947, he made use of his driving skills and army training on the hilly roads around Wensley, when he became a bus driver for Woolliscroft's Silver Service.

DAVID DEVANEY, ROYAL ARTILLERY

David, son of the Wensley cobbler, John Devaney, was a member of the Territorial Army and the day after war was declared, a motor cyclist collected him to take him to his unit.

He was a gunner in an anti-aircraft (ack-ack) regiment and was based on the east coast in the Hull area, where its job was to

Anti-aircraft searchlight unit near the river Humber, helping David Devaney's regiment near Hull. Figure on the left is Harold Boswell, future husband of Wensley girl, Mary Evans

guard the important fishing port from air attack and protect the coast from invasion in the early days of the war.

Whilst in service on the Humber he met Sally, a local Hull girl and after marriage, she came to live with David at Rose Cottage in Wensley Square.

CLIFFORD AND ERIC WRIGHT

Clifford and Eric were sons of Walter Wright of Eagle Terrace. The elder son, Clifford, served in the infantry and fought in Italy during 1944/45, whilst Eric was called up in early 1944 into the Royal Artillery and served towards the latter stages of the actions in Germany. Whilst in the army he learned the craft of cobbling and could hand stitch a pair of shoes, which he did for his

Clifford and Eric Wright of Wensley

family after the war. Eric's hearing was damaged due to the constant firing of the guns and he suffered from some loss of hearing. Before he was released from the army he spent some time in Palestine, at the start of the 'troubles' between Jewish activists and the British Authorities.

FRED NEWTON, ROYAL ARTILLERY

Brother-in-law to the three Taylor brothers, Fred served as batman for an officer in the Royal Artillery at Church Stretton in Shropshire, but was discharged from the army before the war ended, due to ill-health.

*Fred Newton of Wensley,
Royal Artillery*

We know that this list of 'survivors' is not exhaustive and we apologise to those veterans whose stories we have not been able to research. However, we trust that this chapter clearly illustrates that South Darley 'parishioners', 'did their bit' to safeguard democracy for future generations. As their story passes into history we salute their sacrifice and hardships. **They have been 'remembered'.**

CHAPTER SIX

A RETURN TO PEACE

The war had ended in victory for Britain and its Allies in August 1945 and South Darley families could look forward to a return to peacetime conditions. Throughout late 1945 and 1946, servicemen and women began their return to civilian life and husbands, sons and daughters readjusted to the novel experience of being back permanently within the bosom of their families.

There was sadness, though, within the parish and especially within the hearts of members of those families who had lost their loved ones. Five parishioners had not returned, and although the number of killed did not reach the horrendous scale of the First World War, when South Darley's casualty list totalled 22 names, five families mourned the loss of their menfolk.

A welcome sign of the return to some form of normality was seen in 1945 when the people of the parish of St. Mary the Virgin observed the centenary of their parish church with joy and thanksgiving, and raised £600 to install in the belfry a carillon of eight bells. The work was carried out by John Taylor of Loughborough. Back in June 1940 the Reverend Simmons's wish for the 'Prayer Bell' to be rung had been prevented by government decree, but now the new peal of bells could truly proclaim that the 'torch of Justice, Freedom and Truth' had been kept alight.

Peace also brought about changes in working patterns, resulting from the demobilisation of servicemen, for many men expected to be able to return to the jobs they had before their enlistment, jobs that had often been taken on by women during the wartime years. By 1944 there had been an acute shortage of people for work and great pressure was placed on women to fill these posts. The 'Grannies call up' had resulted in many women up to 50 years of age being made to take on war work. These slightly older women, such as Margery Boden and Mrs. George Tomlinson on Oker Road, had to participate in munitions work at Lammon Archer and Lane during the last year of the war. Though many of the returning men did replace some women during 1946/47, the fact that women had proved themselves capable of doing such work contributed to a change of attitude and the start of a very slow, general trend towards a greater freedom for women to compete with men in the jobs market.

In some aspects of life, conditions worsened after August 1945 as rationing remained in force and became ever tighter and more restrictive than in wartime years. Rationing was a fact of life throughout the late 1940's and early 1950's and austerity was the watchword. There was little choice in the shops and for most families it was a case of buying "Utility" clothes and furniture with their coupons.

Another aspect of wartime remained to remind South Darley folk of those five fateful years of conflict. Prisoners of war, especially those from Germany, could still be found working within the parish during the latter part of 1946 and into the severe winter months of 1947.

In 1946 Eberhard Hans Wilhelm Ruthenburg, better known as Jack, was working as a POW labourer on Enthoven's land near Darley Bridge. Born in Stralsund on the Baltic coast, the son of a policeman, his family moved to Stettin when he was six. He was called up late in 1943 and joined a Panzer armoured regiment. He was wounded during the Allied invasion of Normandy, and after recovery was later involved in action in Belgium and Holland, where once again he was wounded. Jack was brought back to a German hospital in Goslar and was receiving attention there when it was captured in the Allied advance.

As the war ended, the older prisoners of war and those with homes to return to, were released but Jack was young and his former home was now in Russian occupied Poland. Therefore, in early 1946, together with many others, he landed at Tilbury and eventually arrived at Heage, the main POW camp in Derbyshire. Civilian drivers

Left: Helmut Hergerfeld
Right: 'Jack' Ruthenberg

were responsible for taking German work parties to distant farms, where they helped with turnip picking and digging drainage ditches.

The regime was very relaxed and although a fence surrounded the camp, there were holes to be found in it. By this time he had become acquainted with a Darley Bridge woman, Dorothy Wood (nee Boam), whilst working nearby and she provided him with an old bicycle. On one or two occasions, until he was discovered, he went through a gap and cycled to meet her at Darley Bridge.

During the terrible winter of 1947, Jack and his POW colleagues were taken to Biggin, near Hartington, to help in combating the isolation of the villagers. Plane loads of food were delivered and the POW's attempted to keep the roads clear to Friden brickworks.

By April 1948, Jack was released from POW status to become a civilian worker in agriculture and horticulture. At this point, many such prisoners returned home but Jack remained, for he had fallen in love with Dorothy and in any case his family in Germany had been uprooted as they fled to West Germany. He came to Bridge Farm, where he worked for Sydney Wildgoose and eventually Jack and Dorothy were married and a son, Eric, was born at Darley Bridge.

Sydney Wildgoose had arrived at Bridge Farm around 1947. The farmhouse by this time was dilapidated, infested with rats and required a great deal of repair. Mixed farming was officially undertaken, but

Bridge Farm, Darley Bridge 1950. Working on the turnip clamps.
L-r: Sydney Wildgoose, Jack Ruthenberg, Jim Gregory

Bridge Farm, Darley Bridge. Early 1950's.
Left: Stooks in field (now planted with trees)
Right: Sydney Wildgoose on the right

Christmas party provided by Sydney and Patience Wildgoose at Bridge Farm, 1950.
Back, l-r: Sydney Wildgoose, Mrs Simcock, Margaret Wildgoose, Joan Else, Patience
Wildgoose, Zena Beck, Carol Taylor
Middle: Peter Else, David Pritty, John Pritty, ? Else, George Harrison, Bryan
Wildgoose, Richard Beck, Faye Wildgoose, Muriel Taylor
Front: Sylvia Taylor, Susie Harrison, Roy Wood, Janet Needham, Alistair Cameron

because of the continuing problem of belland (lead poisoning), crops provided the main source of income. By now, Enthovens were owners of the farm and Sydney acted as farm bailiff, until he bought it off them in 1957. As on all the farms in South Darley, the main change occurring in these early post war years was in the increased use of mechanisation, with the tractor displacing the horse. We can see the extent of this change when we look at the photograph of the ploughing competition, held in the early 1950's at Megdale, near Snitterton.

We have seen that during 1946/47 German POW's were brought from Heage to work at Enthoven's lead smelter works. Frank Toplis and his son Harold would travel with a van from their Two Dales based haulage fleet to transport as many as 12 of them to and from the site, where they worked on labouring jobs within the plant and on the land.

Another POW who travelled from Heage to Enthovens was Helmut Hergerfeld, a young German born in Bremen and captured by the Americans. His sister had been killed during an Allied air raid on the port. Jim Taylor from Tiersell View, Wensley, had been demobbed from

Ploughing competition early 1950's at Megdale, Snitterton. Oker and Okerside in the background

Lobby Farm
Left: Carl Boden, with Ron Greatorex hand shearing sheep in Wensley Dale, early 1950's
Right: Ron Greatorex driving a tractor, early 1950's

the Army and was driving for George Siddall of Darley Bridge. Jim was in charge of a party of POW's including Helmut, dressed in their brown overalls with a yellow star on the back, who were directed to lay drainage pipes along Dudwood Lane, Elton.

Ivan Greatorex and Roy Marsden delivering milk in Oker Road, early 1950's

It was during this period that Jim and Helmut became friendly and when, eventually, the

Frank Toplis's garage 1938. Now the site of Loggins and Two Dales petrol station

prisoners were allowed to leave the camp each Sunday, Jim and his wife Daisy would invite Helmut to their house. Jim would meet him off the train at Darley Station and eventually he was allowed by the authorities to stay with them overnight, each weekend. Jim Taylor would often provide Helmut with an old suit and they both travelled into Bakewell.

Whilst working at Dudwood Lane, Elton, Daisy remembers using coupons to buy sausages off Blackburns, the butcher, and cycling with the package to where Helmut was working in order for him to take the food to his camp Eventually, it was time for Helmut Hergerfeld to be released and Daisy and Jim waved him goodbye from Belper station. Within a few weeks he had written to them from Germany and corresponded regularly throughout the following years. Together with his parents, he later ran restaurants in the port of Bremen and, at his invitation, Daisy and Jim were able to spend an enjoyable holiday with him in Bremen.

Enthovens c1949

It is worth noting that during 1947 an orchestra of German POW musicians from Heage Camp came to the Cross Green schoolroom to provide an orchestral concert for parishioners. It was very well received and a vote of thanks was given in German by a teacher from St. Elphin's School.

Throughout the late 1940's and early 1950's H.J. Enthoven and Sons continued in its role as a smelter and refiner of lead obtained from batteries and scrap lead. In those early days it was a dirty, forbidding place and the work was hot, dusty and dangerous, a legacy of the dark days of the war.

Lead based scrap was recycled to produce a range of alloys manufactured to a high degree of refinement. Most of the raw material intake comprised lead pipe and sheet which was readily dealt with by being melted down. This was a dirty job, but much less hazardous than dealing with the batteries.

These were collected and turned over to spill out the acid electrolyte, which trickled away down the nearest drain. The casing was then smashed and picked out to become part of an enormous pile, which, when fired, gave off a vast volume of black smoke.

The lead baring battery plates were fed to three Newnham Hearth furnaces, specifically designed for the smelting of lead ore at Mill Close Mine, but not very efficient for their new role. The Newnhams were each served by two men working turn about for spells of 30 minutes. Sweat would pour from their bodies, which became covered in dust. In order to rid some of the lead dust absorbed, the manager encouraged the men to sup plenty of ale at the Three Stags Head public house, Darley Bridge, where he made sure that there would be a few free pints. Medical belief at the time also suggested that milk provided some protection and the entire labour force was each given one pint a day.

As the War Department could at last begin the process of selling off equipment no longer required for the war effort, some material came the way of Enthovens. Very memorable were the huge submarine batteries, some of which were made at the D.P. Batteries at Bakewell. Several loads of pipes were delivered that had been recovered from the English Channel, part of PLUTO, the fuel pipe that was laid to supply the armed forces in Europe after the Normandy landings of June 1944. More exciting were cartridge cases collected at firing ranges, which, to win back the lead, were thrown on to a pot of molten lead. These were live rounds! Eventually, bright brass and copper was recovered.

During the period that German POW's were working for Enthovens, they made wooden toys, such as small forts and lorries, in the joiner's shop, and presented them to employees' children at the Christmas party.

With a work force of over 70 employees, it can be seen that Enthovens had partially taken the place of Mill Close Lead Mine as a major employer of men from the district but for a while a few returning servicemen also found work in recovering the waste product of the old lead mine spoil heaps within the parish. In Cambridge Wood, near Wensley, Frank Taylor and a few other men were employed from 1946 to 1954 by George Harry Key of Hopton Mining Company in spar and barytes mining and retrieving minerals associated with lead mining areas. Our photographs show that work was on a small scale and use was made of fairly crude equipment, but it still provided employment for these men during the early years of peacetime.

Just beyond Wensley Reservoir, behind the Red Lion Inn, the public footpath goes steeply down the hillside through Cambridge Wood, passing a small pond before reaching the valley bottom and climbing again through the old spoil heaps towards Clough Wood. The miners used picks and shovels in Cambridge Wood and loaded the material onto an old lorry that carried it to the top of a cable railway, sited near

Picking out minerals from surface workings of old lead mines in Cambridge Wood area, c1948

Working surface workings of old lead mine areas, Cambridge Wood, c1948. Railway line in background

the pond and constructed to run to the valley floor. A hand operated 'Manchester wheel' (a wheel with a cable wrapped around it, with a handle brake attached, as a steadying mechanism) operated the movement of the wagons. A loaded wagon would travel downhill on the cable and its weight would pull two empty wagons up the hill on another set of rails. Material was 'dumped' on the valley floor and lorries transported it away.

Such quarrying and mining activities had to come to a temporary halt when Derbyshire faced the worst winter ever experienced, during February and March 1947. For three consecutive days, snow blizzards caused drifting, with the blocking of road and rail links, isolation of towns and villages, severed telephone lines and the delay of deliveries of fuel and food. In the Matlock district, drifts of six to ten feet blocked the roads to outlying villages, including for awhile Winster, Elton and Birchover. Only the 'valley' bus service was maintained in those first few days and trains ran many hours late.

During the next few weeks, icy, snow laden blasts swept over the hills, undoing time and again the arduous work of keeping open the roads. Longnor was in a desperate plight, with fuel and food scarce until a plane dumped supplies by parachutes, guided by a large black cross, drawn in soot on the snow covered surface. At Biggin, 54 German POW's played a prominent role. After two weeks, Orme and Co. and Naylors the butchers, of Bakewell, delivered supplies to Friden brickwork's by lorry and villagers and POW's pulled sledges of

Winter, February 1947. Eric Smith of James Smith's nurseries on Sydnope Hill

supplies from there to Biggin. A 'ski-plane', chartered by the Daily Mail, eventually landed with more supplies for the inhabitants.

By the third week of icy conditions, coal merchants at Matlock Station yard were unable to reach outlying clients. From the higher parts of Winster, Elton, Wensley, Hackney and Tansley came a daily procession, mainly of women and children, to carry back to their empty hearths in shopping bags, sacks, boxes or tins the coal supplies due to them. Some had sledges on which to carry their bundles. On a number of occasions local taxi driver, Des Turkington, pulled a train of five such sledges from Darley Station up Toll Bar Hill to Wensley.

By the 8th week Matlock had already 80 POW's helping, whilst 150 British troops and 100 more POW's were to be brought in to clear the roads. Twenty five of these POW's were employed on Butcher's Lane, North Darley, in a determined effort to relieve Mr. and Mrs. Hubert Mills at Moor Farm, who had been almost completely cut off for some weeks. This was regarded as a desperate case for Hubert had several hundred gallons of milk which he had been unable to deliver.

Wensley and Winster were without the benefit of Silver Service buses during the first few days of the blizzards and when the service was resumed the bus tyres had chains around them to provide a better grip on the road surface. On Eversleigh Rise, Toll Bar Hill and on Main Street, Wensley, cinders and ashes from peoples' hearths were scattered on the icy roads but most of the ash and cinders were brought by Council lorries from the Gas Works on Bakewell Road, Matlock. Conductors such as Lucy and Ethel Wain and May Wayne needed to be capable of wielding a shovel on certain difficult stretches of the route. Passengers were told to disembark at times and a number of Birchover residents provided them with welcoming 'tots' to warm their hearts. Before the war Mr. Peter Wood from Gurdhall Farm had brought his horse and snow clearing apparatus (a large triangle of wood) to clear the Wensley roads but by 1947 the Council were more closely involved with snow clearance operations.

Almost a year earlier, South Darley School, Cross Green, had witnessed the conclusion of an era when Headmaster David Chapman Parsons retired on the 20th December 1946, after twenty two years service at the school. Replacing him was a native of Sheffield, Ken

Gillies, who was to steer the school through a vital seven year period when educational changes in secondary education were very much at a transitional stage.

Minister of Education R.A.B. Butler introduced the Education Act of 1944 which reorganised secondary education and introduced the 11 plus selection examination. Selection to grammar school at eleven years of age was made possible for anyone passing the examination and in April 1947 the leaving age was raised to 15 years. During the early 1950's a rapid building programme provided secondary modern accommodation for those who 'failed' the exam at eleven years, but for the intervening period whilst these schools were being constructed, those who did not pass on to grammar school remained at schools such as Cross Green. However, in January 1953, Darley Dale Secondary Modern School was opened at Greenaway Lane, under Headmaster Joseph Hancock. The development of separate primary and secondary educational establishments was realised and Cross Green School now became part of the primary system, with pupils leaving at the age of eleven.

During late 1945 and 1946 older pupils travelled once again to the Two Dales centre to participate in woodwork or domestic science, but by 1948 they were able to take these lessons in the newly built Horsa buildings at Darley Council School, Greenaway Lane. The new innovation of school meals was also introduced.

Until the time when the school catered only for primary age children, the older boys continued to have gardening lessons at first on the Wenslees, but with the arrival of Ken Gillies, the venue for such activities changed. Part of the small field between the Church and Lumb Cottage was dug over by the pupils until a suitable plot was created, so enabling the gardening lessons to be conveniently closer to school. The tools could now be stored in part of one of the old air raid shelters in the school yard.

Innovations, such as a school magazine, 'The Stag', produced by older pupils, a greater number and variety of school trips, the wearing of school uniform and the introduction of a school 'house system' were all welcomed by the pupils. School teacher 'Wilfy' Warren was a fine addition to the teaching staff and the school benefited from his expertise as a music teacher. Annual sports days were held in the splendid setting of Wensley Dale, with long crocodiles of children and helpers carrying chairs, forms and equipment through the fields on what are remembered fondly as sunny June – July days. Sport was encouraged by Ken Gillies, who had played professional football for Sheffield United.

In early February 1953, Mr. Gillies left Cross Green to become Headmaster of the new County Junior Mixed School at Birley, near Sheffield. At a leaving assembly on the Friday, a gift of a portable typewriter was presented by 11 year old George Harrison, the first scholar to be admitted to school by Mr. Gillies. South Darley Primary School now passed into the hands of a new Headteacher, Mr. Wilkinson.

The people of Darley could see another positive sign of a return to normal life with the relinquishing of the Whitworth Institute and grounds by the Army in 1946 and its restoration during 1947/1948, in preparation for the long anticipated reopening to the public.

By 1946, servicemen were returning to their jobs at the Matlock firms of John William Wildgoose on Rutland Street and 'Hall and Co'. of Dale Road and these two firms were to the forefront in the reinstatement project, aided by a compensation grant from the Ministry of Defence. All of the joinery work was dealt with by Fred and Arthur Gregory of Warney Road, Two Dales. There was certainly a great deal of restoration work required because the amount of damage caused during the Royal Army Service Corps tenure was considerable.

Throughout the period of restoration these firms were also involved in constructing the 'temporary' Horsa building at the Greenaway Lane Council School (now housing Mencap) and providing a school kitchen for the introduction of school meals.

1947 saw the effort concentrated on the Whitworth Institute buildings. Army boots had damaged many floor surfaces. New block floors were laid and others were renovated. The temporary floor of the

South Darley School Christmas parties c1948
Top: The infants
Bottom: The seniors

South Darley School 1948
Back row, l-r: Tom Concannon, Geof Taylor, Mervyn Wright, Carl Boden, Alan Shaw,
John Marsden, Bill Daniels. Middle row: Alan Bagshaw, Jim Grimshaw, Jim Taylor,
Denis Shaw, Geoffrey Needham, Bill Winthrop, Ken Gillies. Front row: Wendy
Henstock, Shirley Bain, Pam Henstock, Pearl Dobson, Joan Masters, Norma Holmes,
Sheila Dowling

South Darley School 1948
Back row, l-r: Jim Grimshaw, Alan Shaw, Tom Concannon, Bill Daniels, Alan
Bagshaw, Geoffrey Taylor, Ken Gillies. Front row: Mervyn Wright, Bill Winthrop, Jim
Taylor, Carl Boden, Dennis Shaw

South Darley Infants class c1948/49
Back row, l-r: Gerald Stafford, John Pritty, Roy Wood, Robert Winthrop, Keith
Stanbrooke, George Harrison, Gordon Shimwell, Ian Fern, Tony Shaw, Gloria Palk
(school secretary). Middle row: Peter Dunn, Janet Furniss, John Masters, Peter Willis,
Janet Needham, Janet Haynes, Alan Ainsworth, John Wright. Front row: Valery Roose,
X, X, Ann Sanders, Joan Flint, Jennifer Wright, Elizabeth Saunders

South Darley School c1951
Back row, l-r: John Pritty, Robert Winthrop, Gordon Shimwell, Miss Renshaw, Ann
Sanders, Geoffrey Gregory, Susan Cunningham. Middle row: Peter Willis, Richard
Beck, John Wright, Doreen Chandler, Mary Dunn, Jennifer Nixon, Clive Hardy. Front
row: Bryan Wildgoose, David Pritty, Raymon Else, Gerald Stafford, Rosemary Corker,
Janet Glenn

South Darley School 1950
Back row, l-r: Alan Bagshaw, Billy Daniels, Jimmy Taylor, Tommy Concannon, Jimmy
Grimshaw, Billy Wintrope. Middle row: Peggy Wright, Shirley Bain, Pamela Henstock,
Sheila Dowling, Joan Masters, Margaret Dunn, Wendy Henstock, Eileen Wain, Jean
Fern, Paul Dobson. Front row: Dennis Shaw, Alan Shaw, Graham Stone, Teddy
Corker, Ken Gillies, Valerie Watkins, Geoffrey Taylor, Carl Boden, John Marsden

George Harrison presents the leaving present to headteacher Ken Gillies, February
1953

South Darley School's winning choir at Matlock School's Festival, Matlock Bath 1952
Back row, l-r: Wilfred Warren, David Jaina, Robert Winthrope, Richard Beck, Richard Kneale, Raymon Else, David Pritty, John Arnold. Middle row: John Cauldwell, Alan Ainsworth, John Wright, Norman Concannon, Bryan Wildgoose, Ian Fern. Front row: Mary Dunn, Jane Arnold, Susan Goodwin, Irene Wheeldon, Maureen Devaney, Mary Widdison, Janet Dunn, Faye Wildgoose

Matlock Bath Music Festival c1953
Back row, l-r: Richard Beck, John Wright, Ian Fern, Wilfred Warren, Alan Ainsworth, Bryan Wildgoose. Third row: John Arnold, Norman Concannon, Robert Winthrope, Richard Kneale, Raymon Else. Second row: Susan Goodwin, Jane Arnold, Mary Dunn, Janet Dunn, Irene Wheeldon. Front row: Faye Wildgoose, John Cauldwell, David Pritty, David Jaina, Maureen Devaney, Mary Widdison

School Pantomime 'Aladdin' in the schoolroom c1950
Back row, l-r: Peggy Wright, Mavis Boam, X, Margaret Dunn, Sheila Dowling, Eileen
Wain, John Dunn, Shirley Baynes, Joe Goodwin, Roy Taylor, Billy Winthrope, Bryan
Wildgoose, Daphne Wragg, X, Jean Fern, Margaret Daniels. Middle and front rows:
Ann Smedley, Vivienne Shepherd, Ann Shimwell, Valery Watkinson, Shirley Stevenson,
Isobel Winthrope, Shirley Grubb, X, Rex Concannon, Derek Grimshaw, Geof Trickett,
Eddie Shaw, Alan Marsden, Pat Haynes, Margaret Clay

South Darley School Netball Team 1951
Back row, l-r: Margaret Daniels, Mavis Boam, Miss Ward, Eileen Wain, Ann Smedley
Front row: Jean Fern, Margaret Dunn, Peggy Wright

1954-55
Back row, l-r: Peter Else, David Taylor, John Cauldwell, Geoff Gregory, Dennis Masters, Brian Chadbourne, Peter Bailey, Richard Beck. Front row: Mr Gregory, John Taylor, Malcolm Boden, Graham Haynes, Norman Harrison, Edwin Moseley, Mr Wilkinson

1954-55
Back row, l-r: Mr Wilkinson, Thelma Whitehead. Front row: Faye Wildgoose, Christine Wilmot, Maureen Devaney, Janet Dunn, Mary Widdowson, Margaret Elliot, Susan Goodwin

School Sports in Wensley Dale 28th June 1955
L-r: Ann Blaydon, Christine Boswell, Jennifer Taylor, Pat Concannon

South Darley School Sports Day in Wensley Dale 28th June 1955. The trophy was presented to the Derwent captain, Faye Wildgoose
Back row, l-r: Chris Moseley, Stuart Masters, David Evans, Peter Else, Norman Harrison, Graham Haynes, X, Brian Chadbourne, X, Susan Goodison, Malcolm Boden, Janet Dunn, Michael Wheeldon, Dennis Masters, John Devaney, Edwin Moseley, John Taylor, Richard Beck, David Taylor, David Jaina, Margaret Elliot, Gill Pritty, Faye Wildgoose, Joan Chadbourne, Irene Wheeldon. Middle row: Linda Devaney, X, X, Linda Holmes, Pat Concannon, Jennifer Taylor, Jennifer Price, Patricia Pritty, X, Ann Blaydon, X, Pam Hodgkinson, Christine Boswell, Eric Ruthenberg. Front row: Malcolm Concannon, Keith Wright, John Turkington, David Allen Jane Siddall, Lucille Siddall, Josie Cook, X, Pam Richardson, Janet Blaydon, Margery Fawley, Christopher Wright, Francis Smith

Sports Day in Wensley Dale 1956
Back row, l-r: Mrs Gladwin, Edwin Moseley, Mrs Simcock, Mrs Winthrope, X, John Pritty, ? Pritty, Pat Pritty, Mr Wilkinson, Mrs Wilkinson, Mr Boden, Mrs Boden, Mrs Cunningham, Betty Shimwell. Third row: Keith Wright, Peter Bailey, Malcolm Concannon, Peter Else, John Taylor, David Taylor, Malcolm Boden, David Jaina, David Evans, Paul Gleeson, David Devaney, Maureen Stevenson, Laura Belk. Second row: X, Mrs Price, Mrs Tomlinson, Edie Cook, Vera Fawley, David Boswell, Mona Richardson, Valery Fawley, Audrey O'Connor, Anne Howes, X, Mrs Hodgkinson, Patricia Pritty, Mary Smith. Front row: Margery Fawley, Susan Wood, Christine Fawley, Pam Richardson, Carol Richardson, Lucille Siddall, Gillian Pritty, Maureen O'Connor, Kathleen Cunningham, Joan Chadbourne, Pam Hodgkinson, Peter Stevenson, Francis Smith

swimming bath room was taken up and water once again began to flow. The Institute and grounds had its own water supply from one of three large underground reservoirs in the fields behind Darley Hall. One fed the Stancliffe Stone works and its laundry, the second fed Darley Hall and the third fed the Institute, hotel and lake. The water flowed under great pressure through a three inch cast iron main. During 1947/48 this

Laying the water main on A6 road near the Whitworth Institute c1900

system had to be shut off and the Institute converted to mains water. However, the reintroduction of a swimming pool did not come to fruition as the project would have proved too costly in meeting new health and safety guidelines.

Nailed boots had also done damage to many steps inside the buildings, including the staircase to the ballroom. Wildgoose employed four stonemasons to put in new insets of York stone. A great number of stained glass windows had been cracked or smashed and glaziers were involved in replacing these with clear glass.

The Naafi, which in pre-war years had housed the Museum, was now prepared for use as the venue for meetings by the British Legion. The four Nissan huts were taken away, with two being brought for a total of £30 by Two Dales farmer, Stanley Wagstaffe, and converted into Dutch barns for storing hay. The old Tea Room, used by the R.A.S.C. as a cookhouse and mess, was brought up to standard and remained on site until the early 1960's, when it was demolished and the stone re-used by Johnson's Flour Mill for extending Warney Mill to four storeys in height.

The grounds of the Whitworth Institute c1890. Workmen excavating the site of the boating lake. Darley Station is shown in the background to the right and Darley railway sidings to the left

Unfortunately, the puddled clay base of the former boating lake had deteriorated and it was felt that reinstatement was not viable, financially. After water was pumped away, it was filled in slightly and developed into a sunken garden. Barrons of Borrowash (landscape designers) planted trees inside the dried out lake, restored the roads to their pre-war width by re-turfing and added a new feature by creating a crown green bowls green. The boathouse was renovated and reglazed and used as a shelter. By 1949 the reinstatement work was completed and the public did not have long to wait before the gates could be re-opened to them.

This occurred in February 1949 after the opening of the wing that became known as the British Legion Hall (now the Terrace Room and formerly the Naafi) and on Sunday November 5th 1949 the Armistice Service was held at the Cenotaph, combined with a special service of dedication of the plaque bearing the names of the fallen 1939-45. The Reverend R.J. Stanford conducted the service and flag bearers of the British Legion were in attendance.

It was not until a year later, on Remembrance Day Sunday November 12th 1950, that the unveiling and dedication service of the South Darley memorials to the dead of the 2nd World War occurred.

Armistice Service in the Whitworth Park 5th November 1949, combined with the special service of dedication of plaque bearing names of the Fallen 1939-45. Reverend RJ Stanford conducting the service

February 1949. Re-opening of the Whitworth Institute after being in the hands of the War Department during Second World War. Members of the British Legion after opening of the wing that became known as the British Legion Hall. (Now the Terrace Room and formerly the NAAFI in the war years.)

Two unveiling ceremonies took place at South Darley on that Sunday morning.

At the existing war memorial outside St. Mary's Church, a tablet bearing the names of those who fell in the last war was unveiled by Colin Hadfield, an ex-serviceman, and dedicated by the Archdeacon of

Unveiling and Dedication Service 12th November 1950. Colin Hadfield unveils the tablet bearing the names of former comrades in arms who fell in the 1939-45 war

Derby, the Reverend H.E. FitzHerbert. The Last Post and Reveille were sounded by Murray Slater.

Homage was read by Dr. E.D. Forster and wreaths were laid by members of the British Legion, Councillor F.R. Rhodes, relatives of the fallen, Red Cross (Mrs. G. Tomlinson), choir (Arnold Wright), Enthovens Ltd. (Mr A. Taylor) and the Women's Institute.

Mr. Ken Gillies, Headteacher of Cross Green School, was the Marshall and a procession then filed into Church for the unveiling of the memorial window to the dead of both wars by Neville Siddall, another ex-serviceman. The window, which was the work of Abbot and Company, of Lancaster, had been subscribed for by the residents of South Darley through the efforts of the War Memorial Committee, with Mr. Tom Spencer as Chairman, Ken Gillies as treasurer and the Reverend I.O. Evans as secretary. A coloured panel bore the traditional

Wensley Hall. St Elphin School boarders, September 1949 to July 1950. Mrs Muriel Bowser second from left, seated. Eleanor Bowser seated in front of her

figure of St. George and a smaller panel showed Oker tree. Abbot and Company worked on the image of the tree from a photograph taken one winter's day in 1949 by Dennis Wright of Thorntrees, Oker Road.

The Archdeacon performed the dedication and gave the sermon and lessons were read by Tom Spencer and Member of Parliament, E.B. Wakefield. In announcing the anthem, Stainers "What are these", the vicar, the Rev. I.O. Evans, referred to the tragedy at Mill Close Mines many years ago when one victim of an explosion, Mr. Needham, was identified by the copy of the anthem which was found in his pocket, after proceeding to work from a choir practice.

A wreath was laid in the window by Councillor Tom Spencer. The Church was filled to over flowing and some thirty extra chairs had to be placed in the aisle.

At a time when the ending of wartime hostilities should have brought fresh hopes to all families within the parish, the Bowser family at Wensley Hall Guest House suffered a sad loss. In October 1945, Eric Bowser travelled by car to Sheffield to complete the buying of Wensley Hall from Edith Marshall. The next day he died, as the result of a heart attack, leaving a widow, two young daughters and a large guest house still to be run.

This, Muriel Bowser did by herself for a number of years. However, her daughters attended St. Elphin's School, Darley Dale, and through this connection a change came about in the business arrangements at Wensley Hall. Up until 1952, it changed from being a guest house to providing accommodation seven days a week for twelve St. Elphins schoolgirls. Meals had to be prepared and the girls' welfare and recreation catered for by Muriel Bowser and a matron, who lived in. For these girls it seemed a less regimented life than within the school itself, providing a freer childhood and a 'home from home', although there was always a seriousness of purpose behind all activities.

Memories of the girls are of playing in the Hall's orchard, or in Wensleydale, helping in the milking parlour of nearby Green Farm and taking riding lessons at the Red House Stables. From 1945 and through-out the 1950's, domestic work at the Hall was undertaken by locals from Wensley, including Ethel Corless, Dorothy Flint, Sally Evans and Mary Boswell. Ruth Annison (nee Bowser) recalls how, after the death of her father, these adults meant so much to her and sister Eleanor, providing much kindness and a continuity of adult presence within their home.

By the early 1950's Muriel was also studying typing and shorthand at Derby, working in the Express Dairy offices, Rowsley, and helping out at North Darley School. It was here that she realised that she could provide for her family more easily by taking up a temporary teaching post at Ernest Bailey Grammar School in the late 1950's and renting out a wing of the Hall as accommodation. This 'temporary' teaching post was to last till 1973. Writing about Muriel Bowser has certainly brought back memories to me, for as a teenager in the 1960's I was taught by her, and have every admiration for the way she worked to provide for her family.

Change also occurred during this period in the one remaining village shop in Wensley, with the retirement of Richard Hodgkinson and the arrival of Mr. and Mrs. Crapper at the post office. Sadly, with the early death of Mr. Crapper, his wife was left to run the business by herself, which she did for a number of years. The long standing Crown Inn Licensee, Mrs. Briggs, also stood down, to be replaced by Mr. and Mrs.

Stan Willis, whilst in late 1949, the Belfield family arrived at the Red Lion, a 400 year old coaching inn, after the departure of Wensley landlady, Mrs. Cauldwell.

For Harold Belfield, a former coalminer from the Ripley/Butterly area, his wife Elizabeth, son George and daughter Barbara, this was to be a fresh venture. Told of a farm for sale with good grazing land and a fully licensed pub attached to it, they travelled to take a look at the place. They moved in on Armistice Sunday 1949. "Bitter was 1/3d a pint in those days", recalls George. Having been in farming since leaving school, George, together with his father, concentrated on building up the farm, which had become rather neglected since the death of Jesse Cauldwell. Basic machinery was bought, together with an old horse from a Shottle farmer, barns and outbuildings repaired, a dairy herd developed and cattle reared. During the early 1950's milking was still by hand, until George purchased second hand milking equipment.

Meanwhile Elizabeth and Barbara concentrated on running the public house. The old Club Room was repaired, with a new floor laid and Old Time dancing reintroduced. Fresh milk produced on the farm was sold in the pub, with milk shakes made for children and fresh milk mixed with Guinness stout.

Ben Clay, former Wensley shopkeeper and now a Matlock Market stall holder hit the headlines of the big daily newspapers in 1949 under the name of "Barrow Boy Ben". He had started selling fruit and veg from a barrow at Park Head and many Matlock councillors objected. When one morning the council workmen erected a barricade of planks and

A pint of milk at the Red Lion public house. Billy Clay with drinking companions Frank Newton and George ? from Winster

273

drainpipes round Ben's 'pitch', the incident was exploited by the newspaper men. During the next few months "Barrow Boy Ben" was asked to leave the Park area. He certainly moved when asked to do so, but only by a couple of yards.

'Barrow Boy' Ben Clay in Matlock, 1949

Eventually, Ben's son Billy joined his father in the business and became as well known locally as Ben, partly due to his market repartee and his trademark, a large eleven inch handle-bar moustache. Whilst at Cross Green School in the late 1930's and early 1940's, Billy had probably received the cane from Headmaster David Parsons more than most local lads. One afternoon, many years

Billy Clay, son of Ben, on Matlock open air market, now the site of Somerfields supermarket

after Mr. Parson's retirement, Billy was serving on the market stall when he heard a familiar voice behind him say, "How are you, Clay?" Without turning round to see who it was, he told his assistant to take over the stall as he was going to take his former head teacher for a drink at the Railway Inn. Bill had obviously not forgotten the voice of his Nemesis.

In 1945, Len Riley was still using the front room of his cottage at No.17, Darley Bridge, as a greengrocers shop and transporting his goods around the district on his cart, pulled by Dolly the horse. The former butcher's shop next door now belonged to him but he never used it. A change came about, however, when his nephew, Cyril Stevenson,

Left: Peter Stevenson and Maureen sitting on a window ledge of Darley bridge shop
Right: Shopkeepers Cyril and Kathleen Stevenson, Darley Bridge

together with wife Kathleen, moved into this dwelling and from 1950 began using it as a shop to sell sweets, bread and general provisions. By the mid 1950's Len Riley began to wind down his green grocery business and his nephew Cyril added green groceries to items that could be purchased from the shop. From 1957 onwards, Len's brown Morris Commercial van with canvas roof, which he had never learned to drive, was used by Cyril to take green groceries around Oker, Snitterton, Wensley and Stanton Lees.

Relative newcomer, shopkeeper Mary Jane Bell at Riverside Cottage, was well respected, but her husband Vincent was not so popular with the local school children, nor they with him. The situation was not helped by the children's use of the nickname 'Ding Dong' Bell and their routine, daily prank of ringing the shop doorbell and then running off, much to his annoyance.

The years shortly after the conclusion of the war also saw a change in the use of 'Dale View', Sitch Lane, Oker. The Evacuation Nursery and its young charges had returned to London by 1945 and the requisitioned house soon came onto the market, to be bought by David Clifford and his wife Winnie, who were members of a Christian

*Dale View Bible College, Sitch Lane, Oker. A party of students in the grounds, 1950's.
The owner, Mr Clifford, is at the back, in the centre*

religious group known as the Plymouth Brethren. 'Dale View' was run
first as a Christian guest-house and conference centre, with well-known
Christian speakers attending. For a number of years Doris Walker from
number 3 St Mary's View worked there as a cook.

A change occurred when the Cliffords began operating the premises
as a Bible and Theological College, running it as Matlock Bible
College. Accommodation was always a problem and numbers of
students slept in the garages and large greenhouses in the grounds of
'Dale View', as well as high up in the attic. Guests could also be
catered for at Doris Walker's home. Many of the students were women
and their training was aimed at enabling them to serve overseas as
missionaries. However, by the mid 1950's the Bible College was
closed, and, due to the unfortuante danger from subsidence on the shale
covered slopes of Oker Hill, 'Dale View' was demolished in the 1960's.

One area of the parish, however, where change was not easily
noticeable in the 1940's and early 1950's was in Wensleydale, and in
particular the cottages belonging to the Haywood and Phinney Charity.
In an earlier chapter we saw how Edith Knowles (previously Gillatt)
lived in one of these tiny cottages and each year Roy Gillatt, her son,
would bring his family to stay with her. An account of this adventure is

related by Edith's grand daughter, Stella Dawson:-

"As young children during the 1940's, my brother and I would eagerly look forward to our annual holiday, spending just one week, along with our parents, at the home of our paternal grandmother.

We'd catch the Manchester train from Derby and if it stopped at Darley Station we would walk the rest of the way to granny's, but if the train only stopped at Matlock we'd take the Silver Service bus to Wensley Square.

Granny's cottage was a semi-detached one up and one down with a tiny lean-to kitchen at the rear. She had no gas or electricity, no running water and the lavatory was an earth closet across the yard, complete with scrubbed wall to wall wooden seat and the cut up Radio Times hanging on a nail.

There was always a fire in the black-leaded range and this heated the water on one side and provided heat for the oven on the other side. Some cooking, like fry-ups, was done on a Primus stove.

Water for washing was rain water collected in a large barrel at the back of the cottage and drinking water came from a spring which emptied into a shallow well, just a few yards away from granny's front gate.

Oil lamps provided the lighting, whilst the wireless worked on wet batteries, which regularly needed re-charging. I can still recall listening to the commentary on the FA Cup Final of 1947, which Derby County won and we had fingers crossed not only for the Rams but praying also that the batteries held out.

The bedroom contained two double beds; my brother and I shared one, our parents used the other and poor granny had to sleep downstairs on a settee. It wasn't until several years later she told me that often in the night she felt mice running over the eiderdown on one of those double beds.

How we loved those holidays — the sun always seemed to shine and every year our dad used the lens from binoculars to burn the date on the wooden frame of granny's old deck chair. We'd collect watercress from the stream, watch fox cubs playing in the woods and enjoy endless games of cricket with the village kids. It was an adventure to walk the half mile there and back to the nearest farm to fetch milk.

Granny taught me how to skin a rabbit and would recite poems which were miles long and which I wish I could remember now, to tell my grandchildren. And the puddings we had were never to be forgotten — rhubarb pies, slit open with a generous dollop of 'conny' (condensed milk) inside. We lived like kings.

Towards the end of the holiday dad would dispose of the contents of the earth closet down an old uncapped mine shaft in the nearby 'Dungeon'. We would then spend half a day in the woods collecting kindling so that granny had a plentiful supply to last all winter. We'd return to Derby to a house with 'all mod cons' but never for one moment did we think that we'd suffered hardship at granny's cottage.

Oh! Those happy days".

We see in Stella's account how little had changed, for water still came from the well and 'night soil' was deposited in the mine shaft. For most of Wensley, however, some changes gradually occurred in relation to both of these matters.

The water supply to the rest of the village was fed by gravity from Stanton Moor to Wensley reservoir, and rarely ran dry. However, this did happen on occasions when the 3 inch cast iron main fractured underground, where it was buried in ground made unstable by mine workings and deposition of spoil heaps in Cambridge Wood. The ground in this location was so porous that no trace of leakage could be seen on the surface.

The main problem came, however, in the 1950's as Enthoven's lead smelter works began to expand and more water was required in certain work processes. The company 'tapped' into the 3 inch main and this resulted over the following years in periods when the flow of water from Wensley Reservoir was not sufficient for the need of the village inhabitants. This was certainly the case when combined with the increasing number of reported fractures of the pipe within Cambridge Wood, where the pressure in the pipe was greatest when raising the flow of water uphill.

A booster pump was therefore built on Toll Bar Hill, near Field Farm, Wensley, which forced water from the mains pipe serving Oker Road, uphill, to fill the reservoir during the low usage night time period. At last there was sufficient water in the reservoir during daytime hours to cater for the needs of Wensley and the source of water from Stanton Moor was no longer of any consequence.

The late 1940's and early 1950's saw the Urban District Council taking direct responsibility for the removal of 'night soil' from the earth closets of South Darley households. Instead of Tom Wigley arriving with his horse and cart, as in pre-war years, a council lorry arrived with a cylindrical metal container on the back. The Sanitation wagon or 'Violet wagon' as it was dubbed by certain residents, arrived at Wensley on a Thursday night during the 1950's and the driver and his mate would slake their thirst in the Crown Inn, after the odorous task had been completed. Whilst the pair stood at the bar, everyone made sure they kept their distance.

A far pleasanter and salubrious account of South Darley life can be provided when we examine the post-war leisure time activities of its inhabitants. The Church was still to the fore in social activities and this is well illustrated by the photograph of St. Mary's Church Choir dinner of 1951, with 37 members, relatives or friends on view, whilst newspaper reports tell of well-attended fetes and garden parties still being held in the grounds of Eversleigh House. Strong support for the church is also to be seen in the spirited parish contribution towards the instalment of a carillon of eight bells in 1945, a stained glass window dedicated to the memory of the fallen in both World Wars in November 1950 and the clock in the tower, presented by James and Mary Trickett on 24th May 1950.

The Reverend I.O. Evans was instrumental in fostering keen support for both church and parish activities. It was his enthusiasm and energy which helped to bring together like minded thespians in forming an amateur dramatic society known as 'The Oker Tree Players', which performed well received productions throughout the late 1940's and

St Mary's Church Choir dinner 1951

Back row, l-r: Dennis Wright, Roy Marsden, Mervyn Wright, David Crapper, Joan Simcock, Ray Slack, Billy Winthrope, Ron Greatorex, Reverend IO Evans.

Third row: Eileen Wright, George Wright, Jack Taylor, Mrs Crapper, Mr Kean, Bert Buxton, Mrs Shepherd, Arnold Wright, Harry Taylor, Reg Boden, Tim Simcock, Mrs Smith, Mabel Taylor

Second row: Mrs Evans, Mrs Taylor, Mrs Kean, Mrs Bowler, Miss Walker, Mrs Simcock, Mrs Furniss, Mrs Haynes, Mrs Wright

Front row: Shirley Evans, Margaret Bowler, Eileen Wain, Sheila Smith, Mary Fawley

Oker Tree Players performing 'When we are married' by JB Priestley at Cross Green School in April 1949, and later at the Ritz Cinema

Back row, l-r: Reverend IO Evans, Roy Watkinson, Tom Simcock, Mr Bennett, Audrey Shimwell, Wilson Gaythwaite, Joan Simcock, Archie Smedley Hill

Front row: Mary Wright, Mrs Gilbert, Maud Allen, Zoe Bark, Kathleen Shepherd

1950's. The schoolroom was used to house the performances, though great excitement was generated when in 1949 they appeared before a large audience at the Ritz Cinema, Matlock. By 1953 the Players were able to make use of the newly built Village Hall.

To lighten the gloom of the austerity years and to raise money for the provision of a new South Darley Village Hall, a committee was set up in 1949 to organise the first post-war Wensley Carnival for Saturday 16th September 1950. It proved an outstanding success. Except for a shower, which marred the crowning of Queen, Margaret Daniels, by post mistress, Mrs. Crapper, the weather was fine and the fancy dress parade attracted many entrants.

In early September 1951, the second annual carnival took place and on this occasion Mr. and Mrs. J.S. Wain crowned the mock King and Queen of Wensley, Tom Simcock and George Tomlinson, whilst in support were their attendants, Arnold Wright and Joe Devereux. After the crowning, the fancy dress parade was judged and then the Royalty made their speeches. In the procession which followed there were seven decorated lorries carrying tableaux. The first prize was won by one

First Wensley Carnival Summer 1950
Back row, l-r: Dot Flint, Mrs Willis (Crown Inn), Mr P Armstrong (Secretary),
Margaret Daniels, Mrs Crapper (post office), Irene Newton, Neville Siddall
(chairman), X, Mrs Salt. Front row: Ann Shimwell, Maureen Devaney, David Taylor,
Irene Wright, Jennifer Wright

Wensley Carnival, September 1951
Top: Arnold Wright, Tom Simcock, George Tomlinson, Joe Devereux

Bottom: Mr JS Wain, Irene Wheeldon, Arnold Wright, Tom Simcock, Joe Devereux,
George Tomlinson, Mrs Wain

representing " Snow White and the Seven Dwarves" and the second prize went to " Christmas Morn", both of them having been performed by the school during the year. Later a grand dance was held in the schoolroom and the " Queen" led the first old fashioned waltz.

On the evening of Saturday 23rd August 1952, in the presence of a large crowd, John Hadfield, Chairman of Derbyshire Stone Ltd., officially opened the new Village Hall. The door was unlocked by a beribboned key handed to Mr. Hadfield by Jennifer Wright. The cost of this 60 foot by 24 foot hall, £1900, had been met by the National Council for Social Services, acting in cooperation with Derbyshire Rural Community Council, but over £520 had been raised by South Darley Village Hall Committee to defray the cost of furnishings and extras.

Work on the hall had been done by voluntary labour on a 'From each according to his ability' basis and the opening ceremony saw the culmination of a six year effort, which had as its driving force the Reverend I.O. Evans.

A.G. Bennett, Chairman of the Village Hall Committee traced the history of the venture from the first meeting convened by Matlock Urban District Council in Autumn 1946. The hall was the fifth and last hall to be provided in Derbyshire, under the Temporary Halls Renting Scheme.

Entertainment by local artists contributed to a most enjoyable programme at the concert which followed. Singing by a choir of ten

Carnival Tableau, 1951, 'Christmas Morn'
Back row: Hazel Hardy, Mavis Boam, Peggy Wright
Front row: Vivienne Shepherd, Margaret Dunn, Tom Shepherd, Barbara Gregory

Opening ceremony of Village Hall, 23rd August 1952. Jennifer Wright, carrying the key, leads John Hadfield to the Village Hall

Committee members of opening ceremony of Village Hall, 23rd August 1952
George Shimwell, Norman Taylor, Tom Spencer, Annie Pepper, Mrs Marshall, Tom Simcock, George Tomlinson, John Hadfield, Arthur Bennett, James Bark, Arnold Wright, Mrs Harrison, Mrs Boam, Mrs Hothesall, Bill Taylor, Jennifer Wright

young local women, accompanied by Minnie Potter, was delightful, and two plays presented by South Darley W.I. and 'The Oker Tree Players' were well received. Community singing led by George F. Potter completed the programme.

The hall was packed again on Sunday night for a sacred concert, organised by Mr. H. Trickett and Arnold Wright as St. Mary's contribution to carnival week.

The culmination of Carnival Week, 1952, was on Saturday 30th August in Wensley Square. The newspaper account reports ;-

"It was at once apparent on entering South Darley by way of Darley Bridge that something special was afoot for most of the houses were gaily decorated with garlands, festoons, flags and gay ribbons. It was the day of the carnival procession, climax of a week of special events. A charming and unusual feature of the decorations was that many people had decorated their gate posts with flowers.

The proceedings began when Councillor Tom Spencer as the Town Crier, complete with purple cloak, cocked hat and bell, led the "royal" procession from the Reading Room to the Square at Wensley, where the crowning of the richly apparelled comic King and Queen by Mr. and Mrs. Taylor of Cowley Hall took place on a decorated lorry outside the post office.

The royal party, with Gerald Fletcher as parade Marshall, headed a procession led by Darley Dale Silver Prize Band round the village, then on to Oker, Darley Bridge, via the gated road, and back to the Village Hall. The lorry bearing the Rose Queen, Daphne Wragg, and her attendants, made a charming tableau. Teas and refreshments were provided in the hall by the South Darley W.I. The early evening was occupied by a programme of sports in the field adjoining the hall and later on a social in the hall drew a large audience. The carnival concluded with a dance, for which Billy Hodgkinson of Winster supplied the music".

Other events earlier in the week included a men versus women comic football match on Thursday, in the field behind St. Mary's View, where the women from Rowsley beat the men of Cross Green 6 – 5,

South Darley Carnival, 30th August 1952
Back row, l-r: Mr Taylor (Cowley Hall), Tom Harrison, Horace Woodhouse, Mrs Taylor
Front row: King George Agutter, Queen Charlie Tomlinson

with Mrs. J. Bark acting as referee. A concert in the Village Hall by Jack Smedley's Concert Party followed, with the day's proceeds amounting to £16. There was a full house for an old time dance in the hall on Friday, with Tom Simcock and D. Kean (Darley Bridge Post Office) as M.C.'s.

January 1953 saw the older residents of the parish catered for with a meeting in the Village Hall to establish a Club for South Darley's Darbies and Joans, the forerunner of the present Over 60's Club, which, at the time of writing, still meets at the same venue. A photo observes some of the newly enrolled members enjoying a hand of whist.

1953 also witnessed an important social event in the life of the parish when, on Tuesday 2nd June, South Darley celebrated the coronation of Queen Elizabeth II.

A United Service at 9 am., held at St. Mary's Church, marked the opening of Coronation Day. Between 2pm and 2.45pm selections by Darley Dale Band were to be played on the Sports field, kindly loaned by Mrs. Clay of Field Farm. However, due to the inclement weather, the sports for all ages were transferred from the field to Oker Road, to be run on the tarmac surface.

At 4 p.m. the new Village Hall, gaily decorated, provided an attractive venue for teas for more than 250 old people and children. At 7.00pm South Darley parishioners could choose between attending a

Wensley Carnival 30th August 1952
Town crier Tom Simcock

Crowning of King and Queen

Top; Mens v ladies football match at Wensley Carnival Week in field behind St Mary's View, 30th August 1952

Bottom: Back row, l-r: X, Len Riley, Alf Smith, X, Tom Simcock, Horace Woodhouse, James Bark.
Front row: X, Jack Smedley, John Smedley

Crowning of the Rose Queens at Eversleigh House
Top: July 1949. Back, l-r: Councillor Rhodes, Shirley Grubb (Rogers), Mavis Boam,
Sheila Dowling, Mrs Rhodes, Margaret Dunn, Isobel Winthrope, Reverend Evans
Front: Jennifer Wright, Janet Furniss

Bottom: 1952. Back, l-r: Jim Bark, Arnold Wright, Patience Haynes, Mrs Wakefield,
Daphne Wragg, Isobel Winthrope, Mr Wakefield (MP), Reverend Evans
Front: Susan Woodhouse, Doreen Chandler, John Pritty, Janet Haynes, Rita Masters

*Whist drive for newly enrolled members of South Darley Darby and Joan Club,
January 1953, in the Village Hall*

concert in the Village Hall, arranged by Mr. and Mrs. G.F. Potter or a
whist drive held in the schoolroom. Proceedings for this special day
ended with a dance and running buffet in the hall at 10 p.m., which
lasted until early Wednesday morning.

Two Dales celebrations had begun with hymns and prayers in
Whitworth Institute pavilion, with sports taking place on the football
pitch. After a tea in the park's Tea Room, Mr. Eddie Shimwell
presented a gift of souvenir silver spoons to all those under eighteen
years and Old Age Pensioners. Rain marred the evening programme
planned for the Field, Two Dales, but it was re-run on the following
Saturday evening, with sports, followed by a bonfire and fireworks.

During these same early post-war years of the 1940's and 50's, the
Wensley Red Stars Football Team once again joined the Matlock and
District, Bakewell and District, and later, the Hope Valley Leagues,
with junior members competing for a while in the Rowsley Youth
League. The Youth team, captained by Joe Greatorex, competed at
Causeway Lane, Matlock in the final of the Rowsley and District Shield

Coronation Day, 2nd June 1953 at St Mary's View, Oker Road. Getting ready for the races.

competition against Hackney Foresters in 1948, beating the opposition 4 – 0 in the process. It is certainly worthwhile noting that an estimated crowd of three thousand watched the match.

The teams produced some fine players, competing in home matches on the same field as the Wensley Wuffets of old, behind the Red Lion Inn, before moving down to a pitch along the Wenslees. With David Devaney and Les Masters running the teams and Jack and Harry Taylor running the line as trainers, Wensley were a match for most teams in the district. The Club also played a social role within the parish, for they attracted much support, and annual club dinners and meetings at the Crown Inn were welcome additions to the social calendar.

By 1953, a sign of the times for the people of South and North Darley was the lessening of the burden of post-war austerity measures and the prospect of happier times at the onset of what was hoped to be a new 'Elizabethan Age'. A greater security of employment and the benefit of holiday pay resulted in more families taking a break by the seaside. In Derbyshire, however, the first National Park in the country,

*1947 Cricket Season. Darley Dale play Derby Club and Ground. Derby bring the FA
Trophy they have recently won.
Back row, l-r: X, Tommy White (groundsman), Ben Gregory, Cyril Howse, Cyril
Taylor, X, X, X, X, X, X, X, X, X, X, X, X, Fred Smith
Front row: Bill Allen, X, Louis Jacques, Raich Carter, X, Charlie Lymn, Derbyshire
Captain, Reg Boden, Alfred Smith, X, Noel Jacques*

*Church play at St Elphin's School c1949
Back row, l-r: Sheila Smith, Mrs Evans, Josie Palk, Reverend Evans, Mary Fawley, Jim
Grimshaw, Betty Shimwell, Pearl Dobson
Front row: Eileen Wain, Joan Simcock, Jean Fern, Ann Shimwell, Valerie Watkinson,
Norma Holmes, Noreen Wain*

Gathering of Wensley residents c1950
Back row, l-r: Barbara Cooper, Arthur Slack. Middle row: Arthur Devereux, Malachi Concannon, John Charles Bishton, Joseph Slack, Mary Flint, Mrs Crapper. Front row: Michael Cooper, Jack Flint, Joan Chadbourne

Oker Institute c1950 performing 'Butterflies in the Rain'
Back row, l-r: Hazel Hardy, Minnie Potter, Margaret Walker, Wendy Henstock, Margaret Dunn, Brenda Petts, Dinah Petts, Sheila Dowling, Mavis Boam, Pamela Henstock
Middle row: Joan Taylor, Marion Taylor, Barbara Gregory, Ann Smedley, Eileen Dunn, Valerie Watkinson, Ken Walker
Front row: Joe Goodman, Raymon Else, Brian Smedley, Clive Hardy, Peter Dunn, Alan Ainsworth, Muriel Walker, Susan Goodison, Pat Goodison, Maurice Dowling

Cutting of harvest loaf by Harvest Queen, Eileen Wain, October 1951
Back row, l-r: Joan Simcock, Mrs Linnell, Hazel Hardy. Front row: Eileen Wain, Derek
Grimshaw, Arnold Wright, Reverend Evans

Wensley Reading Room Billiards and Snooker Team. Champions of league and 1951
Cup winners. Back row, l-r: E Chadbourne, Alf Smith, Bill Shepherd, Bert Wheeldon,
Norman Taylor, H Moseley. Front row: Cecil Wright, Gill Andrews

South Darley Church Christmas Bazaar. Village Hall 1953. X, Reverend Cyril Cave,
Reg Boden, X, Hannah Chell, Pam Hodgkinson, Arnold Wright, Lindsey Cave, Mrs Cave

South Darley Women's Institute meeting at the Village Hall c1954. Back row, l-r: Mrs
Holmes, Mrs Boam, Mrs Kean, Mrs Tomlinson, X, Mary Neville, Miss Walker, Middle
row: Mrs Bowler, Mrs Siddall, X, Mrs Lawman, X, X, Mrs Roose, X, Mrs Cowley, Mrs
Bark, Mrs Silverwood, Mrs Watkinson, Mrs Harrison, Mrs Boden, Mrs Newton, Mrs
Kemp, Mrs Hadfield, Mrs Evans. Front row: X, Mrs Pepper, Annie Harrison, Mrs
Morrisey, Mrs Marshall, X, X, Mrs Bagshaw, Mrs Malachi Concannon, Mrs Joby
Taylor, X

the Peak District National Park, was established on April 15th 1951, providing a leisure time haven for those who wished to visit and stay in an area of outstanding natural beauty. Much of South Darley parish lay within the Park's boundaries.

It was to be in the Darley area that one man had the vision to see how this new interest in leisure time pursuits within the countryside could be catered for. In 1953, at Two Dales, Herbert Hardy provided the first caravan camping site in Derbyshire to be approved by the Town Planning authorities, known as 'The Cara-Hols' and situated on the site of the present D.F.S. Furniture Store complex.

Herbert had sold Dene Quarries, Cromford and bought a house in Scarborough. After three years at the Yorkshire coastal resort he travelled back to Derbyshire and saw that Walton Mill House, Two Dales, virtually derelict for the previous eight years, was on the market. He had seen at Scarborough the potential for holidays by caravan and believed such a site would be a good business venture, close to the newly established Peak Park, with its potential for tourism.

Wensley Red Stars, 1951-52 at Crown Inn, Wensley
Back row, l-r: Harry Taylor, Ken Fletcher, Alf Bowler, Mervyn Wright, X,X, Graham
Brookhouse, Joe Greatorex, Dennis Allwood, Peter Sellors, Peter Yates, Brian Boam,
Harold Boswell, Norman Peach, Stan Willis, Mrs Willis, Reverend Evans
Front row: Les Masters, Bernard Cooper, Ivan Greatorex, Doug Ryder, Bill
Richardson, Tony Evans, David Devaney

Wensley Juniors 1949-50 seaon
Back row, l-r: Joe Webster, H Grimshaw, G Webster, H Gilbert (sec), J Allwood, A
Bowler, R Webster, T White, H Taylor, W Newton, Bob Glenn, D Allwood, R Greatorex
Front row: Birdie Stone, Ivan Greatorex, G Boden, H Loxley, G Dakin

1949 Wensley Juniors, winners of Rowsley Youth League Shield
Back row, l-r: Charlie Tomlinson, Bryan Allwood, George Boden, Harold Grimshaw,
Denis Allwood, Roy Webster, Alf Bowler, Jack Taylor
Front row: Paul Boden, Ivan Greatorex, Joe Greatorex, Keith Riley, George Dakin

Wensley Team 1951-52 season, Crown Inn
Back row, l-r: Wilf Jordon, Graham Brookhouse, Denis Allwood, Peter Yates, Peter Sellors, Brian Boam. Front row: Bernard Cooper, Ivan Greatorex, Doug Ryder, Bill Richardson, Tony Evans

Wensley Football Team and supporters, Crown Inn 1950's
Back row, l-r: Harry Taylor, Graham Stone, David Devaney, Mr & Mrs Hawsworth, Mrs Daniels, Ted Daniels, Sarah Devaney, Neville Siddall, Bert Wheeldon, Betty Siddall, Mr Peach, Cecil Wright, Ida Greatorex, Mabel Taylor, X, X, Mary Wright, Harry Grimshaw, Ken Hardy, Les Masters, Graham Brookhouse, Mrs. Brookhouse. Front row: Buddy Grindy, Barry Daniels, Tony Evans, Tom Concannon, Joe Greatorex, Mervyn Wright, Mick Cooper, ? Baker, Frank Taylor

Football group, Wensley, c1948
Back row, l-r: ? Slater, Roy Marsden, Roy Webster, Ken Fletcher, Mervyn Wright,
Freddy Grubb (Rogers), Glynn Evans (vicar's son), Ivan Wright, Alf Bowler, Ray
Howse, Graham Allsop, X, X, Norman Stone, Ivan Greatorex, Freddy Newton, George
Storer, X. Middle row: Billy Winthrop, Rev IO Evans, Tommy Concannon, Doug Ryder,
Joe Webster (Bunt), Les Masters, David Devaney, Dennis Allwood, Joe Greatorex, Jack
Taylor, Harry Taylor. Front row: Carl Boden, Eileen Wain, Sheila Smith, Mrs Mary
Wain, Mrs Smith, Mabel Taylor, Eileen Taylor (Wright), Marion Taylor, Sally Evans,
Florence Taylor

Whilst his wife, Edith and three children, Ivan, Stewart and Keith remained at Scarborough, Herbert employed eight men for six months to refurbish the house and attack the neglected gardens. The seven foot wide track was widened by 20 feet of land bought off farmer Howard Wagstaffe. As planning permission was being sought, a petition was raised in the area against the venture and Herbert was advised to plant quick growing poplar trees around the site, as this would be considered in his favour.

The five acre model park developed by Herbert Hardy was officially opened on Saturday August 15th 1953 by Alderman C.F. White, Chairman of the County Council and of the Peak Park Planning Board. Seventy guests heard Alderman White emphasise that while he and his

View of Two Dales Cara Hols, Darley Dale near Matlock

Alderman CF White cutting the ribbon to open Cara-Hols. To the left of Alderman White is Herbert Hardy with his younger son, Stewart. Ivan Hardy, aged 9, handed the scissors to Alderman White

Herbert Hardy talking to holidaymakers in 1953

"Come in number seven, your time is up!"
Herbert and holidaymakers by the boating lake, 1953

colleagues were prepared to give every encouragement to enterprises such as 'Cara-Hols', they still regarded uncontrolled caravanning as a menace.

Asserting that he was a great believer in the open-air life, Alderman White said he would like to see a dozen such sites throughout Derbyshire. "This is the first recognised site in Derbyshire; we shall have another soon in the Peak Park". Alderman White opened the caravan park by cutting a white tape at the entrance with scissors handed to him by Mr. Hardy's eldest son, Ivan, aged nine.

Then the guests had the opportunity to inspect the site which already had ten caravans, with space to accommodate sixty. The old mill house and grounds had been transformed. Stone outbuildings, once used as barns and cattle shelters, had been converted into up-to-date wash houses, with hot and cold water, showers and heated drying and laundry rooms.

Waist high bracken and undergrowth had been cleared from a section of the site which had been untouched for many years and the wilderness had become a picturesque old-world garden. There was a rustic bridge thrown across a stream, and where this met a second stream, a paddling pool and boating lake had been constructed. Swings and see-saws were provided and above all, there were to be no "Keep

Facing page: A once-in-a-lifetime picture evoking memories of memories... For it was taken back in 1952 at a unique get-together of couples-who had been married at St. Mary's Parish Church, South Darley in the 38 years from 1914.
The gathering was inspired by the Rev IO Evans, then Vicar of South Darley, who later in the same year moved on to become Rector of Pilling, near Fleetwood.
Mr Evans is pictured in the front row. To his right are the oldest couple involved, Mr and Mrs Sam Edge, who were married at St Mary's in 1914.
Back row: left to right: Mr and Mrs H Taylor, Mrs Newton, Mrs H Boden, Mr and Mrs D Marsden, Mr and Mrs R Furniss, Mr and Mrs A Vardy, Mr and Mrs G Andrews, Mr and Mrs D Wright, Mr and Mrs G Smith. Middle row: Mr and Mrs F Davison, Mr H Chell, Mr and Mrs A Wright, Mr and Mrs Taylor, Mr and Mrs Beese Mr and Mrs J Bardsley, Mr and Mrs N Silverwood, Mr and Mrs Gladwin, Mr and Mrs J Webster. Front row: Mr and Mrs Towndrow. Mr and Mrs A Evans; Mr and Mrs B Walker, Mr and Mrs Edge, the Rev Evans, Mr and Mrs Tom Spencer. Mr and Mrs J Bark. Mr and Mrs Downs-Rose.

Off the Grass" signs.

The caravan park itself was spacious, with the ground allotted to each caravan clearly defined and with taps and drains placed at regular intervals. A warden was also in attendance at the nearby office.

As the brochure reported:-

"All this, and 'Heaven' in the form of Haddon Hall, Chatsworth, High Tor, Via Gellia, Ladygrove, Stanton Moor, Clough Wood, Robin Hood's Stride and Rowtor Rocks awaited all who were fortunate enough to caravan in the Darley area".

We can see, therefore, that a mood of optimism was gaining ground, for by the end of 1955, a decade of peace had been achieved since the ending of World War Two, and now with hindsight we know that a whole generation of British people has continued to be blessed by this legacy of peace.

The generation dealt with in our book was not so fortunate. Many people within the parish of South Darley experienced two world-wide conflicts which helped to shatter the fabric of their lives. We hope that in our book and its companion 'A Derbyshire Parish at War – South Darley and the Great War 1914 – 1919', we have been able to observe their fortitude and determination in difficult circumstances and pay respect to those who lay down their lives for their country.

And yet it is also our wish to have observed and recorded the rich vein of parish life to be found in that 'slower moving age'. The pace of life, though changing, was more gentle and 'characters' abounded. We hope these books have reflected those now far off days and that we have placed South Darley's story in its historical context.